Beyond Grits and Gravy

The South's All-Time Favorite Recipes

Beyond Grits and Gravy

The South's All-Time Favorite Recipes

GWEN McKEE and
BARBARA MOSELEY

QUAIL RIDGE PRESS

Preserving America's Food Heritage

Library of Congress Cataloging-in-Publication Data

McKee, Gwen
    Beyond grits and gravy : the south's all-time favorite recipes /
Gwen McKee and Barbara Moseley.
       p. cm.
    Includes bibliographial references and index.
    ISBN 1-893062-47-3
    1. Cookery, American—Southern Style. I. Moseley, Barbara. II. Title.

TX715.2.S68M334 2004
641.5975—dc22   2003070680

Manufactured in the United States of America.
Book design by Cynthia Clark
Cover photos by Greg Campbell

On the cover: Fresh Strawberry Pie (p. 236), Butter Cookies (p. 208),
Louisiana Swamp (p. 256), Buttermilk Biscuits (p. 36),
Tomato Gravy (p. 40), Southern-Style Greens (p. 112),
Mamean's Buttermilk Corn Bread (p. 47), Black-Eyed Susan Salad (p. 74),
The South's Best Shrimp and Grits (p. 129).

QUAIL RIDGE PRESS
P. O. Box 123 • Brandon, MS 39043
info@quailridge.com • www.quailridge.com

Contents

Preface 7

Wet Your Whistle 9
    Beverages...10
    Hors D'Oeuvres.......................................18

Rise and Shine....................................... 35
    Breads 36
    Breakfast..49

Soup's On! 57
    Soups...58
    Chowders, Bisques 62
    Gumbos 64
    Stews..66

Salad and All the Fixins' 69
    Salads...70
    Condiments, Pickles...............................84
    Preserves 89

Eat Your Vegetables!............................... 91
    Vegetables..92
    Side Dishes..116

Gone Fishin' 121
    Fish...122
    Seafood 127

What's for Supper? 139
    Meats (Beef, Pork, Venison, Squirrel) 140
    Poultry (Chicken, Turkey, Quail, Duck) 167

Just a Sliver, Please 183
    Cakes...184

A Little Bite of Heaven........................... 205
    Cookies 206
    Candies 218

Did You Save Room for Dessert? 225
    Pies 226
    Other Desserts.......................................242

List of Contributing Cookbooks.................. 261

Extra Help.. 271

Index.. 275

Best of the Best State Cookbook Series 286

Gwen and Barbara take a moment from testing recipes to enjoy a round of golf. With pleasant temperatures nearly year-round, golf is a favorite sport in the South.

Preface

At the mere mention of southern cooking, people perk up with interest. The reaction is more than just favorable . . . there is almost an excitement . . . like, "I know it's going to be really good . . . tell me what it is!" And it rarely disappoints. Well, okay, so what makes southern cooking so good?

First of all, food in the South is a revered thing. It welcomes people. It celebrates occasions. It goes with us to parties and picnics and socials. It helps to comfort. And it even manages to find its way into most conversations.

Like many things in the South, cooking is usually not a hurried thing. Giving the flavor time to really soak in is standard procedure. In Louisiana, they say, "Let it sit . . . give the flavors time to marry." For sure, the word "al dente" is rarely used. But it is certainly more than merely time. It's the flavor, with generous seasonings used to elevate any kind of dish.

And it's the texture, too. Southerners go for soft insides, but crisp outsides. Sauces are important, and gravies are served with just about anything! And of course, fresh-out-of-the-garden vegetables and just-picked fruits make for superb vegetable dishes and jellies and jams, and translate into divine desserts, too.

There's another ingredient, I think, that plays a big role in southern cooking . . . pride. Southerners are so darn proud of their cooking that they want everybody to eat every last bite of the dish they bring to the church supper! They love to be asked for their recipe. And they see no need to be "uppity" about what they put in it to make it taste good—canned soups and packaged goods and just a tad of bacon grease might be just what is needed for the right taste.

We had a hard time deciding what area to include in "the South," so we decided to draw the line close to where Mason and Dixon did, thereby stretching the Deep South to the Mid-South to the Coastal South to the Virginian South and everything in between.

The recipes are the ones people told us they love to use and always get them rave reviews. Some recipes may not have even originated in the South, but were "adopted" from wherever, as something southerners think they *should* have created and are proud to serve (like Red Velvet Cake). So the selections herein are our choices of delicious dishes that were chosen from our favorite southern cookbooks, our families and friends all across the South, and even include some of our own personal favorites. These recipes stretch *Beyond Grits and Gravy* to include up-to-date specialties and easy-do marvels for today's busy lifestyles, as well as the traditional cook-it-all-day southern favorites.

In the course of our research, and in listening to our many cookbook friends, we have found delicious new recipes that were perhaps perfected from an original southern standard. But then we give you the old way in a sidebar, or suggest slight changes or substitutions that we have found are also quite enjoyable in our Editor's Extras. We like shortcuts and pass them on, too. And though most of these traditional recipes do not address diet concerns, there are times when we do. We offer substitution and cooking suggestions that we have tried, and that work for us without loss of the recipe's texture and taste. And you will also note that we could not resist telling a few of our "southern stories" that go along with some of the recipes.

We hope you will enjoy our selections which we think portray the essence of true southern cooking. These all-time favorite recipes go *Beyond Grits and Gravy*, spanning the generations, embracing old favorites, and welcoming new creations in the South.

Supper's ready . . . y'all come serve your plate.

Gwen McKee & Barbara Moseley

Wet Your Whistle

Beverages & Hors D'Oeuvres

I come from a family where gravy is considered a beverage.

— Erma Bombeck

Summer Mint Tea

7 cups boiling water
6 tea bags
Juice of 6 lemons
Hulls of 3 lemons
8 sprigs of mint
2 cups sugar

To boiling water, add tea bags, lemon juice, hulls, and mint. Remove from heat and let steep 10 minutes. Add sugar and stir to dissolve. Strain into 1-gallon jar and add water to fill gallon. Chill and serve over ice.

Any Time's a Party!

Editor's Extra: The secret to real southern iced tea is to dissolve sugar thoroughly in hot tea. Serve over lots of ice in tall glasses.

Southerners drink iced tea year-round, and have been doing so since the 19th century when ice became readily available. Order tea in a southern restaurant and you will likely receive sweet iced tea. However, outside the southern states, order tea and you will most likely get a cup of hot tea. If you request iced tea, it is served unsweetened, and you will only find it available in the summer.

Summertime Citrus Tea

6 tea bags
4 cups boiling water
1 (6-ounce) can frozen orange juice (or limeade) concentrate, thawed and undiluted
1 (6-ounce) can frozen lemonade concentrate, thawed and undiluted
10 cups water
1½ cups sugar

Steep tea bags in boiling water, about 5–7 minutes; discard tea bags. Add remaining ingredients. Serve over ice. Yields 1 gallon.

Cooking with Tradition

Anycolor Punch

The addition of Jell-O makes it possible to vary the color and flavor—an all-occasion punch.

4 cups sugar
12 cups water
1 (3-ounce) package Jell-O
1 (46-ounce) can pineapple juice
Juice of 12 lemons
1 teaspoon almond extract

Bring sugar and water to a boil and add any flavor Jell-O (for color) to dissolve. Add pineapple juice, lemon juice, and almond extract. Add enough water to make 2 gallons of punch. Serves 35.

Hors D'Oeuvres Everybody Loves

Editor's Extra: I like to float pineapple slices on top for garnish.

Southern Champagne Punch

2 fifths champagne
1 fifth Chablis
1 pint vodka
1 (28-ounce) bottle soda water
1 (12-ounce) can frozen lemonade concentrate, undiluted

Chill all ingredients and mix. Can be served from pitcher garnished with fresh fruits, or from a punch bowl with an ice ring. If using an ice ring, do not use lemonade in punch, but dilute and make ring, adding fresh or canned fruit for decoration. Yields 15 servings.

Note: A moderately strong punch can be made by using $1/2$ pint vodka.

The Alabama Heritage Cookbook

Bourbon Punch

1 (12-ounce) can frozen
   pink lemonade, undiluted
1 (2-liter) bottle 7-Up
1 (10-ounce) jar
   maraschino cherries
1 cup bourbon

Mix all ingredients in large bowl. Freeze in quart containers. Serve slushy.

Somethin's Cookin' at LG&E

Joy's Bay Pointe Margaritas

Easy to make . . . delightfully refreshing.

Every year our club hosts a ladies golf tournament, our Fall Fiesta. The margaritas are a traditional part of the celebration after play. No matter how good or bad your game might have been, the laughter and fun and camaraderie—and the margaritas—are all the best.

—*Gwen and Barbara*

1 (6-ounce) can frozen
   lemonade
1 can water
1 can tequila (or less)
¹/₂ can Triple Sec
1 teaspoon lime juice
   (optional)

Put all in blender. Fill with ice to slush. Serve in stemmed glasses. Pass a slice of lime around the rim and dip in coarse salt, if desired.

Joy Hinders

The Bay Pointe Ladies enjoying Joy's (second from right) margaritas.

Mimosas

A southern tradition at bridal luncheons and showers.

¼ cup sugar
¼ cup Grand Marnier
1 fifth champagne
1 quart orange juice

Put sugar and Grand Marnier in separate small dishes. Dip the rim of champagne flutes (or wine glasses) in Grand Marnier, then sugar. Pour champagne into flutes, then orange juice. Makes about 8 servings.

Heather Creel

Kentucky Mint Julep

Traditionally, this is served in a frosted silver mint julep cup.

For nearly a century, the mint julep has been the traditional beverage of Churchill Downs and the Kentucky Derby. Over 80,000 mint juleps are served over the two-day period of the Kentucky Oaks and Kentucky Derby.

SIMPLE SYRUP:
1 part boiling water
2 parts sugar

Combine boiling water and sugar; stir until dissolved.

Mint leaves
Crushed ice
100 proof Kentucky
 bourbon
Simple Syrup

Place 3–4 mint leaves in julep glass. Add crushed ice. Press down with spoon to bruise leaves. Add 1 ounce bourbon and ½ ounce Simple Syrup; stir well. Pack glass with crushed ice and fill with bourbon. Garnish with mint leaves.

To Market, To Market

Hilton Head Freeze

A great drink created as a tribute to a very elegant island. . . . The island is posh and beautiful, the drink is savory and delicious.

¹/₂ ounce medium ripe
   banana (about ¹/₄
   banana)
1¹/₂ ounces light rum
2¹/₂ ounces orange juice
1¹/₂ ounces coconut cream
¹/₂ ounce grenadine
Cherry for garnish

Put banana in blender; add next four ingredients. Add ice (half blender or so). Blend until creamy and stiff. Makes one 12-ounce serving. Garnish with cherry. Equally excellent without alcohol.

Pool Bar Jim's

Peachy Keen Banana Smoothie

A delicious way to start the day . . . or end it . . . or anytime in between.

¹/₂ cup orange juice
¹/₂ cup milk
1 pint vanilla ice cream
   (or frozen yogurt)
1 cup peach yogurt
1 ripe banana

Blend on high till very smooth.
   Good to add ¹/₃ cup protein powder for a great power drink to get you going. Adding slices of fresh peeled peach makes it even better. Serves 2–3.

Gwen McKee

Bloody Mary

This is a real eye-opener when spiced up with Louisiana's own Tabasco sauce.

4 cups good quality, thick tomato juice
1 teaspoon salt
1 teaspoon black pepper
$\frac{1}{2}$ teaspoon celery salt
1 tablespoon Worcestershire sauce
8 dashes Tabasco sauce
2 teaspoons fresh lime juice
4–5 jiggers vodka
Lime wedges to garnish

In a large pitcher, combine all ingredients and chill for at least one hour. Stir again before serving. Pour into tall glasses over chipped ice; garnish with lime. Makes 4 (8-ounce) cocktails.

Who's Your Mama, Are You Catholic, and Can You Make a Roux?

Christmas Eggnog

The old-fashioned Cabaniss recipe for Christmas eggnog was used each year to celebrate Christmas. It was served not only to the family, but to all the servants as well, and thus caused a delay in the serving of Christmas dinner.

12 eggs, separated
12 tablespoons sugar
12 tablespoons whiskey
1$\frac{1}{2}$ quarts whipping cream
1 tablespoon vanilla

Beat egg yolks; add sugar and whiskey gradually. Chill. Whip cream and add flavoring. Whip egg whites until stiff; gradually add egg whites and whipped cream to egg mixture. If mixture is too thick, add a little milk or half-and-half.

Suggestion: For serving over a prolonged period, float a half gallon of vanilla ice cream in the punch bowl.

Twickenham Tables

Keeping milk was a problem in the steamy summers of old New Orleans, since the iceman only came once a day. So my grandma always kept condensed milk in a jar on the table. Everybody put a spoonful of it into their coffee—and they had milk and sugar at the same time!

—*Gwen*

Coffee Liqueur

A delicious homemade Kahlúa.

$^1\!/_3$ cup instant coffee
3$^1\!/_2$ cups sugar
2 cups water
1 fifth vodka
3 tablespoons plus
   1 teaspoon vanilla

Combine coffee, sugar, and water. Heat until dissolved; cool. Add vodka and vanilla. Pour into half-gallon glass container. Age 2 weeks. Use as is for Kahlúa, or serve mixed with milk.

A Taste of the Holidays

Coffee Punch

2 quarts strong coffee
1 pint cold milk
2 teaspoons vanilla extract
$^1\!/_2$ cup sugar
2 quarts vanilla ice cream
$^1\!/_2$ pint whipping cream
Ground nutmeg

Combine coffee, milk, vanilla, and sugar; chill. (This mixture may be made a day ahead.) Break ice cream into chunks in punch bowl just before serving; pour chilled coffee mixture over ice cream. Whip cream; spoon into mounds on top of punch. Sprinkle with nutmeg. Serves 15–18.

The Alabama Heritage Cookbook

Editor's Extra: Good to use half or all chocolate ice cream, too. It also lends itself deliciously to a little spike of bourbon, rum, or amaretto in the cup.

Café au Lait *(kah-fay oh-lay)*

At some time in your French Quarter wanderings, you always find your way to the coffee shops for that special coffee of New Orleans—café au lait. You can almost recreate the Vieux Carré atmosphere by brewing some right in your own kitchen.

Like Mardi Gras and jazz music, coffee is a way of life in New Orleans. The French first introduced coffee to America by way of New Orleans during the mid-1700s. As a result, the Port of New Orleans is the nation's largest coffee port. Traditionally, a visit to the city of New Orleans must include a leisurely breakfast of café au lait and beignets (page 49).

Hot whole milk or cream

Coffee and chicory (or dark roast coffee)

Sugar or sweetener (optional)

Heat milk or cream and beat with rotary beater (or whisk) till foamy. Pour equal amounts of coffee and milk into cup at same time. Sweeten to taste.

The Little New Orleans Cookbook

The Café Du Monde in New Orleans serves countless beignets and cups of café au lait all through the day and night.

Mini Bite-Size Crawfish Pies

Jambalaya, crawfish pie, filé gumbo . . . Well, here's the best crawfish pie you'll ever taste.

PIE DOUGH:

1 cup (2 sticks) margarine, softened

2 (3-ounce) packages cream cheese, softened

2 cups flour

1/2 teaspoon salt

Cream margarine and cream cheese until well blended. Add flour and salt. Mix well. Refrigerate for one hour.

FILLING:

1 medium onion, chopped

1/2 cup chopped green onions

1/2 cup chopped celery

2 cloves garlic, chopped

1/4 cup oil

1 pound crawfish tails, cooked and ground

1/4 cup bread crumbs

1 cup water

Salt and pepper to taste and/or Tony's Creole Seasoning

Sauté onion, green onions, celery, and garlic in oil until tender. Add crawfish; sauté about 5 minutes and remove from heat. Add bread crumbs and water. Mix well, season to taste, and set aside.

Take a small ball of Pie Dough and work well with the thumb into mini-muffin tin to form a thin shell. Using a teaspoon, fill each shell with Filling about 3/4 full. Bake at 350° for 15–20 minutes or until golden brown. Cool slightly before removing. Yields about 4–6 dozen.

Straight from the Galley Past & Present

Crabmeat Canapés

6 ounces shredded crabmeat

1 cup mayonnaise

1/2 teaspoon lemon juice

1/4 cup chopped Vidalia onion

1 egg white

Ritz Crackers

In a small mixing bowl, combine crabmeat with mayonnaise, and season with lemon juice. Add chopped onion. Beat egg white until stiff (not dry) and fold into crabmeat mixture. Place approximately 1 teaspoon crab mixture on each Ritz Cracker and cook 45–60 seconds on HIGH in microwave, or until heated thoroughly. Serve immediately. Yields 25 canapés.

The Original Vidalia Onion Cookbook

Hot Crab Dip

This is one of the best dips you will ever eat.

1 (8-ounce) package cream cheese, softened

1 (7-ounce) can king crab

⅛ teaspoon garlic powder or 1 clove garlic

½ cup mayonnaise

1 teaspoon minced onion or 1 teaspoon onion juice

1 teaspoon dry mustard

1 teaspoon powdered sugar

Pinch of salt

White wine

Combine ingredients and melt over low heat. Mix until smooth. Add 2 tablespoons white wine before serving. Lower heat; keep warm for serving. An electric fondue pot could be used for making this dip. Use potato chips or dried bread cubes as dippers.

A Taste from Back Home

Scrumptious Shrimp Appetizer

When "salt and pepper to taste" are called for in a recipe, don't be afraid to experiment with red or white pepper, or even mixed seasoning. Always start lightly.

My chef nephew, Brett Ransome, believes no recipe should give exact seasoning measurements, that you should taste as you go. And if a recipe calls for a seasoning you don't like, use a different one.

—Gwen

12 ounces cream cheese, softened

1 tablespoon mayonnaise

1 teaspoon curry powder

Salt and pepper to taste

1 (7-ounce) can whole baby shrimp, drained

4 green onions, minced

2 hard-boiled eggs, chopped

Combine cream cheese, mayonnaise, curry powder, salt and pepper. Place on a flat dish or platter and sprinkle the shrimp on top; then the green onions, and chopped eggs. Serve with assorted crackers. Serves 12.

Standing Room Only

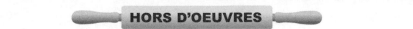

Marinated Shrimp Biloxi

An easy, make-ahead, feed-a-crowd hors d'oeuvre.

4½ pounds shrimp
1 small jar capers
Celery seed to taste
4–5 lemons, sliced thin
3 large onions, sliced thin
1 tablespoon horseradish
2 (16-ounce) bottles Italian dressing (pour oil off one bottle)
½ cup red wine vinegar

Cook and clean shrimp. Cool. In a shallow glass dish, put 1 layer each of shrimp, capers, and celery seed. Completely cover with lemon slices and onion slices which have been separated into rings. Repeat until all are used. End with lemon slices on top. Mix horseradish, Italian dressing, and vinegar. Pour this marinade over shrimp and chill at least 24 hours. Remove from marinade and serve with toothpicks.

Hors D'Oeuvres Everybody Loves

Marvelous Seafood Mornay

Sheer elegance.

1 stick butter
1 small bunch green onions, chopped
½ cup finely chopped parsley
2 tablespoons flour
1 pint half-and-half
½ pound grated Swiss cheese
1 tablespoon sherry
Red pepper to taste
Salt to taste
1 pound white crabmeat or boiled, deveined shrimp

Melt butter in heavy pot and sauté onions and parsley. Blend in flour, half-and-half, and cheese until cheese is melted. Add remaining ingredients and gently fold in crabmeat or chopped boiled shrimp. Serve in pastry shells or in chafing dish with Melba rounds.

The Country Mouse

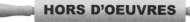

Shrimp Dip

Simply divine.

1 (7-ounce) can shrimp, drained and mashed
1 (8-ounce) package cream cheese, softened
1 (16-ounce) container sour cream
1 package Italian dressing mix
2 tablespoons lemon juice

Mix all together and chill several hours before serving. Good with vegetables.

Favorite Recipes

Shrimp Mousse

Out of this world! Good served with crackers as an hors d'oeuvre or as a luncheon salad.

The first time I encountered this enchanting dish was at a pre-football-game party. It had been formed in a fish mold and placed on leafy greens. The fish had a little red-pepper-ring eye. It attracted me in appearance. Then I tasted it on a cracker . . . and another . . . and another. I finally moved away out of embarrassment. "The fish" shortly disappeared.

—*Gwen*

2 cups sour cream
1 pound cream cheese, softened
1 cup mayonnaise
1/2 cup chili sauce
1 teaspoon salt
1/8 teaspoon Tabasco
1 tablespoon Worcestershire
1/2 cup finely minced bell pepper
1/4 cup finely minced pimiento
2 tablespoons unflavored gelatin
1/4 cup cold water
Juice of 2 lemons
6 cups finely chopped cooked shrimp

Cream together sour cream, cream cheese, and mayonnaise. Add all seasonings and vegetables. Dissolve gelatin in water and lemon juice. Heat in a double boiler 5–10 minutes. Gradually fold this into cheese mixture. Add shrimp and blend very well. Pour into well-chilled (spray with a non-stick cooking spray) ring molds and chill overnight.

Frederica Fare

Editor's Extra: Makes a lot; easy to halve.

Dairy Dip with Parmesan Potato Wedges

Crunchy, flavorful potatoes with a smooth rich dip.

DAIRY DIP:

2 cups cottage cheese

$^1/_2$ cup blue cheese, crumbled

$^1/_2$ cup sour cream

2 tablespoons lemon juice

1 teaspoon Worcestershire sauce

2 tablespoons green onions, sliced

Blend Dairy Dip ingredients until almost smooth. Chill. Serve as a dip with Parmesan Potato Wedges. Makes 3 cups.

PARMESAN POTATO WEDGES:

2 cups puffed rice cereal, crushed

$^1/_4$ cup grated Parmesan cheese

1 teaspoon salt

1 teaspoon paprika

6 baking potatoes

3 tablespoons butter or margarine, melted

Mix crushed puffed rice, Parmesan cheese, salt, and paprika. Scrub, dry, and cut potatoes into wedges. Dip each wedge into melted butter, then roll in rice cereal coating. Place wedges on a buttered 10x15x1-inch pan and bake at 425° for 15 minutes. Makes 8 servings.

Home for the Holidays

On her grandmother's heirloom table, Gwen's daughter, Heather, beautifully presents party food in lovely serving dishes, some of which are treasured family pieces she carefully packs between uses. Many of the recipes are treasured family favorites, too. Preserving America's Food Heritage is truly a delicious affair.

Broccoli Dip

This has been on many a pre-game buffet table and is still popular.

3 (10-ounce) packages
    frozen chopped broccoli

1 stick margarine

1 small onion, minced

1 (6-ounce) roll garlic
    cheese

1 ($10\frac{3}{4}$-ounce) can cream
    of mushroom soup

1 (4-ounce) can sliced
    mushrooms, drained

Cook the broccoli according to package directions. Drain and set aside. Melt margarine in saucepan and sauté onion. Add cheese, stirring until it melts. Add soup and mushrooms, mixing well. Add drained broccoli to cheese mixture. Serve hot in a fondue, chafing dish, or crockpot with Fritos.

To serve as a vegetable, place in casserole dish, then sprinkle with herb-seasoned stuffing mix or crushed Fritos. Bake in 350° oven for 20 minutes.

Canopy Roads

Hot Beef Dip

An easy-pleasy dip.

$\frac{1}{4}$ cup chopped onion

1 tablespoon butter

1 (8-ounce) package cream
    cheese

1 cup milk

1 (4-ounce) can
    mushrooms, drained

$2\frac{1}{2}$ ounces smoked dried
    beef, chopped

$\frac{1}{4}$ cup Parmesan cheese

2 teaspoons chopped
    parsley

Sauté onion in butter. Add cream cheese and milk; stir over low heat until cream cheese melts. Stir in rest of ingredients. Serve hot with chips or crackers.

The Colonel's Inn Caterers'

Perfect Pimento Spread

Our friend, Debbie, always brought a cooler of drinks to our golf outings, and when we opened it, we hoped to find a container of pimento cheese on top. Debbie sometimes used chopped roasted red bell pepper and a little sour cream. It was always an instant hit. Yum!

—Gwen and Barbara

8 ounces sharp Cheddar cheese, grated, room temperature
1 tablespoon finely chopped onion
1 tablespoon Worcestershire
1 (4-ounce) jar pimentos
4 tablespoons mayonnaise
Salt to taste
Red pepper to taste

Whip till fluffy. Refrigerate 24 hours. Add more mayonnaise or a little milk to soften before spreading.

The Country Mouse

Vegetable Spread

This is just like eating peanuts—you can't stop eating this. And with a food processor, it's so easy to make.

1 tablespoon plain gelatin
¼ cup cold water
¼ cup boiling water
1 cup mayonnaise
½ teaspoon salt
1 large tomato, chopped
½ cup finely chopped celery
1 small onion, chopped fine
1 large carrot, grated
½ cucumber, peeled, chopped and drained
½ bell pepper, chopped, and drained

Dissolve gelatin in cold water; add hot water and allow to cool. Mix with mayonnaise and salt. Add vegetables. Refrigerate overnight.

Spread on rounds of bread for party sandwiches, and garnish with a tiny sprig of parsley. Serve as a mold with crackers, or stuff in a juicy red summer tomato as a salad. Makes 4 cups.

The Alabama Heritage Cookbook

Spinach in a Bread Bowl

A classic . . . it never fails to be a hit.

1 cup mayonnaise
1 cup sour cream
1 envelope dry vegetable
  soup mix
2 tablespoons fresh minced
  onion
1 (10-ounce) package
  frozen chopped spinach,
  thawed and drained
1 (5-ounce) can water
  chestnuts, chopped
2 loaves round crusty
  bread

Combine all ingredients except bread. Cut circle in top of one loaf of bread; hollow it out. Put filling inside bread. Cut remaining loaf into cubes. Serve with small knife to spread filling on cubes.

Sunny Side Up

Editor's Extra: The variations on this popular bread bowl recipe are endless. Try adding grated Cheddar or Swiss cheese, a little Dijon, Tabasco, some slivered almonds . . . also offer other dippers such as celery and carrot sticks, crackers or Frito scoops. And use different kinds of bread bowls: Hawaiian, French, sour dough, rye. . . . You could use Miracle Whip for the mayo, too. Great, pretty green dip!

Vegetable Sandwiches

Cool and refreshing.

3 carrots, scraped
1 cucumber, peeled
1 onion
1 bell pepper, seeded
1/4 teaspoon salt
1 (3-ounce) package cream
  cheese, softened
1/2 cup mayonnaise
1 loaf sandwich bread,
  crusts removed

Grind vegetables (or process) and put in strainer. Press out all the juices. Mix vegetables with softened cream cheese and mayonnaise. Will spread one loaf of sandwich bread. Will keep in refrigerator for 5–6 days. Mellows with age.

Head Table Cooks

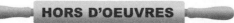

Cucumber Sandwiches

A really cool party sandwich.

1 large cucumber
1 (8-ounce) package cream
  cheese, softened
¹/₂ cup mayonnaise
1 tablespoon fresh lemon
  juice
3 small green onions and
  tops, finely chopped
Tabasco sauce to taste
Garlic salt to taste
Seasoned pepper to taste

Peel, seed, and coarsely grate cucumber. Wring out excess cucumber juice in clean towel (or paper towels). Cream cheese with mayonnaise and lemon juice. Add cucumber, onions, and seasonings to taste. Serve on party rye slices. Also good as a dip. Keep refrigerated.

Prairie Harvest

Cheese Straws

¹/₄ pound butter, softened
¹/₂ pound sharp Cheddar
  cheese, grated, softened
1¹/₂ cups all-purpose flour
1 teaspoon salt
¹/₂ teaspoon red pepper
1 egg, beaten
Pecans (optional)

Mix well all ingredients except egg and pecans, and roll into 1¹/₂-inch roll (about the size of a half-dollar). Refrigerate.

Slice in ¹/₄-inch sections. Brush each slice with beaten egg and place pecan half on top, if desired. Also, may be shaped over a stuffed olive and rolled into balls. Bake at 350° for 10–12 minutes and serve warm.

Seasons of Thyme

My mother-in-law, Frances, made incredibly delicious crispy cheese straws—they were a work of art. She laid them out in ribbons, perfectly fanned out one on top of another in a tin that we could not wait to open. Her secret was adding a little dry mustard and a shake or two of Tabasco, then baking them in a slow oven (275°) for 50 minutes. My son still makes them this way . . . that's what PRESERVING AMERICA'S FOOD HERITAGE is all about.   —*Barbara*

Sweet Potato and Peanut Chips

Nice appetizer . . . or accompaniment to ribs or chicken.

$^1\!/_2$ **cup honey roasted peanuts**

2 large sweet potatoes, peeled

$^1\!/_2$ **cup unsalted butter, melted**

Salt to taste

Preheat oven to 475°. Line 2 large baking sheets with foil. Lightly butter the foil. Process the peanuts in a food processor fitted with steel blade until finely chopped, but not powdered. Transfer to a bowl. Slice potatoes to $^1\!/_8$-inch thickness, and dip in melted butter to coat both sides. Arrange slices on baking sheets. Sprinkle top with peanuts. Bake chips until the tops are lightly browned and potatoes are tender (15–20 minutes). Watch carefully to prevent burning. Transfer to paper towels and drain. Let cool 5 minutes. Salt to taste. Yields 4 dozen.

The Enlightened Titan

Potato Skins

4 (2- to 2$^1\!/_2$-pound) russet potatoes, baked

$^1\!/_2$ **cup butter or margarine, melted**

1 small clove garlic, minced

$^1\!/_8$ **teaspoon paprika**

Salt and pepper to taste

6 ounces Swiss cheese, sliced $^1\!/_8$ inch thick

Chopped chives

Preheat oven to 450°. Quarter potatoes lengthwise. Carefully scoop pulp from skins, leaving $^3\!/_8$- to $^1\!/_2$-inch-thick shell. Reserve pulp for other use.

Combine butter, garlic, paprika, salt and pepper. Brush over inside of skins. Place skins on cookie sheet. Bake at 450° for 10 minutes or until crisp. Remove from oven. Top each with a slice of cheese and sprinkle with chives. Bake 2–3 minutes longer or until cheese melts. Yields 16 servings.

Per Serving: Cal 121; Pro 4g; Fat 6g; Chol 18mg; Fiber 1.2g.
Percent of Calories: Prot 14%; Carb 43%; Fat 43%.

Palmetto Evenings

Editor's Extra: Use other kinds of cheese for variety. We like Pepper Jack. And bacon bits, too!

Spinach Cheese Squares

4 tablespoons butter

3 eggs

1 cup flour

1 cup milk

1 teaspoon salt

1 teaspoon baking powder

1 medium onion, grated

1 pound sharp cheese, grated

2 packages chopped, frozen spinach, thawed and well drained

Preheat oven to 350°. Melt butter in 9x13x2-inch pan in oven; remove. In mixing bowl, beat eggs, flour, milk, salt, and baking powder; mix well. Add onion, grated cheese, and drained spinach. (If you further chop the spinach in a food processor, it makes a better texture.) Pour into pan; bake for 35 minutes. Cool thoroughly; cut into squares. This freezes well.

The Bonneville House Presents

Growing zucchini in your garden means you will have a handy vegetable that is extremely versatile. It can make appetizers, breads, all kinds of vegetable dishes, and even cakes. The leaves are so big (the size of this page), that I often miss one hiding under a leaf. Last year one of my grandkids came running in the house all excited: "Gran, come quick! We've got a watermelon in the squash patch!"

—*Barbara*

Zucchini Bites

4 small zucchini, unpeeled and grated (about 3 cups)

1 cup biscuit mix

$\frac{1}{2}$ cup finely chopped onion

$\frac{1}{4}$ cup Parmesan cheese

1 tablespoon dry parsley flakes

$\frac{1}{2}$ teaspoon seasoned salt

$\frac{1}{2}$ teaspoon oregano

$\frac{1}{4}$ cup vegetable oil

4 eggs, slightly beaten

1 cup sour cream

Combine all ingredients. Pour into greased 9x13x2-inch pan. Bake at 350° for 30 minutes or until golden brown. Cut in 1-inch squares. Yields 4 dozen.

The Market Place

BLT Bites

Talk about impressive!

16–20 cherry tomatoes

1 pound bacon, cooked and crumbled

¹/₂ cup mayonnaise or salad dressing

¹/₃ cup chopped green onions

3 tablespoons grated Parmesan cheese

2 tablespoons snipped fresh parsley

Cut a thin slice off each tomato top. Scoop out and discard pulp. Invert tomatoes on a paper towel to drain.

In a small bowl, combine all remaining ingredients; mix well. Spoon into tomatoes. Refrigerate for several hours. Yields 16–20 appetizers.

Dutch Pantry Cookin' Volume II

Editor's Extra: A fun way to serve these is to lightly steam an artichoke, cool, put on a pretty plate, then place the BLT Bites between the spiky leaves.

Bacon Roll-Ups

¹/₄ cup butter

¹/₂ cup water

1¹/₂ cups herb-seasoned stuffing

1 egg, slightly beaten

¹/₄ pound hot pork sausage

²/₃ pound sliced bacon

Melt butter in water. Remove from heat; stir in stuffing, then egg and sausage. Blend thoroughly. Chill for an hour.

Shape into small balls. Cut bacon strips into thirds crosswise. Wrap bacon around dressing mixture and fasten with toothpick. Place on rack in shallow pan and bake at 375° for 35 minutes or until brown and crisp. Drain on paper towels and serve hot. May be made ahead of time and frozen before baking. Yields 36 appetizers.

The Hors D'Oeuvre Tray

Sweet and Sour Sausage

1 cup sugar
4 tablespoons cornstarch
4 tablespoons soy sauce
$^2/_3$ cup vinegar
$1^1/_3$ cups water
2 bell peppers, cut in pieces
1 (20-ounce) can pineapple
   chunks, drained
$2^1/_2$ pounds link sausage,
   cut into bite-size pieces,
   cooked and drained

Mix all ingredients except peppers, pineapple, and sausage in a large skillet. Cook over low heat until thick. Add bell peppers and continue to cook on low. Add pineapple chunks and sausage, and heat thoroughly. Serve hot in a chafing dish with party picks. Serves 12.

Southern Generations

Sausage Balls with Jezebel Sauce

A favorite that is exceptionally easy.

1 pound hot bulk sausage
1 (8-ounce) package extra
   sharp Cheddar cheese,
   shredded
2 cups biscuit mix

Mix sausage and cheese together. Thoroughly knead biscuit mix into sausage and cheese. Shape into small balls the size of a big marble. Bake in preheated 350° oven for 20 minutes. Serve with or without Jezebel sauce. Makes 80–90 balls.

JEZEBEL SAUCE:
1 (12-ounce) jar pineapple
   preserves
1 (12-ounce) jar apple jelly
1 (5-ounce) jar prepared
   horseradish
3 tablespoons dry mustard
1 teaspoon black pepper

Mix Jezebel Sauce ingredients. Store in refrigerator. Will keep indefinitely.

Hors D'Oeuvres Everybody Loves II

Sweet and Sour Meatballs

1 pound ground beef
1 egg, beaten
¼ cup finely chopped
  onion
1¼ cups bread crumbs
1 teaspoon pepper
1 tablespoon parsley flakes
1 (16-ounce) jar apricot
  preserves
¾ cup hot barbecue sauce

Mix together beef, egg, onion, bread crumbs, pepper and parsley; form into bite-size meatballs. Brown in large skillet. Drain and place in baking dish.

Mix apricot preserves and barbecue sauce; pour over meatballs. Bake at 350°, uncovered, for 30 minutes. Serve hot in chafing dish.

Cookin' Along the Cotton Belt

Editor's Extra: Crushed cornflakes sub well for the bread crumbs. We sometimes add a little garlic salt, too.

Tasty Chicken Wings

These fly away in a hurry!

3 pounds chicken wings
Salt and pepper to taste
½ teaspoon paprika
½ cup honey
¼ cup soy sauce
4 tablespoons brown sugar
1 clove garlic, crushed
¼ cup catsup

Place cleaned, disjointed wings in foil-lined 9x13-inch pan. Sprinkle with salt, pepper, and paprika. Combine honey, soy sauce, brown sugar, garlic, and catsup. Pour over wings and bake uncovered, turning and basting every 15 minutes with sauce. Bake at 400° for one hour. Serves 10–12.

The Crowning Recipes of Kentucky

Sesame Chicken Nuggets

Disappearing-ly delicious!

NUGGETS:
1 egg, slightly beaten
¹/₂ cup water
³/₄ teaspoon salt
¹/₄ cup sesame seeds
¹/₂ cup flour
3 whole chicken breasts, skinned, boned, and cut into 1-inch pieces
Vegetable oil for frying

Mix egg, water, salt, sesame seeds, and flour to make a batter; stir in chicken pieces. Heat oil to medium. Carefully add chicken pieces, one layer at a time, frying until golden, about 3–5 minutes on each side. Drain on paper towels. Serve hot with toothpicks for dipping. Yields approximately 50 nuggets.

Note: Nuggets may be frozen after frying. Thaw and reheat on a cookie sheet at 375° for about 10 minutes.

SAUCE PIQUANT:
¹/₂ cup apricot-pineapple preserves
2 tablespoons prepared mustard
2 tablespoons horseradish

Mix sauce ingredients in a small saucepan and cook for 3 minutes. Serve warm. Yields ³/₄ cup.

Out of This World

French Fried Dill Pickles

Dill pickles
¹/₂ cup flour
¹/₄ cup beer
1 tablespoon cayenne pepper
1 tablespoon paprika
1 tablespoon black pepper
1 teaspoon salt
2 teaspoons garlic salt
3 dashes Tabasco

Cut dill pickles in slices as thick as a silver dollar. Mix the rest of the ingredients together. Dip pickle slices in batter and quick-fry at 375° in grease until the pickle slices float to the top, or about 4 minutes.

A Man's Taste

Boiled Peanuts

A soft southern favorite.

**2 pounds fresh raw
peanuts in shells
(available in many
supermarkets in the fall)**

**3 tablespoons salt, or to
taste**

At many crossroads in
the South, you will find
a "peanut man" selling
boiled peanuts out of
his truck along the
highway. Because the
peanuts are so juicy,
they are usually
enjoyed outdoors.
Some people take them
to football games.
Indoors on newspaper
is nice, too . . . have
paper towels handy.

Wash peanuts well. Place them in a huge cast-iron pot, or the biggest pot you have. Pour in enough water to almost fill the pot. Add salt and stir. Cover and cook over high heat. Bring to a rolling boil. Reduce heat only enough to prevent water from boiling over. Add water as needed to keep peanuts under water. When adding water, increase heat to high until peanuts are boiling again. Boil for $3^{1}/_{2}$–4 hours.

Test to see if they are done by spooning out a peanut, cooling briefly, opening the shell and biting into it. Boiled peanuts should be soft, not crunchy or hard. Drain and cool slightly before serving. Store in plastic bags in refrigerator or freezer.

Barbara Moseley

Editor's Extra: A variation is to add crab boil to the water for a spicier flavor.

Trash the Party Mix

Southerners call snack mix "trash." This is make-do easy. The seasoning is perfect!

1 stick margarine

2 tablespoons lemon juice

1½ tablespoons seasoned salt

1 teaspoon onion salt

2 teaspoons garlic powder

2½ tablespoons Worcestershire sauce

2 cups broken pretzel sticks

2 (12-ounce) cans mixed nuts

12 cups crispy cereal*

Mix first 6 ingredients in saucepan while heating oven to 250°. Mix pretzels, nuts, and cereal in an 11x15x2-inch baking pan. Pour hot mixture over and stir gently to distribute. Bake 45 minutes, stirring twice during baking. Cool, then store in airtight containers.

Note: Everybody I know loves trash, and most recipes call for things you have to make a special trip to the grocery store to get. So this gives you some interesting options that you can be very creative with. If you don't have a can of mixed nuts, use shelled pecans or roasted peanuts . . . I sometimes throw in the honey roasted variety. The cereal* is best with a mixture. My latest batch had 8 cups Crispix, 2 cups Waffle Crisp, and 2 cups Cocoa Puffs—because this is what my grandkids like and I had on hand. I have used Corn Chex, Golden Grahams, Cheerios, Honey Combs . . . you name it. I don't recommend fruity or flaky cereals or tiny ones like Rice Krispies, and best to use no more than ½ sugared cereal. But anything goes as long as it's crispy. Wow, this is good!

Gwen McKee

Rise and Shine

Bread & Breakfast

Bread is like dresses, hats and shoes—in other words, essential!

—Emily Post

Buttermilk Biscuits

Every recipe you have ever read will tell you to serve biscuits wrapped in a napkin or such and then put in a basket. I'll tell you a little secret: Reach in that oven, take the pan out and put a biscuit on everybody's plate and stick the rest back in the oven. 'Course you know to turn that sucker off! When everybody has lapped up that biscuit, go get 'em another one.

Biscuits are good with anything, anytime, but if you want a real treat, set that bucket of molasses and the peanut butter jar on the table. Let each one mix up about half and half of syrup and peanut butter. Talk about good! After you have made these biscuits a time or two, you'll sure chunk rocks at canned biscuits.

2 cups self-rising flour
Pinch of soda
3 tablespoons oil
¾ cup buttermilk

Mix all this together. Dough should be soft and sticky. Scrape out on a floured board. Now get your hands covered in flour and knead all that mess around and over till you have a dough that is not sticky. Pat out till it's about a ½ inch thick. (This is more or less, just depends on how thick you like biscuits.)

Cut the biscuits out with a biscuit cutter. Now you can buy a nice biscuit cutter or use an old cookie cutter, or a water glass. I use a little canned milk can that has had one end melted off so it leaves a nice-slice cuttin' surface, and some holes punched in the other end to let air out. After you cut the biscuits out, get a glass pie pan or a cake pan or a cookie sheet or whatever. Don't make much difference as long as the oil won't run off the edges, cause I want you to pour enough oil in the pan to cover the bottom, and then take them biscuits and sop the top in oil; turn it over on its bottom and set it down.

Cook 'em about 20 minutes in an oven that is close to 375°. Now keep watchin' 'em cause when they get the shade of brown you like, they'll be done.

Sunday Go to Eatin' Cook Book

Editor's Extra: You can bake these delicious biscuits a little quicker at 400°. Great biscuits!

Sweet Potato Biscuits

So flavorful, you don't need to butter them.

1 egg, slightly beaten
1 cup cooked, mashed
    sweet potatoes
$^1/_4$–$^1/_2$ cup sugar
2 tablespoons butter or
    margarine, softened
3 tablespoons shortening
2 cups self-rising flour
    (approximately)

Combine egg, sweet potatoes, sugar, butter, and shortening in a mixing bowl; mix well. Stir in enough flour to make a soft dough. (Dough will be softer than regular biscuit dough.) Turn out on floured surface; knead lightly a few times. Roll to $^1/_4$-inch thickness. Cut with a 2-inch biscuit cutter. Place on ungreased baking sheet and bake at 350° for about 15 minutes. Yields about 16 (2-inch) biscuits.

Hors D'Oeuvres Everybody Loves II

Derby Breakfast Yeast Biscuits

1 package yeast (or cake)
1 cup warm buttermilk
$^1/_2$ teaspoon baking soda
1 teaspoon salt
2 tablespoons sugar
$2^1/_2$ cups self-rising flour
$^1/_2$ cup shortening
4 tablespoons melted
    butter

Dissolve yeast in warm buttermilk; set aside. Sift soda, salt, sugar, and flour in a bowl; cut in shortening. Add yeast mixture. Stir until blended. Knead and roll $^1/_2$ inch thick. Cut biscuits and dip in melted butter. Place on greased pan. Let rise one hour. Bake at 400° for 12 minutes.

Kentucky Kitchens

Mayonnaise Biscuits

**2 cups self-rising flour,
   sifted**
1 cup milk
2 tablespoons mayonnaise

Grease a 12-tin muffin pan. Mix well the flour, milk, and mayonnaise. Spoon evenly into muffin tins. Bake at 425° for 18–20 minutes or until done.

Gwen McKee

Country Fried Ham Biscuits
with Red-Eye Gravy

If you can sit down to eat this breakfast, fill your plate with leftover biscuits and hot gravy—delicious!

**3 slices country ham,
   ¹/₄ inch thick**
¹/₄ cup coffee (or water)
¹/₄ teaspoon sugar
6 large biscuits, cooked

Fry ham on each side in greased heavy skillet (iron). Remove ham from skillet. Stir in coffee and sugar. (Scrape bottom of skillet to release ham flavor.) Put ham back in gravy. Simmer till hot. Split biscuits open on plate. Put ham in them and 1–2 teaspoons gravy each. Serves 6.

Betty Talmadge's Lovejoy Plantation Cookbook

I loved to watch my grandmother make biscuits in the big wooden dough bowl shaped like a canoe. Her hands worked the dough so fast and lightly, and when she pinched off some dough and patted it in her hands, it magically became a perfect biscuit. Though I have mastered the taste, I never learned to make mine look like hers—in fact, mine sometimes look more like turtles with warts. Of course, once the gravy goes on top, it really doesn't matter what they look like.   *—Barbara*

Edinburg Mill Restaurant's Sausage Gravy

. Bring on the biscuits!

1 pound mild sausage

4 tablespoons finely chopped onion

2 tablespoons sugar

1 teaspoon salt

¹/₂ teaspoon pepper

2 tablespoons Worcestershire sauce

¹/₄ cup plain flour

¹/₂ cup water

¹/₂ cup milk

Dash of Kitchen Bouquet

Brown sausage in a skillet, adding one tablespoon at a time to prevent sticking. When sausage is browned, add onion, sugar, salt, pepper, and Worcestershire sauce, and simmer for 2 minutes. Add flour, sprinkling evenly on top of sausage. Add water and milk gradually until the right consistency is achieved. Add a dash of Kitchen Bouquet for color. Simmer for 10–15 minutes. Serves 6–8.

Virginia's Historic Restaurants and Their Recipes

Saw Mill Gravy

This gravy gets its name from the saw mill camps that were in the Smoky Mountain area years ago. Saw mill gravy was also made from bacon the same way as from sausage in the camps. Gravy was always served for breakfast and sometimes other meals.

1 pound bulk sausage

2 tablespoons flour or more (depends on how much you want to make)

Milk

Salt and pepper to taste

Make sausage into patties and fry in moderately hot skillet until brown and cooked done. Put sausage patties on paper towels to drain grease. Use about ¹/₂ of the grease in skillet to make gravy. Brown flour in grease, stirring constantly. Add about 1¹/₂ cups milk and enough water to make gravy as thin as you like. Break up about 2 of the cooked sausage patties and crumble in the gravy, if desired. Salt and pepper to taste. Serve over hot biscuits.

Gatlinburg Recipe Collection

Tomato Gravy

A southern favorite; especially good on a cold night with hot biscuits.

Southerners will smother anything in gravy. But it has to be good, tasty gravy. Good drippings and seasoning, and getting the right smooth consistency are equally important, and it takes a little practice.

I remember going to church with Mama one Sunday when she had put a roast in the oven that would be ready when we got home. So Papa volunteered to make the gravy—after all, he had seen her do it so often, it couldn't be very difficult. Well, she didn't tell him how much flour to stir into the drippings, and when he used cups instead of spoons, he ended up with a very thick goo. So he watered it down, and when it was too thin, he added more flour . . . and on and on. When we got home, he had a huge pot of very white "gravy" . . . that not even the dogs would eat.

—*Barbara*

1 pound bacon or salt pork, cooked crisp
¼ cup bacon drippings
1 medium onion, finely chopped
¼ cup flour
1 cup water
2 (14½-ounce) cans diced tomatoes
Salt to taste
½ teaspoon black pepper
2 teaspoons sugar

Fry bacon in cast-iron skillet, and save drippings; set bacon aside. In same skillet, sauté onion until translucent, then remove from skillet. Add ¼ cup flour to drippings and brown, stirring constantly. Immediately add onion, water, and tomatoes (I like to whirl tomatoes in food processor a time or two) and stir. Add seasonings and simmer for about 15 minutes. Serve with hot biscuits and bacon on the side. If desired, bacon can be crumbled into gravy.

Note: If using salt pork rather than bacon, you might want to leave out the salt. Also, one can of Ro-Tel tomatoes to replace one can diced tomatoes gives an extra zip to this treat—but leave out the black pepper.

Barbara Moseley

Southern Popovers

1½ cups all-purpose flour
1½ cups milk
3 eggs, slightly beaten
½ teaspoon salt

Combine all ingredients in blender and blend until smooth. Place well-buttered muffin tins in oven at 450° for 3 minutes or until a drop of water sizzles when dropped in them. Remove tins from oven; fill ⅔ full with batter. Bake at 450° for 30 minutes; reduce heat to 300° and bake an additional 10–15 minutes. Serve immediately. Yields one dozen.

A Taste of South Carolina

Monkey Bread

Light pick-off dinner rolls you will make again and again.

1 envelope yeast
¾ cup warm water
2½ cups biscuit mix
Dash of salt
5 tablespoons sugar
1 stick margarine, melted

Dissolve yeast in warm water and stir slightly to mix. Combine other ingredients except margarine; mix with yeast. Knead 1 minute on surface sprinkled with extra biscuit mix. Roll out dough to about about ½-inch thickness. Grease Bundt pan with melted margarine. Cut dough into irregular pieces, dipping each piece into margarine, and lay in pan—about 3 layers. Let rise in warm place 1 hour. Bake in preheated 400° oven for about 25 minutes. Turn over on a plate and pick off rolls.

Any Time's a Party!

Granny's Best Dinner Rolls

Real light with a soft texture—old-fashioned goodness made so easy with instant potatoes and no kneading. Homemade rolls will give your guests double pleasure—the aroma while baking and the delicious taste. As my grandchildren hit the door, I hear them say—mmmmm, it smells like Granny's kitchen.

2 cups milk
$^1/_2$ cup margarine
$^1/_2$ cup sugar
$^1/_4$ cup instant potato flakes
1 tablespoon salt
2 packages dry yeast (2 tablespoons)
$^1/_2$ cup lukewarm water
2 teaspoons sugar (to feed yeast)
2 eggs, beaten
$5^1/_2$–6 cups all-purpose flour, divided

Scald milk; add margarine, $^1/_2$ cup sugar, potato flakes, and salt. Cool to lukewarm. Soften yeast in lukewarm water with 2 teaspoons sugar; let sit until foamy, about 8 minutes. Add yeast to milk mixture with eggs and 3 cups flour. Beat with electric mixer until smooth and light (about 5 minutes).

Stir in enough flour to make a soft dough, just until dough leaves side of bowl. (Do not get too stiff; dough will be sticky, but will stiffen in refrigerator.) Cover and let rise about 30 minutes. Punch down and refrigerate until cold, or overnight.

When needed, shape into rolls as desired. (I make mine Parker House style.) Place into greased pans; let rise until double in bulk (about $1^1/_2$ hours). Bake at 400° for 15 minutes or until golden brown. Brush tops with melted butter or margarine as removed from oven (to give a pretty "glow"). Serve hot. Makes 4–5 dozen delicious rolls.

Variation: To make Whole-Wheat Dinner Rolls, substitute brown sugar for sugar and half whole wheat flour for half of the all-purpose flour.

Tip: I bake extra rolls, cool and roll in foil. Freeze. When ready to serve, I heat them in a 325° oven (leave in foil) for about 15 minutes (longer if rolls are still frozen). They taste like fresh baked rolls. Great to have in the freezer.

Holiday Treats

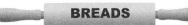

In-A-Hurry Rolls

Delicious homemade yeast rolls in less than an hour.

1¼ cups milk
2½ tablespoons sugar
1½ teaspoons salt
¼ cup shortening
¼ cup warm water
2 envelopes yeast
3¼ cups sifted flour

Scald milk. Stir in sugar, salt, and shortening. Cool to lukewarm. Place warm water in large mixing bowl and add yeast. Stir until dissolved. Add lukewarm milk mixture and flour. Stir only to mix flour well. Fill well-greased muffin pans half full. Cover and let rise in warm place until doubled in bulk—about 35–45 minutes. Bake in 425° oven till brown—about 15 minutes. Serve immediately. Makes 18.

Any Time's a Party!

Tangy Butter Fingers

Great with meals, or eat 'em like snacks.

2 cups buttermilk biscuit
  mix
1 egg
½ cup whole milk
½ cup margarine
1 teaspoon minced onion
1 teaspoon garlic powder
1 teaspoon parsley flakes
½ teaspoon celery seed
½ teaspoon sesame seed
1 teaspoon paprika

Combine biscuit mix, egg, and milk; beat vigorously. Turn out onto a lightly floured board; knead lightly. Roll out in 1 (12x8-inch) rectangle; cut with a floured knife; into 4x1-inch fingers. Melt margarine in jellyroll pan. Lay fingers in melted margarine, turning once to coat. Sprinkle a mixture of onion, garlic powder, parsley flakes, celery seed, sesame seed, and paprika over top of fingers. Bake at 450° for about 12 minutes or until brown. Yields 2 dozen fingers.

Mountain Laurel Encore

Short'nin Bread

Most folks have heard of this but never eaten it. It is simple but delicious with tea or coffee. More like a cookie than a bread, Mammy's little baby loves it!

1 cup light brown sugar
4 cups flour
1 pound butter, softened

Combine sugar and flour. Add butter and mix well. Place on floured board and pat to thickness of ½ inch. Cut into shapes as desired and bake in a moderate (325°-350°) oven for 25 minutes.

Kum' Ona' Granny's Table

Mississippi Hush Puppies

So good with fried Mississippi catfish.

It is generally thought that hush puppies originated in Florida around 1918 from southerners on hunting or fishing trips frying their catch over a campfire. They made little cakes with the cornmeal used for frying, and combined it with some milk or water, then fried it with the fish. What was leftover, they threw to the yelping dogs, crying, "Hush, puppies!" These little cakes have become a staple with fried fish, and they are still made with leftover cornmeal.

1 cup self-rising cornmeal mix
½ cup self-rising flour
1 large egg
½ cup milk
½ cup diced onion
½ cup chopped bell pepper
1 jalapeño, seeds removed, chopped

Mix cornmeal and flour in large bowl. Make a well in the center of mixture. Combine egg and remaining ingredients; mix well. Add egg mixture to dry mixture, and stir until moistened. Heat oil in large pot to 375°. Drop batter by rounded tablespoonfuls into hot oil and fry in batches, 2 minutes on each side until golden brown. Drain on paper towels; serve hot.

Tasteful Treasures

Squash Puppies

We grow squash every year in our garden. I look forward to my squash coming in so I can make yummy dishes like squash puppies. Everybody loves these.
—*Barbara*

5 medium yellow squash
1 egg, beaten
¹/₂ cup buttermilk
1 onion, chopped
³/₄ cup self-rising cornmeal
¹/₄ cup all-purpose flour

Slice squash and cook until tender. Drain squash and mash. Combine squash and remaining ingredients. Drop mixture by tablespoon into hot oil. Fry 5 minutes or until golden brown. Makes about 2¹/₂ dozen puppies.

Third Wednesday Homemakers Volume II

Editor's Extra: A dash or two of Tabasco adds a nice zip to both of these recipes.

Corn Fritters

1 cup sifted flour
1 teaspoon baking powder
¹/₂ teaspoon salt
4 tablespoons sugar
1 egg
5 tablespoons milk
1 tablespoon melted fat
**1²/₃ cups fresh cut corn, or
  1 can whole-kernel corn,
  drained**

Sift dry ingredients together; add beaten egg to milk and melted fat; mix with dry ingredients. Beat until smooth, and stir in corn. Drop by tablespoon into hot fat, 375°–385°; fry until golden brown. Makes 24 fritters.

Treasured Tastes

Bacon Spoon Bread

This hearty main dish soufflé makes a simple supper with a salad and fruit—also good for a breakfast party.

¾ cup cornmeal
1½ cups cold water
2 cups shredded sharp
    Cheddar cheese
¼ cup soft butter or
    margarine
2 cloves garlic, crushed
½ teaspoon salt
1 cup milk
4 egg yolks, well beaten
½ pound bacon, crisp-
    cooked and drained
4 egg whites, stiffly beaten

Combine cornmeal and water in large saucepan; cook, stirring constantly, until the consistency of mush. Remove from heat; add cheese, butter, garlic, and salt. Stir to melt cheese. Gradually add milk. Stir in egg yolks. Crumble bacon, reserving some for garnish, if desired, and add to cornmeal mixture. Fold in egg whites. Pour into greased 2-quart soufflé dish or casserole.

Spoon into warm dishes; top with butter and serve with a spoon. Serves 6.

Feasts of Eden

Southern Spoon Bread

This is soft; though cutable, it is served with a spoon.

1 (8½-ounce) box corn
    muffin mix
1 cup sour cream
2 eggs, beaten
1 stick butter, melted
1 cup milk

Mix all ingredients and bake in a 7x11-inch or larger pan at 350° for 45 minutes or until golden brown. Cut into squares and serve hot.

Heather Creel

Mamean's Buttermilk Corn Bread

Whether served with field peas or turnip greens or just by itself, Mamean's corn bread is always a hit!

1 egg
1¼ cups buttermilk
1⅔ cups cornmeal mix
(with Hot Rise)
4 tablespoons oil, divided

Preheat oven to 415°. Beat egg; add buttermilk and mix thoroughly. Add cornmeal mix and 2 tablespoons oil; mix well. Put remaining 2 tablespoons oil in a 12-inch black skillet and heat until oil is hot. Bake at 415° for 12–15 minutes, then turn oven up to 425° and bake until top is brown, about 5–10 minutes.

Barbara Moseley

Light Corn Bread

A perfect thin and tasty corn bread.

When Barney and I return from a trip, we both crave a home-cooked southern meal. On one such occasion, the greens were almost done when I reached for my egg carton— and it was empty! Well, we simply don't do greens without corn bread! So I used a heaping tablespoon of mayonnaise instead— worked just fine . . . a tad flatter, but the crustiness was a good trade-off. We call this "make-do."

—*Gwen*

1 tablespoon plus ¼ cup
canola oil
½ cup skim milk
1 egg
⅔ cup yellow self-rising
corn meal
1 tablespoon flour
½ tablespoon sugar

Preheat oven to 450°. Heat 1 tablespoon oil in 8-inch black skillet. Mix remaining ingredients by hand (batter will be thin.) Pour into hot oil and bake 12–15 minutes. Serves 2–3. (If doubled, bake in 12-inch skillet.)

Note: Sometimes I use 1 egg white or 2 tablespoons egg substitute for the egg. Just as good! This recipe makes 7 crispy corn sticks (1 pan).

Gwen McKee

Augusta's Best Strawberry Bread

3 cups all-purpose flour
2 cups sugar
1 teaspoon baking soda
1 teaspoon salt
1 teaspoon cinnamon
4 eggs, beaten
1¼ cups vegetable oil
2 (10-ounce) packages
  frozen strawberries,
  thawed and chopped
1 cup chopped pecans

Sift flour, sugar, baking soda, salt, and cinnamon into large mixing bowl. Make well in center. Combine eggs, oil, strawberries, and pecans. Add to sifted ingredients, stirring until well combined. Spoon batter into 2 greased and floured 9x5-inch loaf pans. Bake at 350° for one hour. Cool bread in pans 10 minutes. Remove bread from pans. Cool completely on wire racks. Yields 2 loaves.

Second Round, Tea Time at the Masters©

Banana Bread

The easiest of all banana breads. You don't need to beat the eggs, nor add ingredients in any particular order. Just toss it all together, stir to mix, and bake.

Freeze excess ripe bananas by peeling, cutting in chunks, and wrapping well. Ready to use in smoothies. Thawed, they are ready to use in recipes that call for mashed bananas.

Also, if you don't have a fresh orange available, substitute ½ cup orange juice and 1 teaspoon dried orange peel.

2 cups flour
1 cup sugar
½ cup shortening
2 eggs
Juice and grated rind of
  1 orange
4 large bananas, mashed
½ cup chopped black
  walnuts (or pecans)
1 teaspoon baking soda
½ teaspoon salt

Mix all ingredients and bake in greased and floured loaf pan for 1 hour at 350°.

Maurice's Tropical Fruit Cook Book

Beignets

So good with Café au Lait (see page 17).

2 cups flour
¹/₂ teaspoon salt
1 teaspoon baking powder
2 eggs, separated
²/₃ cup milk
Oil, enough to deep fry
¹/₂ cup powdered sugar or
    cinnamon-sugar

Sift dry ingredients into a bowl. Add egg yolks to milk; mix well and add to dry ingredients. Beat egg whites until stiff and fold into batter. Heat oil until HOT. Drop by spoonfuls into deep fat. Beignets will float and pop over. Remove when light brown. Sprinkle with powdered sugar or cinnamon sugar.

Variation: Banana Pop-Overs: Dip 1 piece of banana into batter and drop into hot oil.

Cajun Cookin': Memories, Photos, History, Recipes

Skillet Popover

Delight your family with this fancy giant-size popover for breakfast. I serve it with a light sprinkling of cinnamon sugar. You may choose syrup or warmed fruit preserves or lemon juice and powdered sugar. At any rate, it is sure to please. Be careful to follow the directions carefully and be certain to heat the frying pan.

¹/₄–¹/₂ cup butter
¹/₂ cup milk
¹/₂ cup all-purpose flour
2 eggs
Cinnamon-sugar

Place butter in a heavy iron 9-inch skillet. Place the pan in a preheated oven set at 475°. Mix the milk, flour, and eggs lightly to make a batter. After the butter has melted, tilt pan so that the entire surface will be coated with butter. Add batter and bake for 12 minutes. Remove from the oven and invert onto a large plate. Drizzle the butter in the pan over the popover. Sprinkle with cinnamon-sugar. Roll it over in loose jellyroll fashion. Slice and serve. Serves 2–4.

Taste Buds

Editor's Extra: Good with chopped apple mixed in, too.

Christmas Morning Rolls

Perfect to have ready for overnight guests.

Although Christmas morning is exciting and fun discovering what's under the tree, everybody gets hungry. These yummy rolls don't take anybody away from the action. It is always a delight to discover the transformation of these lovely risen rolls. And all they need is popping in the oven! This is the most requested Christmas morning dish in both the Moseley and McKee households.

1 cup chopped pecans
1 (18-ounce) package frozen rolls
¹/₂ cup brown sugar
1 stick margarine (or more)
Cinnamon to taste
1 small package butterscotch (or vanilla) pudding (not instant)

The night before serving, grease the bottom of a Bundt or solid-bottom tube pan. Cover bottom of pan with nuts. Place frozen rolls in pan. Combine sugar, margarine, and cinnamon in saucepan. Bring to a boil, then pour over rolls in pan. Sprinkle dry pudding mix over top. Leave on counter overnight to rise; don't cover. In the morning, bake at 350° for 30 minutes. Remove from oven and invert onto serving platter.

Feeding the Flock—MOPs of Westminister

This is how the rolls have risen when we discover them in the morning.

And this is how pretty they look when all that wonderful coating is now on top! Yummy!

Apple Pancakes
with Cinnamon Cream Syrup

These fabulous pancakes with syrup are a snap to make. We think you'll agree they are among the best you have ever eaten.

APPLE PANCAKES:

1 egg

1 tablespoon sugar

1 tablespoon butter, softened

1 medium apple, peeled, cored, and quartered

1 cup evaporated milk

1 cup packaged pancake mix

Place egg, sugar, butter, apple, and evaporated milk in blender. Cover; process at low speed several seconds or until apple is chopped. Add pancake mix. Cover; process at high speed several seconds, until blended. Pour by $1/4$ cupfuls onto preheated (400°) griddle or electric skillet. Cook until bubbles appear on top of cakes and underside is browned. Turn; brown on second side. (May transfer to electric hot tray for buffet service.) Serve hot with Cinnamon Cream Syrup. Yields 15–20 pancakes.

CINNAMON CREAM SYRUP:

1 cup light corn syrup

2 cups sugar

$1/2$ cup water

2 teaspoons ground cinnamon

1 cup evaporated milk

In medium saucepan combine corn syrup, sugar, water, and cinnamon. Bring to full boil over medium heat, stirring constantly. Boil 2 minutes, stirring constantly. Cool 5 minutes. Stir in evaporated milk. Serve warm over Apple Pancakes.

Note: May place ingredients in a large microwave-safe mixing bowl. Bring to boil on HIGH (5 minutes). Reduce power to MEDIUM; cook 2 minutes, stirring several times.

Perennials

The Best Hot Cakes I Ever Ate

1 cup oats

1¹/₂ cups buttermilk (or milk with 1¹/₂ teaspoons vinegar added)

¹/₄ cup brown sugar

2 eggs

¹/₄ cup margarine, melted

1 cup flour

1 teaspoon baking soda

1 teaspoon salt

Place oats in buttermilk; let stand 5–6 minutes. Stir in sugar. Beat eggs; add margarine and stir into oat mixture. Combine flour, baking soda, and salt; add to oat mixture all at once. Stir lightly until combined (will be lumpy like mashed potatoes). Fry on both sides on hot, greased, griddle.

Our Best Home Cooking

Apple-Filled Oven French Toast

An overnight sensation!

1 (12-ounce) loaf French bread

1 (21-ounce) can apple pie filling

8 eggs

2 cups milk

2 cups half-and-half

2 teaspoons vanilla extract

¹/₂ teaspoon nutmeg

¹/₂ teaspoon cinnamon

1 cup packed brown sugar

1 cup coarsely chopped pecans

¹/₂ cup butter, softened

2 tablespoons dark corn syrup

Slice bread into 1-inch slices. Arrange a single layer of bread slices in bottom of buttered 9x13-inch baking pan. Spread pie filling over bread. Top with another layer of bread slices.

Combine eggs, milk, half-and-half, vanilla, nutmeg, and cinnamon in a blender container and process until well mixed. Pour over top of bread. Refrigerate, covered, 8–10 hours or overnight.

Combine brown sugar, pecans, butter, and corn syrup in a bowl; mix well. Spread over top of bread mixture. Bake at 350° for 60 minutes or until puffed and golden brown. Yields 8–10 servings.

Everything but the Entrée

Sausage Coffee Cake

Definitely a five-star recipe!

1 pound bulk sausage
1/2 cup chopped onion
1/4 cup grated Parmesan
    cheese
1/2 cup grated Swiss cheese
1 egg, beaten
1/4 teaspoon Tabasco
1 1/2 teaspoons salt
2 tablespoons chopped
    parsley
2 cups Bisquick
3/4 cup milk
1/4 cup mayonnaise
1 egg yolk
1 tablespoon water

Brown sausage and onion; drain. Add next 6 ingredients. Make batter of Bisquick, milk, and mayonnaise. Spread half of batter in 9x9x2-inch greased pan. Pour in sausage mixture, then spread remaining batter on top. Mix egg yolk and water and brush top. Bake at 400° for 25–30 minutes or until cake leaves edge of pan. Cool 5 minutes before cutting into 3-inch squares. This recipe doubles easily in a 9x13-inch pan. Freezes well.

Louisiana Entertains

Sausage Grits

A true southern favorite.

1 pound bulk pork sausage
3 cups hot cooked grits
2 1/2 cups shredded
    Cheddar cheese
3 tablespoons butter
3 eggs, beaten
1 1/2 cups milk
Parsley (optional)
Pimento strips (optional)

Cook sausage until brown in heavy skillet; drain well. Spoon sausage into lightly greased 9x13-inch baking dish. Combine hot grits, cheese, and butter. Stir until cheese and butter are melted. Combine eggs and milk; stir into grits. Pour over sausage. Bake at 350° for 1 hour. Garnish with parsley and/or pimento strips, if desired. This can be made ahead and refrigerated overnight, then baked the next day.

CDA Angelic Treats

Plantation Casserole

This can be made the night before or right away.

2 cups croutons
1 cup shredded sharp cheese
4 eggs, slightly beaten
2 cups milk
1/2 teaspoon salt
1/2 teaspoon prepared mustard
1/2 teaspoon onion powder
Dash pepper
8 slices bacon, fried crisp and crumbled

Preheat oven to 325°. In bottom of greased 10x6-inch baking dish, combine croutons and cheese. Combine eggs, milk, salt, mustard, onion powder, and pepper. Mix until blended. Pour over crouton mixture. Sprinkle bacon on top. Bake 55–60 minutes until eggs are set. Serves 6.

Macon Sets a Fine Table

Ham and Eggs Breakfast

This is excellent to fix the night before for house guests.

8 slices white bread
2 or 3 slices ham, hickory smoked, 1/3 inch thick
Cheese, sliced
7 eggs
3 cups milk
1 1/2 teaspoons dry mustard
1 teaspoon salt
3 cups cornflakes
1/4 cup butter, melted

Trim crust from bread. Butter a 9x13-inch casserole. Lay 4 slices bread in dish. Place ham slices on top. Top with slices of cheese and more bread. Beat together eggs, milk, mustard, and salt. Pour over bread. Refrigerate overnight.

Preheat oven to 300°. Crush cornflakes and sprinkle over top of casserole. Drizzle with butter. Bake for 1 hour.

Giant Houseparty Cookbook

Editor's Extra: Other kinds of ham can be used, and I like to strip or cube it for easier distributing. And grated cheese (Cheddar or Swiss) works fine, too.

When I was a little girl, I would go out to the barnyard with Mama and gather the eggs in the bottom of my turned-up shirt. One day a cow wandered into the barnyard and began to chase us! Mama told me to run, then scooted me under the gate to get away from the cow . . . and I broke all my eggs! It was a gooey mess! I never forgave that cow.
—*Barbara*

Egg in a Nest

A good recipe kids love to make and eat.

Bread
Egg
Butter

Cut a circle from the center of a slice of bread. Butter both sides of slice and circle. Place both in frying pan on medium-high heat and drop a little butter in the hole so egg will not stick. Crack shell and very carefully place egg in the hole. Fry for a few minutes until egg begins to set. Carefully turn with a spatula and cook on the other side. The circle will also toast in the frying pan while the egg is cooking.

Look Mom, I Can Cook

A hen and a rooster strut their stuff on the Moseley farm. It's very early and the rooster has just done his crowing—now it's time to fluff and strut!

Light Southern Waffles

If you have more than four people to feed, you'd better get a second waffle iron, cause you can't make these fast enough. Great in-a-hurry meal any time at all.

1¼ cups self-rising flour
1 tablespoon sugar
1⅛ cups milk
⅜ cup vegetable oil
1 egg, separated

Heat waffle iron. Mix flour and sugar, then milk, oil, and egg yolk. Whip egg white till stiff, then fold in.

Scoop a ladle of batter onto preheated waffle iron and cook till done. Yields 4 waffles. Serve with butter and syrup.

Gwen McKee

Pop-in-Your-Mouth Pecan Muffins

So good, they don't need to be buttered or jellied or sauced—and that's saying something in the South.

¾ cup self-rising flour
1½ cups light brown sugar
¾ cup melted butter
2 teaspoons vanilla
1½ cups chopped pecans
3 eggs, beaten

Preheat oven to 350°. Grease non-stick muffin tins. Beat all ingredients well and spoon batter only half full into muffin tins. Bake 20–25 minutes or till browned on edges.

Fun to make in mini muffin tins. Fill full and bake about 15 minutes.

Gwen McKee

Soup's On!

Soups, Chowders, Bisques, Gumbos & Stews

*When the taste changes with every bite and the last bite tastes
as good as the first, that's Cajun.*

—Paul Prudhomme

Vegetable Soup

Serve with cornmeal muffins and salad for a wonderful winter lunch.

1 soup bone (with meat) or
  ³/₄ pound lean meat
¹/₄ stick butter
1 stalk celery, chopped
¹/₂ bell pepper, chopped
1 large onion, chopped
3¹/₂ cups tomatoes
2¹/₂ cups tomato sauce
1 (16-ounce) package
  frozen mixed vegetables
1 teaspoon parsley flakes
1 teaspoon oregano
2 teaspoons salt
1 teaspoon pepper
2¹/₂ quarts water

Brown soup bone and meat in butter in soup pot; remove and reserve soup bone and chop meat. Add celery, pepper, and onion, and cook until tender. Add tomatoes, tomato sauce, vegetables, soup bone, chopped meat, seasonings, and water, and simmer at least 4 hours. Remove soup bone, if used, and serve. Serves 8.

Best of Bayou Cuisine

Editor's Extra: Most southerners think a steaming bowl of vegetable soup will cure what ails you, and this one very well might. Outstanding.

Quick Onion Soup

¹/₈ pound butter (¹/₂ stick)
3 large onions, sliced thin
3 (10-ounce) cans beef
  consommé
¹/₄ cup red wine
1 cup grated Swiss or
  Parmesan cheese
1 cup croutons

Melt butter and sauté onions until clear. Add consommé and wine. Pour into oven casserole, sprinkle with cheese, and bake in a preheated 350° oven for 30 minutes. To brown the cheese, broil for a minute after cooking. Pass the croutons. Serves 4.

Cooking on the Go

Editor's Extra: Pour soup into individual ramekins and top each with cheese before broiling.

Hot Tomato Bouillon

1 (10¾-ounce) can condensed tomato soup

1 (14-ounce) can beef broth

⅓ teaspoon prepared horseradish (wet)

1 dash Tabasco sauce

1 cup water

1 tablespoon sherry (optional)

Dairy sour cream or unsweetened whipped cream

Simmer all but sherry and cream for 5 minutes. Add sherry. Add cream just before serving to float on top of cup. Serves 6.

Atlanta Natives' Favorite Recipes

Peanut Soup à la Crème

¼ cup butter

3 tablespoons flour

2½ quarts chicken stock

2 cups smooth peanut butter

2 cups light cream

Chopped peanuts for garnish

Chopped watercress for garnish

Melt butter in a large, heavy saucepan and stir in flour, mixing well. Gradually add chicken stock. Bring the mixture to a boil, stirring constantly. Reduce heat and add peanut butter. Stir until very smooth. Blend in the cream. Do not boil. Spoon soup into small bowls and top with chopped peanuts and chopped watercress. Serves 10–12.

Note: Fresh chicken stock is best. To prepare, boil a fat hen with 2 medium onions, 2 stalks celery, a grated carrot, and poultry seasoning.

Recipes from the Olde Pink House

Catahoula Courtbouillon

As with bouillabaisse, there are as many recipes for courtbouillon as there are Acadians and Creoles. Papa's version is a thick soup, much like a chowder, and can be made with either fresh or saltwater fish.

$^{2}/_{3}$ cup flour

$^{2}/_{3}$ cup cooking oil

2 medium onions, chopped

1 sweet green pepper, chopped

2 stalks celery, chopped

3 cloves garlic, minced (optional)

1 (1-pound) can whole tomatoes, undrained and chopped

1 (10-ounce) can Ro-Tel tomatoes

1 quart fish stock or water

1 tablespoon salt

1 teaspoon cayenne pepper

$2^{1}/_{2}$ pounds firm white fish, cut into fillets or steaks

1 bunch green onions, tops only, chopped

$^{1}/_{4}$ cup finely chopped fresh parsley

In a large heavy pot, make a dark brown roux with flour and oil. Add onions, green pepper, celery, and garlic; cook for 5 minutes. Add both cans of tomatoes and cook slowly over a low fire. Now, here's the secret to making a good courtbouillon—let it cook until the oil forms a thin layer, like paper, over the top of the mixture. You will have to stir occasionally, but after a half hour or so, the oil will rise to the top. Add warmed fish stock or water and seasonings, and let cook for one hour, stirring occasionally.

Add the fish and cook for 15–20 minutes. Right before serving, add onion tops and parsley. Check seasonings and make any necessary adjustments. (I usually put a bottle of Tabasco on the table for those who wish to make it hotter.) Serve in deep bowls with rice, and of course, French bread. Serves 8.

Who's Your Mama, Are You Catholic, and Can You Make a Roux?

Corn and Crabmeat Soup

1 cup fresh yellow corn
¼ cup butter
¼ cup all-purpose flour
2 cups chicken stock
2 cups half-and-half cream
1 pound lump crabmeat
Garlic powder
Salt and pepper

Cut fresh corn from cob and save scrapings and milk. (Canned or frozen corn may be used.) Melt butter in saucepan. Add flour and blend well. Add chicken stock, stirring constantly. Cook until thick and smooth. Stir in cream, crabmeat, corn, and seasonings. Cook over low fire until corn is tender.

The Best of South Louisiana Cooking

Turkey Gumbo Soup

Roast turkey carcass
½ teaspoon salt (optional)
1 cup sliced okra, fresh or frozen
1 tablespoon margarine
1 cup sliced celery
½ cup chopped onion
¼ cup green pepper
1 teaspoon minced garlic
2 tablespoons flour
1 (16-ounce) can diced tomatoes
½ cup rice
2 tablespoons chopped parsley
¼ teaspoon each: cumin, pepper, Tabasco sauce, thyme
8 ounces cooked turkey

Place turkey carcass in large pot and cover with water. Add salt. Simmer about 2 hours. Pour broth into container and chill. Skim off fat. Remove meat from bones and reserve. Sauté okra in margarine until it starts to turn brown, about 5 minutes. Add celery, onion, green pepper, and garlic. Sauté for about 2 minutes while stirring. Sprinkle with flour. Stir until blended and starting to brown. Add tomatoes. Add broth, rice, and seasonings. Simmer 30 minutes. Add meat and heat 5 minutes. Yields 8 (1½-cup) servings.

Per serving: Cal 115; Chol 15mg; Sat Fat <1g; Fat 3g; Sod 473mg; Pro 9g; Cho 13g. Exchanges: 1 meat, 1 vegetable, ½ bread.

Southern BUT Lite

Corn and Ham Chowder

1 cup chopped celery

¹/₂ cup chopped onion

2 cups diced cooked ham

¹/₂ cup butter

3 (10-ounce) packages
  frozen cream-style corn

1¹/₂ teaspoons salt

¹/₂ teaspoon pepper

¹/₂ teaspoon onion salt

¹/₂ teaspoon celery salt

1 cup milk

Fresh chopped parsley for
  garnish

Sauté celery, onion, and ham in butter. Add remaining ingredients. Heat. Simmer 20 minutes before serving. Garnish with fresh parsley.

Recipes from Miss Daisy's

Golden Glow Corn Chowder

This is wonderful!

6 slices bacon, cut into
  1-inch pieces

2 small onions, peeled and
  chopped

¹/₂ medium green pepper,
  seeded, cored, and
  chopped

4 medium potatoes, peeled
  and cubed

2 cups water

1 (16-ounce) can whole-
  kernel corn, drained

1 cup evaporated milk or
  half-and-half

1 (2-ounce) jar chopped
  pimento, drained

Salt and pepper to taste

In a heavy skillet, pan-fry bacon over medium heat until crisp. Remove and drain on absorbent paper. Sauté onions and green pepper in bacon drippings over moderate heat until tender, but not browned. Drain off excess drippings.

In a heavy 2- 3 quart saucepan, cook potatoes in water over moderate heat until tender. Add onions, green pepper, corn, milk, pimento, salt and pepper to taste. Heat through. Garnish each serving with crisp bacon pieces. Makes 4–6 servings.

Apron Strings

Corn and Crab Bisque

STAGE 1:

1 ounce olive oil
  (2 tablespoons)

1 cup chopped onions

²/₃ cup chopped celery

²/₃ ounce garlic purée
  (about 1 tablespoon)

4 ears corn, cut and
  scraped

3 bay leaves

STAGE 2:

2 cups shrimp stock

¹/₃ teaspoon white pepper

¹/₃ teaspoon black pepper

¹/₃ teaspoon cayenne
  pepper

²/₃ ounce Worcestershire
  sauce (4 teaspoons)

1 pint crab meat

STAGE 3:

2 quarts half-and-half

STAGE 4:

¹/₃ pound butter
  (1¹/₃ sticks)

²/₃ cup flour

Sauté all Stage 1 ingredients until soft. Add all Stage 2 ingredients and let simmer 20 minutes. Add half-and-half and bring to a boil, then simmer.

In a small saucepan, melt butter and add flour. Mix well and let cook for 5 minutes. Add the butter/flour mixture to the soup, stir well, and cook until soup thickens. Remove from heat. Yields 1 gallon.

NOTE: You can substitute corn stock for shrimp stock.

Recipe from The Half Shell, Memphis
Fine Dining Tennessee Style

Editor's Extra: Chicken stock is good, too.

*Barbara's grandsons, Niles, Joseph, and Benton, are
proud to announce: "The corn's ready! Come and get it!"*

Award-Winning Seafood Gumbo

On New Year's Day, it was the family tradition for Mom to serve gumbo. She started days ahead, planning, shopping and chopping. Everybody came around for a bowl of this delicious homemade soup.

2 quarts water
Heads and shells of shrimp
1 large onion
3 cloves garlic
6 ribs celery
1 cup vegetable oil
1 cup all-purpose flour
4 pounds shrimp, peeled and deveined
Cooking oil
Tony Chachere's Original Seasoning , divided
3 pounds Hillshire Farm Smoked Sausage, cut into quarters
1 pound andouille sausage, cut in bite-size pieces
2 cups chopped onions
2 cups chopped celery
2 cups chopped green onions
1 (106-ounce) can whole tomatoes, cut in small pieces
2 cups chopped bell peppers
1/4 cup filé
1 teaspoon thyme
1 teaspoon garlic powder
1/2 teaspoon oregano
1/2 teaspoon cayenne pepper
Salt and pepper to taste
1 (16-ounce) bag frozen cut okra
1 pound jumbo lump crabmeat

Bring water to boil, and boil heads and shells of shrimp, large onion, garlic, and celery for about 1 1/2 hours (liquid will reduce; do not let liquid go below 1 quart). Strain seafood stock; cool and refrigerate until ready to use.

Heat 1 cup oil in large heavy skillet over high heat until it begins to smoke. Gradually add 1 cup flour, whisking constantly. Continue cooking and whisking until roux is dark brown (about 4 minutes). Set aside.

Sauté shrimp in a little oil; sprinkle with Tony's. Set aside. Sauté sausages until done; add chopped onions, chopped celery, green onions, tomatoes, and bell peppers; sauté.

In large stockpot, add 1 quart seafood stock, cooked sausage mixture, seasonings, and okra. Add shrimp and crabmeat; add roux as desired. Reduce heat and simmer for 2 hours. Additional stock may be added if gumbo becomes too thick. Serve over steamed rice. Enjoy!

Lagniappe: Secrets We're Ready to Share II

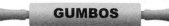

Roux

A roux is used as a base for most Creole dishes. The quantity of fat and oil may vary from recipe to recipe, but the method of cooking remains the same.

3 tablespoons bacon
   drippings or shortening
3 tablespoons flour
Heavy black iron pot or
   other heavy skillet

Melt fat in heavy skillet and stir in flour. Continue to stir over low heat until flour is dark brown. (The slow dry heat fragments the starch molecules in the flour and develops a nut-like flavor that gives body to soups and stews. It also reduces thickening power of the flour.)

'Tiger Bait' Recipes

Microwave Roux (with Vegetables)

Grandmother would even be fooled by this one!

²/₃ cup vegetable oil
²/₃ cup flour
²/₃ cup chopped onion
²/₃ cup chopped celery
²/₃ teaspoon minced garlic
²/₃ cup chopped bell pepper
²/₃ cup chopped green
   onions (optional)
²/₃ cup hot water

Mix oil with flour in a 4-cup glass measuring bowl. Microwave uncovered on HIGH for 6 minutes. Stir and cook another 30–60 seconds on HIGH till the color of mahogany.

Now you can add your chopped vegetables, stir well, and "sauté" them on HIGH for another 5 minutes till soft but not brown.

Now before stirring, pour oil off top, if desired. Add hot tap water, stirring till smooth. Beautiful! And it freezes for later use.

Note: This recipe can be increased to 1 of everything (rather than ²/₃), but put it in an 8-cup measure and increase the cooking times about 30 seconds each time. Or use ¹/₂. I just love this recipe—it's so easy to remember how much of everything to use! Oh, and frozen chopped vegetables work just fine—they just sizzle a bit more and require a few more seconds cooking time.

The Little Gumbo Book

Flawless Oyster Stew

2 cups milk
2 cups half-and-half
2 dozen small oysters
4 tablespoons butter
Worcestershire sauce
  (optional)
Salt to taste
Celery salt to taste
White pepper to taste
Paprika to taste

Combine milk and half-and-half and scald (this means heating to the point where a film forms on top, not boiling). Set aside. Drain off nearly all of the juice from the oysters into a saucepan, leaving about 2 tablespoons on oysters. Heat the drained-off oyster juice to the boiling point only.

    In separate saucepan add butter to oysters, and a few drops of Worcestershire sauce if you like a dash of piquancy, and place over high heat just long enough for oysters to fatten up and edges begin to curl—no longer, or they will be as tough as shoe leather. Take oysters off stove, add both liquids (milk and juice); stir in salt, celery salt, and pepper to taste. And be sure to taste. Serve immediately, sprinkle with some paprika, and accompany with oyster crackers. Serves 6.

Old Mobile Recipes

Savannah Crab Stew

4 tablespoons flour
1 teaspoon salt
1/4 teaspoon white pepper
1 quart milk
1 tablespoon butter
1 tablespoon
  Worcestershire sauce
1 tablespoon lemon juice
1/4 cup sherry
1/2 pound crabmeat
Dash Tabasco sauce

Combine flour, salt, and pepper. Add mixture to milk in saucepan. Add butter and stir until smooth. Cook over low heat until slightly thickened. Add remaining ingredients and serve at once.

Crab Chatter

Shrimp Stew

My mother came from a family of eight children. Her mother was a very good and innovative cook. Often the cupboard was low on supplies. When they heard Maw Maw say, "Tonight I'm going to have to scrap up supper," they knew they were in for a real treat. Maw Maw could produce the most delicious meal from little tads of leftovers and scraps of whatever she could find. They were regarded as favorite meals.

Most southerners eat "supper" at night rather than dinner. This goes back to farming days when you had a hearty breakfast when the sun came up, then came back to the farmhouse for a big mid-day dinner. When the sun went down, you had leftover corn bread and milk or biscuits and syrup, or the like, for supper.

—Barbara

$^1/_2$ cup flour
3 tablespoons cooking oil
2 medium onions, chopped
2 ribs celery, chopped
$^1/_2$ cup chopped green bell pepper
4 small cloves garlic, peeled and mashed
1$^1/_2$ quarts water
2 bay leaves
2 (6-ounce) cans tomato paste, or 2 fresh tomatoes, chopped
2 pounds raw medium shrimp, peeled and deveined (approximately 40)
Salt and pepper to taste
Hot cooked rice

Make a roux by combining flour and oil in a heavy 4-quart saucepan. Brown over medium heat, stirring constantly to prevent scorching. Add onions, celery, green pepper, and garlic; stir and cook until vegetables are softened. Add water, bay leaves, and tomato paste; simmer slowly for 1$^1/_2$ hours. Remove bay leaves after first 30 minutes. Add shrimp and simmer for 15 minutes; do not overcook. Season to taste with salt and pepper; serve immediately over hot cooked rice. Serves 6–8.

Bluegrass Winners

Magic Beef Stew

Wintertime welcomes the warmth and heartiness of good ole beef stew.

2½–3 pounds lean stew beef
6 large carrots, cut into 2-inch pieces
3 large potatoes, quartered
3 large onions, sliced
5 stalks celery, cut into 2-inch pieces
1 tablespoon salt
1 teaspoon pepper
¼ cup tapioca
2 tablespoons sugar
1½ cups tomato juice
1 cup water

Layer first 5 ingredients in casserole. Sprinkle with mixture of salt, pepper, tapioca, and sugar. Pour mixture of tomato juice and water over all. Seal with foil and lid. Bake at 275° for 4 hours or until beef is tender. Serve with salad and corn bread. Yields 5–6 servings.

Capital Eating in Kentucky

Editor's Extra: Sometimes I turn up the temperature to 325° and shorten the cooking time by an hour or so, but slow cooking is the secret. Adding the potatoes halfway through the cooking is an option that keeps them a little more firm, but stir them in gently so as not to interrupt "the magic."

Salad with All the Fixin's

Salads, Pickles & Preserves

There is as much dignity in plowing a field as in writing a poem.

—Booker T. Washington

Daughter-in-Law Potato Salad

At the Thomas Family Reunion, this is made in much larger amounts and is referred to as "daughter-in-law" salad because the task generally falls to some of the daughters-in-law.

Mayonnaise, to your liking

Salt and pepper to taste

4 cups diced, cooked potatoes

Prepared mustard, small amount

2 hard-cooked eggs

1/2 cup chopped pickle or salad cubes

1/4 cup minced green onions or mild white onion

1/2 cup chopped celery

Diced pimiento (optional)

1/4 cup chopped green pepper

A secret to a good potato salad is to add the mayonnaise, salt, and pepper to the potatoes while they are still hot and will absorb the flavors. Add a small amount of mustard to the mayonnaise to give a nice color. Add remaining ingredients and toss lightly with 2 forks until coated with mayonnaise. Yields 8 servings.

Family Secrets: Famous Recipes from the Homeplace

The McKee barn on "the old place" is perfect for their family reunions. It's a bring-a-dish occasion that nobody wants to miss.

New Potato Salad

Make a day ahead. Absolutely wonderful!

8–12 new potatoes

3 eggs

1 bunch green onions, sliced

3 stalks celery, chopped

Boil new potatoes with eggs until potatoes are done, but still firm; drain and let cool. Peel potatoes, if desired, and cut into chunks. Mix in large bowl with onions, celery, and peeled, chopped eggs.

DRESSING:

1 teaspoon salt

$^{1}/_{2}$ teaspoon pepper

1 teaspoon basil

1 tablespoon Dijon mustard

2 cloves garlic, minced

3 tablespoons red wine vinegar

$^{1}/_{2}$ cup mayonnaise

$^{1}/_{3}$ cup olive oil

Combine salt, pepper, basil, Dijon mustard, garlic, and vinegar in small bowl; whisk in mayonnaise and oil. Pour over potatoes and let sit overnight.

Knollwood's Cooking

Vidalia Onion Potato Salad

This is so good and different from regular potato salad.

$1^{1}/_{2}$ cups mayonnaise

$^{1}/_{2}$ cup oil

$^{1}/_{4}$ cup cider vinegar

3 pounds new potatoes, boiled and sliced

2 or 3 medium Vidalia onions, sliced

Salt and pepper

Fresh parsley for garnish

Beat mayonnaise, oil, and vinegar with a fork until well mixed. Pour over potatoes and onions which have been layered in a bowl and each layer sprinkled with salt and pepper. Refrigerate several hours before serving. Garnish with fresh parsley.

Gran's Gems

Chicken Salad in Raspberry Ring

Spectacular in appearance and taste.

CREAMY MAYONNAISE:

1 cup mayonnaise

$^1/_2$ cup heavy cream, whipped

Combine mayonnaise and whipped cream. Makes 1$^2/_3$ cups.

CHICKEN SALAD:

2 cups cubed cooked or canned chicken

1 teaspoon salt

2 hard-cooked eggs, chopped

$^3/_4$ cup sliced celery

1 teaspoon lemon juice

$^1/_2$ cup Creamy Mayonnaise

Lightly toss all ingredients together. Chill. Serve in Raspberry Ring.

RASPBERRY RING:

3 (10-ounce) packages frozen red raspberries

2 envelopes plain gelatin

$^1/_2$ cup lemon juice

1$^1/_4$ cups boiling water

$^3/_4$ cup sugar

$^1/_4$ teaspoon salt

$^3/_4$ cup cantaloupe balls

Thaw raspberries. Drain, reserving 2 cups syrup (use berries for garnish). Soften gelatin in lemon juice. Dissolve in boiling water. Stir in sugar, salt, and reserved raspberry syrup. Chill till partially set. Add cantaloupe balls. Pour into 5-cup ring mold. Chill till firm.

Serve on a large silver platter surrounded with fruit. Pass additional Creamy Mayonnaise. So pretty.

Old Mobile Recipes

Chicken Salad with Grapes and Almonds

An excellent, impressive salad.

2¹/₂ cups chopped, cooked chicken

1 cup sliced scallions (or less)

1 cup thinly sliced celery

1 cup sliced almonds, lightly toasted

2 tablespoons pimento (optional)

2 cups mayonnaise

1 teaspoon basil

¹/₂ teaspoon thyme

¹/₄ teaspoon garlic powder

1 teaspoon poultry seasoning

2 cups seedless grapes, halved

In a large bowl, combine chicken, scallions, celery, almonds, and pimento. Combine mayonnaise, basil, thyme, garlic powder, and poultry seasoning. Pour over chicken mixture and mix well. Gently fold in the grapes. Serve chilled in a bed of lettuce or stuffed into a pita pocket or a cream puff. Yields 6 servings.

A Taste of Fayette County

Hot Chicken Salad

2 cups diced, cooked chicken

1 cup diced celery

¹/₂ cup diced almonds

³/₄ cup mayonnaise

2 teaspoons grated onion

1 small can water chestnuts, diced

2 tablespoons lemon juice

¹/₂ teaspoon salt

³/₄ cup grated Cheddar cheese

Cracker crumbs

Combine all ingredients except cheese and cracker crumbs. Put in greased casserole dish. Put a layer of grated cheese and crushed cracker crumbs on top. Bake 15–20 minutes at 350°.

The Wyman Sisters Cookbook

Editor's Extra: Although this is a hot casserole that can be a main dish, it can also be served cold on lettuce leaves with fresh fruit as a salad.

Black-Eyed Susan Salad

1 (15-ounce) can black-
eyed peas, drained

1 (10-ounce) package
frozen whole-kernel corn,
thawed

1 small green pepper, diced

1 small sweet red pepper,
diced

$\frac{1}{2}$ cup diced celery

2 tablespoons finely
chopped onion

$\frac{1}{2}$ cup cider vinegar

$\frac{1}{2}$ cup oil

1 tablespoon sugar

2 tablespoons
Worcestershire sauce

$\frac{1}{2}$ teaspoon garlic salt

$\frac{1}{8}$ teaspoon pepper

Combine peas, corn, green and red pepper, celery, and onion in medium-size bowl. Combine remaining ingredients for dressing. Pour over vegetables and toss. Chill several hours before serving. If desired, serve on lettuce. Garnish with pepper rings.

Note: If you don't have sweet red pepper, a good substitute is 3 tablespoons diced pimiento.

Mississippi Stars Cookbook

Summer Corn Salad

8 ears Silverqueen corn,
roasted, cut from cob
(approximately 6 cups)

1 cup diced, seeded tomato

$\frac{1}{2}$ cup minced red onion

$\frac{3}{4}$ cup diced green bell
pepper

2 tablespoons chopped
cilantro

2 tablespoons chopped
parsley

1 teaspoon minced garlic

1 teaspoon cayenne pepper

1 lime, squeezed for juice

1 tablespoon cider vinegar

1 teaspoon salt

$\frac{1}{4}$ cup olive oil

Combine all ingredients and mix well. Refrigerate at least 1–2 hours before serving. Best when made a day ahead. Yields 6–8 servings.

Deep South Staples

Mixed Pasta Salad

Mixed pasta salad is indeed a treat for a hot summer evening meal. This dish has the added attraction of make-ahead preparation (in order for the flavors to mingle). Serve on a bed of lettuce with crusty rolls and butter.

2 cups fresh broccoli florets, blanched

1 cup sliced pitted ripe olives

1½ cups cherry tomatoes, sliced in half

½ cup canned mushrooms

2 green onions, thinly sliced

1 (8-ounce) bottle of oil and vinegar salad dressing

4 ounces spinach fettuccini noodles, cooked, drained, and chilled

4 ounces fettuccini noodles, cooked, drained, and chilled

4 ounces boiled ham, sliced in strips

½ cup grated Parmesan cheese

½ cup crumbled, fried bacon

Marinate broccoli, olives, tomatoes, mushrooms, and onions in the salad dressing at least 5 hours. Drain, reserving the dressing.

Combine the vegetables with noodles, ham, cheese, and bacon. Toss with reserved dressing. Serve on lettuce leaves. Sprinkle with additional cheese, bacon, and parsley flakes, if desired. Serves 6.

Taste Buds

Kudzu covers everything.

When Mamean was first married, she spotted a beautiful vine along the roadside and stopped to pull up some of it to take home. When she proudly presented it to her husband, he nearly had a fit! "Don't you know that's kudzu? It'll take over this farm. I've been trying to kill it for years." Poor Jean was so heartbroken, she cried, but of course didn't plant the cursed kudzu, and she and Papa laughed about this story for years. —*Barbara*

SALADS

Marinated Carrots

Sometimes called "copper penny carrots," this is a long-time favorite.

2 pounds raw carrots
1 medium green pepper, sliced
1 medium onion, sliced
1 (10³/₄-ounce) can tomato soup, undiluted
¹/₂ soup can vegetable oil
1 cup sugar
¹/₂ cup cider vinegar
1 teaspoon salt
1 teaspoon pepper

Cut carrots into thin rounds; cook. Add sliced pepper and onion. Combine soup, oil, sugar, vinegar, salt, and pepper; pour over carrots while still warm. Refrigerate. Let stand overnight. May be used as an appetizer or a vegetable salad.

Gypsy, West Virginia 100th Anniversary Cookbook

Carrot Raisin Salad

A not-too-sweet touch of honey is just right.

3 cups grated carrots (about 5 or 6)
1 cup seedless raisins
1 tablespoon honey
6 tablespoons mayonnaise
¹/₄ cup milk
1 tablespoon fresh lemon juice
¹/₄ teaspoon salt
¹/₄ teaspoon nutmeg (optional)

Toss carrots lightly with raisins. Blend remaining ingredients and stir into carrot mixture. Chill at least 30 minutes before serving. Makes 6–8 servings.

The Wonderful World of Honey

Barbara and I got a big chuckle thinking about "seedless raisins," which are often specified in recipes— we've never run across them any other way.

—Gwen

Hot Slaw

3 slices bacon
1 medium onion, chopped
1 tablespoon sugar
1¹/₂ teaspoons flour
¹/₂ teaspoon salt
¹/₄ teaspoon pepper
1 cup vinegar
1 medium-size cabbage, shredded

Snip up the bacon into snibbles and fry until crisp. Take out and drain on a paper towel. Sauté onion in bacon drippings until it is a golden brown. Combine sugar, flour, salt, and pepper, and stir into the drippings. Gradually add vinegar, and cook slowly until thickened, stirring constantly. Add bacon to the sauce, and heat. Pour over the shredded cabbage and toss to mix well.

You'll find this same dressing good with lettuce, or even on potato salad.

The Courier-Journal Kentucky Cookbook

Wilted Lettuce

Guests will ask for this recipe.

3–4 slices bacon
Grease from bacon
1 egg
3 tablespoons sugar
1 teaspoon salt
Pepper to taste
3 tablespoons vinegar
¹/₄ cup water
1 head lettuce

Fry bacon crisp; break into small pieces, leaving it in bacon grease. Beat egg. Add sugar, salt, pepper, vinegar, and water. Pour this mixture into bacon and bacon grease. Keep heat low and stir constantly until slightly thickened. Pour over lettuce, torn into bite-size pieces. Serve immediately. Easy. Prepare same day. Serves 8.

Culinary Classics

Spinach Strawberry Salad

An unlikely pair that is a real winner!

1 pound leaf spinach
1 pint strawberries, sliced

Tear well-washed and dried spinach into bite-size pieces. Combine spinach and strawberries; add Liz's Dressing, toss and serve.

LIZ'S DRESSING:
$^{1}/_{2}$ cup sugar
1 teaspoon dry mustard
1 teaspoon salt
$^{1}/_{2}$ teaspoon celery seed
3 tablespoons grated onion
1 cup salad oil
$^{1}/_{3}$ cup wine vinegar

Blend dry Dressing ingredients; add grated onion. Beat oil and vinegar together and add. Chill for several hours. Before tossing with salad, beat with whisk or fork until well blended. Dressing keeps well for several weeks. Serves 8.

Lasting Impressions

Mandarin Spinach Salad
with Poppy Seed Dressing

$^{1}/_{3}$–$^{1}/_{2}$ cup white wine vinegar
4 teaspoons sugar
$^{2}/_{3}$ teaspoon dry mustard
$^{2}/_{3}$ teaspoon salt
2 teaspoons fresh lemon juice
$^{2}/_{3}$ cup vegetable oil
1 tablespoon poppy seeds
1 pound fresh spinach
1 large can Mandarin oranges, drained
$^{1}/_{4}$ pound bacon, cooked and crumbled
1 large avocado, sliced
$^{1}/_{4}$–$^{1}/_{2}$ medium red onion, sliced

Mix vinegar, sugar, mustard, salt, lemon juice, vegetable oil, and poppy seeds in food processor. Assemble remaining ingredients and pour dressing over and serve.

The Holiday Hostess

English Pea Salad

3 (15-ounce) cans English peas, drained
1 bell pepper, chopped
1/2 purple onion, chopped (optional)
1 cup mayonnaise
1 cup sour cream
1 (1-ounce) package ranch dressing mix
Shredded Cheddar cheese
Bacon bits

Combine peas, bell pepper, and onion. Mix mayonnaise and sour cream with ranch dressing mix. Combine dressing with peas and mix well. Just before serving, toss with cheese and bacon bits; serve on lettuce leaves.

Barbara's Been Cookin'

Editor's Extra: Interesting to add chopped fresh tomatoes, and a few chopped boiled eggs.

Fire and Ice Tomatoes

This is such a pretty dish. When tomatoes are abundant and you're looking for something a little different to do with them, try this delightful, refreshing dish. Tomatoes are good, no matter how you slice (or not) them. My daddy liked to go into the garden and pluck one off the vine and take a bite right there.
—Barbara

3/4 cup vinegar
1/4 cup cold water
1 1/2 teaspoons mustard seed
1 1/2 teaspoons celery salt
1/2 teaspoon salt
4 1/2 teaspoons sugar
1/8 teaspoon red pepper
1/8 teaspoon black pepper
6 large tomatoes, cut in quarters
1 onion, cut in slices and separated into rings
1 bell pepper, cut in strips

Combine vinegar, water, and seasonings. Boil one minute. Pour over vegetables and chill several hours. Will keep 2–3 days.

The James K. Polk Cookbook

Asheville Salad

The perfect aspic!

1 (10³/₄-ounce) can tomato
   soup
1 (8-ounce) package cream
   cheese, softened
1¹/₂ packages Knox gelatin
¹/₂ cup cold water
1 tablespoon grated onion
¹/₂ cup finely chopped
   pecans
1 cup finely cut celery
¹/₂ cup mayonnaise

Heat tomato soup. Add cream cheese and stir until dissolved. Mix gelatin with cold water and add to hot mixture. Cool. Stir in onion, pecans, celery, and mayonnaise. Pour into mold and congeal. Serves 8–10 people.

Mama's Recipes

Cottage Cheese Salad

1 (3-ounce) box lime Jell-O
1¹/₂ cups hot water
1 (8-ounce) can crushed
   pineapple, drained,
   reserve juice
1 cup cottage cheese
¹/₄ teaspoon salt
¹/₂ cup mayonnaise
1 tablespoon vinegar
1¹/₂ cups diced celery
¹/₄ cup pimiento (optional)
¹/₄ cup chopped nuts
   (optional)

Dissolve Jell-O in water and add ¹/₂ cup reserved pineapple juice. When slightly thickened, whip. Add remaining ingredients and chill. May be prepared the day before using.

Larue County Kitchens

Avocado Shrimp Salad

A little southern elegance . . .

2 ripe avocados, peeled and halved

Lemon juice

1 pound raw, headless, peeled shrimp

1 (8-ounce) can crushed pineapple, drained

1/2 cup finely chopped bell pepper

1/2 cup destringed and finely chopped celery

2/3 cup firm sour cream

1 teaspoon onion salt

1 cup shredded Swiss cheese

Red tip lettuce, washed and drained, for garnish

Coat avocado halves with lemon juice and chill. Cook shrimp in large quantity boiling salted water for 3 minutes. Drain and cool in refrigerator.

Combine pineapple, bell pepper, celery, sour cream, onion salt, and shrimp. Refrigerate for 30–45 minutes.

Scoop out hollow of avocado to allow room for mixture. Mound mixture on halves and cover with shredded cheese. Refrigerate until ready to serve. Serve on bed of lettuce.

Charleston Receipts Repeats

Florida Sunshine Salad

This is good with fowl, pork, or ham. It may also be used at holiday time in place of cranberry sauce. It can be made in one large mold or six individual molds. Beautiful on a lettuce leaf.

1 (12-ounce) can apricot nectar

1 (3-ounce) package lemon gelatin

1 (6-ounce) can frozen orange juice, thawed

1 (3-ounce) package cream cheese

1/2 cup chopped pecans

Heat apricot nectar to boiling point. Dissolve lemon gelatin in this. DO NOT DILUTE. Add can of orange juice, undiluted. Make small balls of cream cheese to which pecans have been added and place 3 small balls in each (individual) mold or scatter throughout large mold. Fill mold with juice mixture and refrigerate until jelled.

Seminole Savorings

Cherry Salad Supreme

1 (3-ounce) package
    raspberry Jell-O

2 cups boiling water,
    divided

1 (21-ounce) can cherry
    pie filling

1 (3-ounce) package lemon
    Jell-O

1 (3-ounce) package cream
    cheese, softened

$^1\!/_2$ cup mayonnaise

1 (8$^1\!/_4$-ounce) can crushed
    pineapple, undrained

$^1\!/_2$ cup Cool Whip

1 cup miniature
    marshmallows

$^1\!/_4$ cup chopped nuts

Dissolve raspberry Jell-O in 1 cup boiling water. Stir in pie filling; chill until set. Dissolve lemon Jell-O in 1 cup boiling water. Beat together cream cheese and mayonnaise; gradually add lemon Jell-O. Stir in undrained pineapple; fold in Cool Whip and marshmallows. Spread on top of set raspberry Jell-O; top with nuts.

Down Memory Lane

Slice of the South Salad

2 (3-ounce) packages
    blackberry gelatin

2 cups blackberries

1 cup chopped pecans
    (optional)

Mix gelatin according to package directions. (If berries are frozen, decrease cold water to $^1\!/_2$ cup.) Add berries and nuts to gelatin and let chill until set.

TOPPING:

1 (8-ounce) package cream
    cheese, softened

$^1\!/_4$ cup cold milk

$^1\!/_2$ cup sugar

1 teaspoon vanilla

2 cups whipped topping

Pecans, chopped (optional)

Mix cream cheese with milk, sugar, and vanilla; fold mixture into whipped topping. Spread on gelatin and chill. Sprinkle pecans on top as a garnish, if desired. Yields 15 servings.

Upper Crust: A Slice of the South

82

Congealed Coca-Cola Cranberry Salad

A Georgia Thanksgiving classic.

- 1 (3-ounce) package orange gelatin
- 1 cup boiling water
- 1 (16-ounce) can whole cranberry sauce
- 1 envelope unflavored gelatin, softened in ½ cup cold water
- 1 (20-ounce) can crushed pineapple, undrained
- 1 tablespoon lemon juice
- 1 tablespoon grated orange rind
- 1 cup chopped pecans or walnuts
- 6 ounces Coca-Cola Classic

Dissolve orange gelatin in boiling water; add cranberry sauce and blend well. Add softened plain gelatin. Add remaining ingredients and stir just to blend. Spray an 8-cup mold with nonstick cooking spray. Pour mixture into mold. Chill. When mixture begins to set, stir to distribute nuts evenly. Continue to chill until firm. Yields 8 servings.

Georgia on my Menu

Editor's Extra: This is fun to mold in a Bundt pan, then turn over onto a lettuce-lined round platter (set pan in hot water for just a few seconds to loosen). You can put the pan back on top of what's left, turn over into the pan, and refrigerate.

VICKSBURG CONVENTION & VISITORS BUREAU

Coca-Cola was invented on May 8, 1886, by Dr. John Styth Pemberton, and first went on sale at the soda fountain in Jacob's Pharmacy, in Atlanta, Georgia. The Vicksburg, Mississippi, site where Coca-Cola was first bottled in 1894 is now the Biedenharn Candy Company Museum.

Blender Mayonnaise

Bring on the homegrown tomatoes!

2 eggs
1¹/₂ teaspoons salt
¹/₂ teaspoon dry mustard
Pinch of white pepper
¹/₄ teaspoon paprika
2 tablespoons fresh lemon juice
1 cup vegetable oil

Blend all ingredients except oil at high speed for about 10 seconds, then add oil in a thin, steady stream. Run blender another minute. Occasionally stop to scrape sides of blender. Makes 1¹/₄ cups.

Any Time's a Party!

Editor's Extra: If you want to make your mayonnaise "lighter," this works just as well with one egg.

Poppy Seed Dressing

You'll want to dress all your salads with this.

3 tablespoons dry mustard
1¹/₂ teaspoons salt
2 cups sugar
1 cup vinegar
3 cups Wesson oil
2 tablespoons grated onion
3 teaspoons poppy seed

Mix mustard, salt, sugar, and vinegar, and beat well. Add oil slowly, 1 tablespoon at a time. When thick, add grated onion and poppy seed. This recipe can be halved or quartered—delicious! Keeps well.

Old Mobile Recipes

Nellie's Pickled Eggs

2 dozen eggs
4 cans whole beets (do not
  use pickled style)
1¼ cups sugar
1¾ cups vinegar

Boil eggs for 20 minutes, then cool and peel. Pour juice from beets into saucepan. Layer eggs and beets in large container (like a gallon jar) with tight lid. Heat beet juice, sugar, and vinegar till it comes to a boil. Pour juice mixture over eggs and beets. Set aside to cool with lid partially on. Then put lid on firmly and place in refrigerator for 2 weeks. Take eggs out and slice or leave whole and serve.

A Taste of Fayette County

When I was eight years old, I went with my best friend, Linda, to a little community in Louisiana called Bachelor. Linda's father had a tiny general store on a gravel road in the middle of nowhere. We had to walk over a cattle guard to get to it from her house, and I was so afraid my skinny little legs would go all the way through the iron bars that seemed so far apart. But the store—I can still remember the wonderful smells—was rich with childhood wonders . . . a chest-type Coke machine full of icy-cold little bottles of Cokes and Grapettes and root beers and cream sodas . . . fresh sliced meats that we were allowed to eat without bread, just rolled up in our hands . . . and rows of jars of candies and gumballs . . . oh my! Then there was that big intriguing jar of purple eggs that many overalled men paid a few pennies to enjoy while waiting for their lunch meat. Good memories. —*Gwen*

South Carolina Cucumber Pickles

An excellent pickle.

7 pounds cucumbers
2 cups pickling lime
2 gallons water
2 quarts vinegar
4½ pounds sugar
1 tablespoon salt
1 teaspoon whole cloves
1 teaspoon celery seed
1 teaspoon pickling spice

Slice cucumbers and cover with a solution made of 2 cups lime in 2 gallons of water. Let soak 24 hours, then rinse well. Cover with clear water and let soak 3 hours. Drain well.

Heat vinegar, sugar, salt, cloves, celery seed, and pickling spice until sugar melts. Put cucumbers in this syrup and soak overnight, covered.

Cook cucumbers in the syrup for 35 minutes at boiling stage. Pour in hot jars while hot. Boil jars to seal for 5 minutes. Makes about 8 pints.

A Taste of South Carolina

Editor's Extra: You might prefer to put the spices in a mesh ball or cheesecloth ball to keep the syrup clean.

Bread and Butter Pickles

1 gallon sliced cucumbers
8 small onions, sliced
2 green peppers, thinly
  sliced
½ cup salt

In a large container, place cucumbers, onions, and green peppers; sprinkle with salt, then soak in ice water for 3 hours (keep adding ice to water, if necessary). Drain and pat dry with clean towels.

SYRUP:
5 cups sugar
1½ teaspoons turmeric
½ teaspoon ground cloves
2 tablespoons mustard seed
1 teaspoon celery seed
5 cups vinegar

When this mixture boils thoroughly, pour pickles in. Scald, but do not let boil. (The cucumbers and onions will begin to look transparent just before boiling.) Pack sterilized jars with pickles, then seal. Do not use pickles for 2 weeks, as this time is required for completing the pickling process.

The Wyman Sisters Cookbook

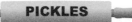

Watermelon Rind Pickles

Deliciously southern.

1 large firm ripe
  watermelon
¹/₄ cup non-iodized salt
4 cups sugar
2 cups white vinegar
2 cups water
1 thinly sliced lemon
2 sticks cinnamon
1 tablespoon whole cloves

Remove the green skin and pink flesh from the white rind; reserve the flesh for another use. Discard the skin and cut the rind into 1-inch pieces and reserve. You should have 8 cups.

In a large lidded container, cover the watermelon rind pieces with water; add salt and mix well to dissolve. Cover, and soak overnight. Drain and rinse well. Place in a large pot and cover with fresh water. Bring to a boil and reduce heat to low. Cook for 5 minutes and drain.

In another pot, combine the remaining ingredients and bring to the boil. Lower the heat and simmer for 20 minutes. Add the drained rind pieces and simmer for 7 minutes. Ladle into sterile, hot jars; cover well with syrup, seal and process for 15 minutes. Makes 6 pints.

The Southern Cook's Handbook

Seven Minute Microwave Dills

1 quart (2- to 3-inch)
  whole cucumbers, or
  ¹/₄-inch unwaxed
  cucumber slices
1 clove garlic, peeled
¹/₂ teaspoon dried dill
  weed, or 1 head fresh dill
¹/₈ teaspoon turmeric
1 hot pepper (optional)
1¹/₂ cups water
¹/₂ cup cider vinegar
2 teaspoons salt, uniodized

Fill sterile 1-quart canning jar with washed and dried cucumbers, garlic, dill weed, turmeric, and hot pepper, if desired. In a 4-cup Pyrex measuring cup, combine water, vinegar, and salt. Microwave on HIGH (100%) 4 minutes until boiling. Pour liquid over cucumbers until covered. Add additional water, if necessary. Cover jar loosely with plastic wrap. Microwave on HIGH (100%) 3 minutes. Cap, leaving plastic wrap in place. Cool and eat! Store in refrigerator for maximum crispness. Will keep 1 year. Yields 1 quart.

Voilà! Lafayette Centennial Cookbook 1884-1984

Sweet Pickled Okra

3 pounds fresh small pods okra

6 cloves garlic

6 teaspoons dill seed

6 teaspoons celery seed

Hot pepper pods as you wish (6 pods for fanatic, 4 for convinced, 2 or 3 for the undecided)

1 quart white wine vinegar

1 quart water

½ cup salt (not iodized)

1 cup sugar

Pack washed okra into 6 pint jars (leave stem ends). Divide garlic, dill, celery seed, and pepper among jars. Put vinegar, water, salt, and sugar into big saucepan; bring to boil. Pour into jars, to within ½ inch of top. Seal jars; place in hot water bath (jars must be covered) 7–8 minutes. Remove to wire racks to cool. Makes 6–8 pints.

Suggestion: Chopped peeled baby turnips and celery, with some of these okra pods sliced on a bed of lettuce hearts, with a lemony mayonnaise make a delicious and unforgettable salad in mid-winter.

Delectable Dishes from Termite Hall

Summer fruits and vegetables get preserved in jars to be enjoyed all winter. Southerners take great pride in their "put-ups."

Strawberry Fig Preserves

Unquestionably the best!

3 cups peeled mashed figs

3 cups sugar

2 (3-ounce) packages strawberry Jell-O

Mix well in saucepan; cook for 10 minutes. Pour mixture into jars and seal.

Flatlanders Cook Book

Pear Preserves

Pear preserves are soothing to eat with breakfast toast on a hot summer morning. If you like, add a stick of cinnamon and cook it with the pears.

16 cups peeled, sliced pears

2 pounds (4 cups) sugar

Juice of 1 lemon

2 cups water

Place pears, sugar, and lemon juice in a large pot and add water. Cook over moderate heat until pears are tender and syrup is thick.

Ladle preserves into hot, sterilized half pint jars and seal. Process for 5 minutes in boiling water bath, if desired. Makes 8–10 half pints.

Note: I like to add about 3 drops of red food coloring to the syrup because it makes the pears look more appetizing.

Aunt Freddie's Pantry

Barbara's Uncle Dan made the best pear preserves . . . his syrup was thick and yummy. We all loved it, and when we asked him why his were so good, he shrugged his shoulders and said, "It just takes a lot of cookin'."

Hot Pepper Jelly

Great on a block of cream cheese with crackers! Good with fowl, lamb or any kind of meat.

3 large firm green bell peppers
18 hot peppers
1½ cups cider vinegar
6½ cups sugar
1 bottle Certo
4 drops green food coloring

Remove seeds from bell peppers; grind peppers and save juice. In saucepan, mix ground peppers, reserved juice, vinegar, and sugar. Bring to good rolling boil for 5 minutes. Cool 2 minutes. Add the Certo. Cool 2 minutes. Then boil 5 minutes. Strain and pour into sterilized jelly glasses. Yields 6 jars.

Easy Livin'

If you have Thanksgiving dinner with Barbara, you'll be offered hot pepper jelly with the turkey and corn bread dressing.

Eat Your Vegetables!

Vegetables & Side Dishes

PHOTO © HORST GOSSMANN

*It's difficult to think anything but pleasant thoughts
while eating a homegrown tomato.*

—Lewis Grizzard

Fried Green Tomatoes

Green tomatoes
Sweet milk
Fish-fry made with corn flour
Vegetable oil
Salt and black pepper

> The most delicious fried green tomatoes I have ever eaten were served with a fantastic sauce made from a few chopped onions sautéed in butter and oil, flour added and slightly browned to make a French Roux, then thickened with heavy cream. It was seasoned with garlic powder, nutmeg, cayenne, salt, and a pinch of sugar. A few crawfish tails sautéed with the onion make it even more interesting. This is served on the side, as the fried green tomatoes should stay crispy. Yum!
> —*Gwen*

Slice tomatoes into approximately $1/8$-inch rounds (2 or 3 slices equal 1 serving). Soak slices for one hour in enough milk to cover completely. Remove and coat generously with fish-fry. Pat fish-fry down on both sides of slices.

Put enough oil in skillet to cover bottom completely and generously, but not enough to lap over sides of slices. Heat oil in skillet to medium high. Oil is properly heated when a pinch of fish-fry sizzles, but does not burn. Add tomato slices in one layer so that sides do not touch. Salt and pepper the top sides.

When coating is barely brown on bottom side, turn slices. Salt and pepper the top sides. Continue turning slices until coating is golden brown. Remove and drain on paper towels. Serve immediately.

Variations: Coating may also be made of 2 parts flour to 1 part fine-grind cornmeal. Finely grated Parmesan cheese and/or paprika may be added to coating.

The Southern Cook's Handbook

Fried Green Tomatoes

The cornmeal version.

6 medium tomatoes (green,
   but turning pink)
1 cup cornmeal
$^{1}/_{2}$ teaspoon salt
$^{1}/_{4}$ teaspoon pepper
$^{1}/_{2}$ teaspoon oregano
Bacon drippings

Cut tomatoes horizontally into $^{1}/_{4}$-inch-thick slices, discarding the top and bottom slices. Mix cornmeal with seasonings. Coat the tomatoes well. In hot skillet containing bacon drippings, add tomato slices in one layer. Lower heat to medium and fry for about 6 minutes, or until golden brown. Drain on paper towels. Repeat with remaining tomato slices. Serves 8.

The Kentucky Derby Museum Cookbook

Scalloped Tomatoes

2 cups thinly sliced onions
2 tablespoons margarine
1 (20-ounce) can tomatoes
3 slices toasted bread,
   cubed
$^{1}/_{4}$ teaspoon pepper
$^{1}/_{2}$ teaspoon celery salt
2 tablespoons brown sugar
1 cup shredded Cheddar
   cheese

Sauté onions in margarine until transparent; remove from pan and drain. Combine tomatoes with bread cubes and add seasonings, sugar, and onions. Pour into buttered casserole. Top with cheese and bake uncovered at 350° for one hour. Yields 6 servings.

Heart of the Mountains

Editor's Extra: You can use fresh sliced or diced tomatoes, too. I like to peel them.

Baked Tomatoes Rockefeller

An impressive luncheon dish with finger sandwiches, and of course, iced tea.

2 (10-ounce) packages
   chopped spinach

2 cups seasoned bread
   crumbs

6 green onions, chopped

6 eggs, slightly beaten

³/₄ cup butter, melted

¹/₂ cup Parmesan cheese

¹/₄ teaspoon Worcestershire
   sauce

¹/₂ teaspoon minced garlic

1 teaspoon salt

¹/₂ teaspoon black pepper

1 teaspoon thyme

1 teaspoon monosodium
   glutamate (optional)

¹/₄ teaspoon Tabasco sauce

12 thick tomato slices

Cook spinach according to directions and drain. Add remaining ingredients except tomatoes. Arrange tomato slices in a single layer in buttered 9x13-inch baking dish. Mound spinach mixture on tomato slices. Sprinkle lightly with more Parmesan cheese. Bake at 350° for 15 minutes. The spinach mixture may be made well in advance, and it freezes well. Yields 12 servings.

Vintage Vicksburg

Southern Tomato Pie

2–3 good-size tomatoes,
   sliced

1 tablespoon Italian
   seasoning or to taste

1 tablespoon oregano or to
   taste

1¹/₂ teaspoons chives or to
   taste

Salt and pepper to taste

1 (9-inch) pie crust, cooked
   until it is light brown

1 cup grated sharp cheese

1 cup mayonnaise

Sprinkle tomato slices with seasoning, oregano, chives, salt and pepper; place slices in pie crust. Combine cheese and mayonnaise to make a thick paste; then, cover tomatoes with paste. Bake at 350° until tomato paste is bubbly and the crust is a deep, golden brown.

Great Flavors of Mississippi

Broccoli and Tomato Casserole

From Dr. Ann Smith of Georgia College, this recipe is often used in this cook's catering service. She always has requests for this recipe.

3 tablespoons butter
2 tablespoons flour
1 1/4 cups milk
1 teaspoon salt
1 cup grated Cheddar cheese
1 tablespoon onion or lemon juice
1 1/2 pounds frozen broccoli
4 ripe tomatoes
1/2 pound bacon

Make a cheese sauce of butter, flour, milk, salt, cheese, and juice. Place broccoli, which has been cooked until tender, in bottom of casserole. Cover with sauce. Cut tomatoes in halves and place on top of sauce and broccoli. Place bacon on top. Bake at 400° until bacon is crisp.

Good Cookin'

Editor's Extra: Broccoli spears and tomato halves make a pretty presentation, but chopped broccoli and sliced tomatoes work just as well and taste just as delicious. Diced bacon cooks more crisply.

Broiled Tomatoes

Quick and delicious.

Tomatoes
Margarine
1/2 teaspoon salt
1/8 teaspoon pepper
1/4 teaspoon basil
1/4 teaspoon thyme
1/4 teaspoon oregano
1/4 teaspoon sugar
Parmesan cheese, grated

Purchase firm ripe tomatoes according to how many you are going to feed. Slice tomatoes in fairly thick slices and place on foil-lined baking sheet. Dot with a little margarine. Combine salt, pepper, spices, sugar, and Parmesan cheese and sprinkle on top. Broil until lightly browned, or grill, or bake at 300° for about 20 minutes. Check frequently.

Gazebo I Christmas Cookbook

Beans Anchored in Bacon

1 (16-ounce) can whole
　green beans
3 strips bacon, cut in half
Salt and pepper to taste
½ bottle Kraft Catalina
　Dressing

Drain green beans and divide into 6 equal portions. Wrap each portion of beans with ½ strip bacon, secure with toothpick. Sprinkle with salt and pepper to taste. Marinate overnight with dressing. Bake in moderate oven for 30 minutes. Serves 6.

Any Time's a Party!

Editor's Extra: I like to gather fresh, tender, young green beans from my garden and steam them for this dish. Nothing like fresh!

Green Beans and Stewed Potatoes

3 slices bacon
3 cups fresh green beans,
　snapped
4 cups water
1 teaspoon salt
½ teaspoon pepper
4 small fresh potatoes,
　scraped
3 tablespoons margarine,
　melted
2 tablespoons flour

Brown bacon in large saucepan. Add green beans, water, salt, pepper, and potatoes. Cover and simmer 40–50 minutes or until potatoes are tender. (Gently stir at 10 minute intervals to prevent sticking. Additional water may be added, if needed.)

After potatoes are cooked, remove ½ cup hot liquid from beans and potatoes. Combine with margarine and flour to make creamy paste. Stir paste into beans and potatoes while still cooking. Simmer 10 minutes, or long enough to thicken liquid. Serves 4.

Dinner on the Ground

Editor's Extra: We always called this green beans and new potatoes, and had a longing for them soon after the fresh snap beans were ready to pick.

Ro-Tel French-Style Green Beans

2 (16-ounce) cans French-
  style green beans
1 (10-ounce) can Ro-Tel
  tomatoes, drained
½ pound mild Cheddar
  cheese
Seasoning to taste

Drain green beans and add water to cover in saucepan. Cook on medium heat about 25 minutes; drain. Add Ro-Tel tomatoes and cook 20 minutes. Slice (or grate) cheese and add with seasoning to green beans. Cook until cheese melts, stirring often. Serve hot. Yields 8 servings.

Festival

Hoppin' John

Hoppin' John is traditionally served on New Year's Day to bring good luck.

1 cup dry black-eyed peas
8 cups water
6 slices bacon
¾ cup chopped onion
1 clove garlic, minced
1 cup regular rice
2 teaspoons salt
¼ teaspoon pepper

Rinse black-eyed peas. In a large saucepan, combine peas and water; bring to a boil, then boil for 2 minutes. Remove from heat and let stand 1 hour. Drain, reserving 6 cups cooking liquid.

In a heavy 3-quart saucepan, cook bacon, onion, and garlic until bacon is crisp and onion is tender, but not brown. Remove bacon; drain on paper towels, then crumble and set aside.

Stir black-eyed peas, raw rice, salt, pepper, and reserved cooking liquid into mixture in saucepan. Bring to a boil; cover and reduce heat. Simmer 1 hour, stirring occasionally. Stir in crumbled bacon. Turn into a serving bowl. Serve immediately. Makes 8 servings.

Tennessee Treasure

Boiled Butter Beans/Lima Beans

Butter beans and lima beans are cooked in the same manner. The lima bean is larger and more mealy. They may be seasoned with butter, ham or salt meat.

2 cups fresh butter beans or lima beans

4 cups water

1 teaspoon salt

1 teaspoon sugar (or more)

2 tablespoons butter, or piece of boiling meat about 2 inches square, 1-inch thick

$^1/_2$ cup milk or cream (optional)

Pepper to taste

Wash and pick over the beans; cover with water in a saucepan with lid. Add salt and sugar. Boil for about 10 minutes, then add the butter; or if meat is to be used, add the meat. Boil slowly until beans are tender, about 45 minutes to 1 hour. If beans become too dry, add a little warm water. There should be a little broth left with the beans. If desired, just before serving, add the milk or cream and season to taste with pepper; reheat. Serves 4–6.

Marion Brown's Southern Cook Book

Field Peas and Okra

1 quart fresh or frozen field peas

$1^1/_2$ quarts water

4–5 slices bacon or salt pork

2 teaspoons sugar

1 teaspoon salt, or to taste

1 teaspoon black pepper

6 pods fresh or frozen okra

Place peas in large saucepan and cover with water. Add bacon or salt pork and bring to a boil. Cook at low boil for about 20 minutes; add seasonings and okra. Turn to simmer and cook for another 30 minutes. Remove okra and continue to cook if peas are not as tender as you want. Watch water level—do not let peas dry out. Taste for seasoning. Serve with hot corn bread—a must!

Barbara Moseley

Country Baked Beans

An absolute necessity with barbecue.

4 pieces bacon, fried and drained (save drippings)

1 (1-pound 15-ounce) can pork and beans, drained

1 (16-ounce) can kidney beans, drained

1 (8-ounce) can lima beans, drained

1 small bell pepper, chopped (optional)

1 medium onion, chopped

2 tablespoons reserved bacon drippings

³/₄ cup brown sugar

1 tablespoon mustard

3 tablespoons Worcestershire sauce

¹/₃ cup catsup

¹/₄ teaspoon pepper

Salt to taste

Fry bacon; crumble and set aside. Mix all beans and chopped bell pepper and place in a 2¹/₂- to 3-quart casserole dish. Brown onion in bacon drippings. To browned onion, add remaining ingredients and cook over medium heat for 10 minutes. Add cooked mixture and crumbled bacon to beans; stir gently. Bake, covered, at 350° for 30 minutes. Remove cover and bake an additional 15 minutes. May be prepared a day or two in advance and refrigerated. Serves 16.

When Dinnerbells Ring

These split rail fences, zigzagging all over the South, were easy to put up, since they require no nails or fasteners of any kind. They are an overall part of the beauty of the Natchez Trace Parkway, which runs 444 miles from Natchez, Mississippi, to Nashville, Tennessee.

Skillet Squash

Easy and so good!

1 medium onion, thinly sliced and separated into rings
2 teaspoons margarine
2 cups thinly sliced zucchini
¹/₂ teaspoon sea salt
Dash coarsely ground pepper
1 medium tomato, cut in wedges
1 cup sliced fresh mushrooms

Sauté onion slices in margarine until tender-crisp. Add squash and cook covered for 6 minutes, stirring occasionally. Add remaining ingredients and continue cooking about 4 minutes. Squash should be tender-crisp. Remove with slotted spoon. Serves 6.

A Great Taste of Arkansas

Squash Soufflé

6 or 8 small yellow squash, sliced but not peeled
1 large onion, sliced
2 tablespoons margarine
¹/₂ teaspoon salt
¹/₂ teaspoon pepper
2 teaspoons sugar
6 double saltine crackers
1 egg, lightly beaten
Paprika

Simmer squash and onion together until tender enough to mash with a fork. Drain, leaving a little of the liquid, and mash. Add margarine, salt, pepper, and sugar. Mix and then stir in crackers crumbled up in your hands (reserve a few for topping). Stir in egg. Pour into a buttered baking dish. Put remaining cracker crumbs and a few dots of margarine over top. Sprinkle a little paprika. Bake uncovered for 20–25 minutes at 375°.

Perfectly Delicious

Seaside Stuffed Squash

An attractive way to serve squash—and good.

1 pound summer squash
¹/₂ cup chopped green pepper
¹/₂ cup grated Cheddar cheese
¹/₂ cup sour cream
¹/₂ cup minced onion
4 slices bacon, cooked and crumbled

Boil squash 10–12 minutes. Slice lengthwise. Scoop out pulp. Add remaining ingredients to pulp and mix well. Fill squash with mixture, placing each in a baking dish. Bake 20 minutes in a 350° preheated oven. May be prepared ahead of time and refrigerated until ready to bake. Serves 6.

Sugar Beach

Squash Dressing

2 cups sliced yellow squash
1 stick margarine
1 cup chopped onion
1 cup chopped celery
3 eggs, lightly beaten
1 (10³/₄-ounce) can cream of chicken soup, undiluted
1 (10³/₄-ounce) can cream of celery soup, undiluted
1 (14¹/₂-ounce) can chicken broth
2 cups crumbled, cooked corn bread
Salt and pepper to taste
Poultry seasoning to taste

Wash, peel, and cut squash into ¹/₄-inch slices. Cook squash in salted, boiling water for 8–10 minutes or until tender; drain well. Mash squash with a fork.

Melt margarine in large skillet over medium-high heat; sauté onion and celery until tender. Combine onion mixture with beaten eggs. Add squash, soups, chicken broth, corn bread, salt and pepper, and poultry seasoning; mix well. (If mixture is too dry, add extra chicken broth.) Pour into a greased 2-quart baking dish. Bake, uncovered, at 350° for 30 minutes or until lightly browned and set.

Treasured Family Favorites

Squash Morelle

Easy-do microwave. An interesting and tasty dish for dinner parties.

2 pounds yellow squash, sliced
1 cup chopped onion
1 teaspoon butter
2 eggs, beaten
1/2 cup sour cream
2 tablespoons butter, softened
1 tablespoon sugar
1 1/2 teaspoons salt
1/2 cup mozzarella cheese
1/2 cup ground almonds

Place squash and onion in a 2-quart casserole dish. Dot with butter and cover tightly with plastic wrap. Microwave on HIGH (100%) 16 minutes. Shake dish once or twice to rearrange contents. (Shaking eliminates removing the cover.) Drain and mash.

Mix together eggs, sour cream, butter, sugar, salt, and cheese and stir into squash. Microwave on HIGH 4 minutes. Sprinkle on ground almonds and microwave on HIGH 4 minutes more.

Tout de Suite à la Microwave II

Zucchini Deluxe

Stuffed squash at its best!

6 large zucchini
1 cup fresh bread crumbs
1/4 cup chopped onion
1 tomato, chopped
1/2 teaspoon salt
1/4 teaspoon pepper
2 tablespoons margarine, melted
1/2 pound Cheddar cheese, grated
1/4 cup milk

Wash and trim ends of zucchini. Cook, covered, in boiling salted water for 5–8 minutes. Drain. Cut in half lengthwise. Scoop out center of each. Chop up pulp and combine with bread crumbs, onion, tomato, seasonings, and margarine. Toss lightly. Fill shells and place in large casserole dish. Heat cheese and milk in saucepan over low heat, stirring until sauce is smooth. Pour sauce over stuffed zucchini. Bake in 350° oven for 25–30 minutes. Serves 6–12.

In Good Taste

Zucchini-Corn Casserole

1½ pounds zucchini or yellow crookneck squash

1 medium onion, finely chopped

½ green pepper, finely chopped

2 tablespoons vegetable oil

2 eggs, beaten

½ cup grated Cheddar cheese

½ teaspoon salt

½ teaspoon garlic salt

¼ teaspoon pepper

¼ teaspoon dried rosemary

1 (16-ounce) can cream-style white shoe peg corn

Crumbled bacon or cubed ham (optional)

Slice zucchini and steam until just tender. Let cool. Sauté onion and pepper in oil until limp. Add eggs, cheese, and seasonings to corn. Fold into zucchini along with sautéed onion and pepper. Pour into buttered casserole and place in pan of hot water. Bake at 350° for 45 minutes or until firm. Crumbled bacon or cubed ham makes a nice addition. Serves 6–8.

Revel

Spinach Soufflé

¼ cup margarine

¼ cup flour

¾ cup milk

Dash of pepper

½ pound Velveeta cheese, cubed

1 (10-ounce) package frozen chopped spinach, cooked and drained

6 strips bacon, fried and crumbled

1 tablespoon finely chopped onion

4 eggs, separated

Melt margarine over medium heat. Add flour, milk, and pepper, stirring till smooth. Add Velveeta cheese; stir until melted. Remove from heat. Stir in well-drained spinach, bacon, and chopped onion. Gradually add slightly beaten egg yolks; cool. Fold into stiffly beaten egg whites; pour into 1½-quart soufflé dish. Bake at 350° for 45 minutes. Serves 8.

Any Time's a Party!

Spinach Madeline

A friend of mine who grew up "in the North" was going to use this recipe for entertaining. She called one night and said she had been to two liquor stores to find "vegetable liquor" and it was not available. Of course, "Down South" we just call it "pot likker," but vegetable liquor is the same thing—any juice that remains after cooking a vegetable.

2 (10-ounce) packages frozen chopped spinach

4 tablespoons butter or margarine

2 tablespoons flour

2 tablespoons chopped onion

$^1/_2$ cup evaporated milk

$^1/_2$ cup reserved vegetable liquor

$^1/_2$ teaspoon pepper

$^3/_4$ teaspoon celery salt

$^3/_4$ teaspoon garlic salt

1 teaspoon Worcestershire sauce

6 ounces jalapeño or Monterey Jack cheese

$^1/_2$ cup toasted buttered bread crumbs (optional)

Microwave frozen spinach in pierced packages for 5–7 minutes on HIGH. Press spinach in a colander to remove moisture, but reserve liquid (vegetable liquor). In large glass measuring cup, melt butter or margarine for 45 seconds on HIGH. Gradually stir in flour, then add onion and cook 2 minutes on 80% power (MEDIUM-HIGH). Add milk and vegetable liquor slowly, stirring until lumps are gone. Cook on HIGH for 3–4 minutes, stirring after 2 minutes, until sauce thickens. Add seasonings and cheese, stirring rapidly until cheese melts. Stir in drained spinach. Pour into greased small glass casserole dish (6-inch-square is nice). Top with buttered toasted bread crumbs, if desired, then reheat on HIGH for 2–3 minutes or until bubbly. Serves 4.

Note: This spinach dish would be nice used as a filling for tomatoes or whole onions, especially Vidalias. Stuff vegetables before final zapping.

The Dapper Zapper

Southern Okra

1 cup cut okra

1 onion, chopped

1 sweet green pepper,
  chopped

$1/4$ cup oil

3 tomatoes, peeled and
  quartered

1 tablespoon sugar

1 teaspoon flour

$1/2$ teaspoon pepper

$1/2$ teaspoon salt

Cook okra in boiling salted water for 10 minutes and drain. In skillet, brown onion and pepper in oil. Add tomatoes and cook 5 minutes. Add other ingredients including okra, and cook, stirring, until done, about 10–15 minutes.

Palate Pleasers

Scalloped Okra and Corn

1 ($14^{1/2}$-ounce) can cut
  okra, drained

4 tablespoons butter,
  divided

1 (15-ounce) can corn,
  drained

2 tablespoons flour

1 cup milk

$1/2$ pound sharp Cheddar
  cheese, shredded

1 cup dry bread crumbs

Stir-fry okra in 2 tablespoons butter for 10 minutes. Place in baking dish, alternating layers with drained corn. Make a white sauce by melting remaining butter in a saucepan over low heat and blending in flour. Milk should be added all at once, cooking quickly and stirring constantly. Cheese is stirred in until blended. Pour this mixture over vegetables, and cover with crumbs topped with dots of butter. Bake at 350° for approximately 45 minutes until the casserole is heated through and the crumbs are brown. Yields 6–8 servings.

Georgia on my Menu

Editor's Extra: This works with fresh, frozen or canned okra—whatever you have available.

Old-Time Fried Okra

Truly southern.

½ cup plain flour
½ cup cornmeal
½ teaspoon salt
⅛ teaspoon pepper
1 quart okra, sliced
crosswise, ¼ inch or less
1 egg, beaten
1 cup shortening

Combine flour, cornmeal, salt, and pepper; mix well. In separate bowl, stir beaten egg into okra. Dredge in flour mixture. Heat shortening in large skillet until hot. Add okra and fry until brown and crisp. Remove from pan and drain well on paper towels.

Encore

Eggplant-Zucchini Parmigiana

The New South often looks to low-fat and easy.

1 medium eggplant, peeled,
cut in 12 slices (¼ inch)
1 tablespoon mayonnaise
or sandwich spread
¼ cup Italian bread
crumbs
1 cup low-fat cottage
cheese
1 egg, slightly beaten
¼ teaspoon garlic salt
1 (8-ounce) can tomato
sauce
2 tablespoons grated
Parmesan
1 cup grated mozzarella
(low-fat)
2 small zucchini, cut in
⅛-inch slices

Put peeled eggplant slices on cookie sheet. Spread with mayonnaise and sprinkle with crumbs. Bake in preheated 475° oven for 10 minutes. Remove and turn oven to 375°.

Mix cottage cheese, egg, and garlic salt. Layer all of eggplant, ½ cottage cheese mixture, ½ tomato sauce, ½ Parmesan, and ½ mozzarella cheese. Top with zucchini and then layer the last ½ of the remaining ingredients. Bake uncovered at 375° for 30 minutes. Let stand for 5 minutes before cutting. Serves 6–8.

Cookin' in the Spa

Editor's Extra: The first time I made this, I mistakenly opened a can of Mexican Hot Tomato Sauce, so I went ahead and used it . . . outstanding! Either way, this is a winner.

Eggplant Creole

Creole [KREE-ohl] cooking is traditionally the combination of French, Spanish, and African cuisines. Cooked with a spicy sauce containing tomatoes, onions, and peppers, probably the most famous dish of Creole heritage is gumbo. The origin of the word Creole dates back to the 18th century when the Spaniards governing New Orleans named all residents of European heritage Criollo. The name, which later became Creole, implied one of refined cultural background.

A combination of French and southern cuisines, Cajun [KAY-jun] food is robust, country-style food brought to Louisiana from the French who migrated to the state from Nova Scotia. Think of heavy, one-pot dishes, like jambalaya or crawfish étouffée, served over steaming rice.

1 medium eggplant, peeled and diced
Salt
4 tablespoons margarine, divided
3 tablespoons flour
3 large tomatoes, peeled and chopped
1 small green pepper, seeded and chopped
1 small onion, peeled and chopped
1 tablespoon brown sugar
1 teaspoon salt
2 cloves garlic, minced
$^{1}/_{2}$ teaspoon ground bay leaves
$^{1}/_{4}$ cup dry bread crumbs

Cook eggplant, uncovered, 10 minutes in boiling salted water. Drain well; place in a greased $1^{1}/_{2}$-quart casserole. In large skillet, melt 3 tablespoons margarine. Add flour and stir until blended. Add to skillet tomatoes, pepper, onion, sugar, salt, garlic, and bay leaves. Cook, uncovered, 5 minutes, stirring occasionally. Pour contents of skillet over eggplant. Sprinkle with bread crumbs; dot with remaining one tablespoon margarine. Bake in 350° oven a half hour.

Just a Spoonful

Mrs. Guerry's Baked Apricots

A little something sweet on the dinner plate.

2 (28-ounce) cans apricot
  halves
1 stick butter (more, if
  needed)
1 (1-pound) box brown
  sugar
Cinnamon (about 2
  teaspoons)
1 (1-pound) box Ritz
  Crackers

Butter the bottom of a large baking dish. Drain fruit, reserving liquid for later, if necessary. Place 1 can apricot halves in baking dish and dot each half with butter. Sprinkle with half the brown sugar and a little cinnamon. Top this with a layer of half the crumbled Ritz Crackers. Repeat the whole process so that you have two layers of everything. You probably won't have to add any juice, but add a small amount since the casserole should be moist and delicious, but not runny. Bake for 30–45 minutes in a 375° oven till nicely browned.

Chattanooga Cook Book

Editor's Extra: Cheese Ritz Crackers are great, too, and lemon juice (3 tablespoons or so) instead of the cinnamon is also nice. Easy to halve.

Hot Hominy

Mamean likes to serve hominy when she has fried ham. She stirs the hominy around in the pan drippings to coat it in the delicious ham flavor. At 87, my mother still tends her garden and plays golf! And oh my, when she cooks, you count yourself blessed to put your feet under her table.

—*Barbara*

2 large onions, chopped
1 green pepper, chopped
2 tablespoons butter
2 (14½-ounce) cans white
  hominy
1 (10½-ounce) can Ro-Tel
  tomatoes
½ pound cooked bulk
  sausage
Salt and pepper
Worcestershire sauce
Tabasco sauce (optional)
Red pepper (optional)
2 cups grated American
  cheese

Sauté onions and green pepper in butter. Add hominy, tomatoes, sausage, and seasonings to taste. Cook 20 minutes or until tender. In greased casserole, alternate layers of hominy and cheese ending with cheese. Bake 15 minutes at 350°. Serves 8.

Variation: You may use ½ measure Ro-Tel tomatoes and ½ plain canned tomatoes, if you do not like a hot taste.

The Jackson Cookbook

Vidalia Soufflé

A great alternative to quiche.

6 ounces stale or day-old French or Italian loaf (cut into chunks)

1/2 cup butter or margarine

3 large sweet onions, cut into thin slices

1 tablespoon fresh thyme or 1/2 teaspoon dried thyme

1 cup grated Swiss cheese

1 pint light cream

3 eggs, beaten

Salt and pepper to taste

Preheat oven to 350°. Place bread chunks in a 1 1/2-quart buttered soufflé dish. Melt butter in a large skillet. Cook onions until slightly limp, or translucent. Pour butter and onions over bread. Scatter thyme and cheese over top. Blend cream into eggs until mixture is light and frothy. Add salt and pepper, if desired. Pour over mixture in soufflé dish. Press down to make sure bread is thoroughly soaked. Bake 45 minutes or until knife inserted in center comes out clean. Serve with a salad. Add ham or bacon for a different flavor, or more onions, if you like! Yields 6–8 servings.

Georgia on my Menu

Baked Vidalias au Gratin

8 medium-size Vidalia onions (about 6 cups), peeled and sliced 1/4-inch thick

2 tablespoons butter, or as needed

1/2 cup heavy cream

1/4 cup dry cocktail sherry

1/8 teaspoon pepper

1/2 cup grated Swiss cheese

1/4 cup grated Parmesan or Romano cheese

Preheat oven to 375°. Sauté half the onions in 2 tablespoons butter in large frying pan over low heat, stirring occasionally. Cook only until limp, 5–10 minutes; do not brown or discolor.

Remove to 1 1/2-quart baking dish with slotted spoon; sauté remaining onions, using more butter, if necessary. Add to onions in baking dish, along with cream, sherry, and pepper. Stir to mix. Top with Swiss cheese, then Parmesan or Romano. Bake until top is a bit brown and all is bubbling hot, 15–20 minutes. Serves 6–8.

Island Events Cookbook

White Corn Casserole

10 strips bacon
1 medium onion, chopped
2 (12-ounce) cans white corn, drained
1 (8-ounce) carton sour cream

Fry bacon crisp; remove and crumble. Sauté onion in bacon grease. Combine 8 crumbled strips bacon, corn, sour cream, and onion. Cook at 350° for 20 minutes or until bubbly. Top with remaining bacon bits. Yields 5–6 servings.

Kitchen Sampler

Corn on the cob can be traced back to the Indians who lived all over the country. But it certainly is a staple on a summer southern table. Anyone can vouch for fresh-from-the-field, right-out-of-the-husk corn being the very best.

Boiling with a tad of sugar in the water "adds to the sweetness," some say. Others say salt "brings out the flavor."

The easiest method is microwaving. Simply put 2 ears of corn (in or out of the husks) and a teaspoon or two of water in a dish, cover, and microwave on HIGH 5–6 minutes. Lavish with butter and chomp in!

Fried Corn

Though not "fried," southerners have long called this fried corn.

8–10 ears fresh corn on the cob
3 tablespoons butter
Salt to taste
1½ tablespoons sugar
¼ cup water

Shuck and clean corn. With a sharp knife, cut the top of the corn kernel into a bowl. With corn tilted into bowl, scrape pulp from cob.

In a heavy skillet, melt butter and add corn. Add salt, sugar, and water. Cook until thickened, stirring often. Add more water, if needed.

Mountain Recipe Collection

Editor's Extra: We always like a little black pepper in our fried corn.

Succotash

¹/₄ pound salt pork, cut up
1 tablespoon shortening
1 large onion, chopped
1 small bell pepper, chopped
1 cup sliced okra, fresh or frozen
1 (8-ounce) can tomato sauce
1 (16-ounce) can cream-style corn, or whole-kernel corn, drained
1 (16-ounce) can lima beans, drained
1 tablespoon sugar

Bring salt pork to a boil in water and scald; drain and fry well in shortening. Add onion and fry lightly; add bell pepper, okra, and tomato sauce; cook at medium heat for about 15 minutes. Add corn, lima beans, and sugar; cook ¹/₂ hour on low heat. If mixture becomes too thick, add water as needed.

Cajun Cooking

Editor's Extra: I like to use a can of chopped tomatoes instead of the tomato sauce. If you like it a little spicy, use Ro-Tel tomatoes. You can also add bite-size chicken pieces for a one-dish meal.

Hot and Spicy Cabbage

2 ounces center-cut smoked ham
¹/₂ cup chopped onions
¹/₂ cup chopped bell pepper
Olive-oil-flavored cooking spray
1 (10-ounce) can chopped Ro-Tel tomatoes
¹/₂ teaspoon sugar
4 cups cabbage, sliced
¹/₈ teaspoon each: white and black peppers

Stir-fry ham, onions, and bell pepper in cooking spray. Add Ro-Tel tomatoes and sugar; simmer 2–3 minutes. Add cabbage and peppers. Simmer 15 minutes. Yields 8 servings.

Per serving: Cal 30; Chol 4mg; Sat Fat 3g; Fat <2g; Sod 244mg; Pro 2g; Cho 5g; Exchanges 1 vegetable.

Southern BUT Lite

Southern-Style Greens

3½–4 pounds collards,
   turnip or mustard greens,
   or a mixture
½ pound lean salt pork or
   smoked ham hock
1 tablespoon sugar
3 beef bouillon cubes
8 cups water
1 tablespoon margarine
Salt and pepper to taste

Wash greens in a sink full of water. Swish greens to remove any grit. Drain and rinse sink. Repeat washing. Lift greens out of water into colander. Remove and discard all large stems.

    Combine pork, sugar, bouillon cubes, water, and margarine in a large soup pot. Bring to a boil over medium-high heat. Boil for 5–10 minutes. Add greens. Reduce heat and simmer, covered, for 1½ hours or until greens are tender. Add salt and pepper to taste. You may peel and quarter turnips and add to the soup pot for the last 30 minutes of cooking. Makes 8–10 servings.

Cooking Wild Game & Fish Southern Style

Editor's Extra: You can substitute a 1-pound bag of frozen greens and cut the entire recipe by one-third, even the time. Fresh is best—frozen is quicker.

Granny Brock's Greens

4 cups early greens
4 slices bacon
3 green onions, chopped
3 tablespoons vinegar
2 teaspoons sugar
½ teaspoon salt
¼ teaspoon dry mustard
Dash of pepper

Gather greens (sheep sorrel, dandelion, poke, dock, lamb's quarters, and other favorites) early in the day, if possible. Wash in pure spring water until all grit is removed. Fry bacon and remove from skillet, leaving fat to cool. Mix chopped onions and greens together in large bowl (and then put in individual bowls, if desired). Crumble bacon over greens. To fat in skillet, add vinegar, sugar, salt, mustard, and pepper. Heat and pour over greens. Toss until wilted. Serve immediately.

*More than Moonshine: Appalachian Recipes and
Recollections*

Ro-Tel Potatoes

8 medium white potatoes

1 teaspoon salt

3 tablespoons margarine, melted

1 large onion, chopped

1 (4½-ounce) jar sliced mushrooms, drained

1 (10-ounce) can Ro-Tel tomatoes and diced green chiles

1 pound Velveeta cheese, cubed

In a large saucepan, cook potatoes in jackets in salted, boiling water for 30 minutes or until tender; drain and set aside to cool. Peel cooled potatoes and dice. Place diced potatoes in a greased 2-quart baking dish.

Melt margarine in a large skillet over medium heat; sauté onion and mushrooms 3–4 minutes or until tender. Add Ro-Tel tomatoes with juice and cheese. Cook over medium-low heat, stirring constantly, until cheese is melted and smooth. Pour cheese mixture over diced potatoes. Bake, uncovered, at 350° for 25–30 minutes or until bubbly.

Treasured Family Favorites

Seasoned Potato Slices

When it's too hot to cook, fix this delicious microwave potato dish.

2 baking potatoes (1¼ pounds)

¼ cup margarine

½ teaspoon seasoned salt

1 tablespoon parsley

1 small onion, sliced in rings

1 tablespoon Parmesan cheese

Scrub potatoes and slice ¼ inch thick. Melt margarine in 2-quart microwave-safe casserole on MEDIUM-HIGH (70%) for 1 minute. Stir in seasoned salt and parsley. Add potatoes and stir gently to coat. Put onion rings on top. Cover. Microwave on HIGH 9–11 minutes, stirring after 5 minutes. Potatoes should be almost tender when you remove them from oven. Let stand 5 minutes. Sprinkle with cheese. Serves 4.

The Microwave Touch

Cottage-Fried Potatoes

¹/₄ cup shortening or oil
6 cups chopped potatoes
1 teaspoon salt
¹/₈ teaspoon pepper

Heat shortening or oil in a 10- or 11-inch pan with a tight-fitting lid. Add potatoes when fat is hot enough to simmer gently around a piece of potato. Season with salt and pepper.

Cover tightly and fry gently until potatoes are brown, turning them occasionally as they cook. Remove cover for last few minutes of cooking time to crisp potatoes. Makes 6–8 servings.

Hint: For variety, add a medium onion, finely chopped, to the potatoes when browned on one side.

Home for the Holidays

Fix-Ahead Mashed Potatoes

3 pounds (about 4 large) potatoes
1¹/₄ teaspoons salt, divided
3 tablespoons butter or margarine, softened, divided
²/₃ cup sour cream
2 (3-ounce) packages cream cheese, softened
¹/₄ cup milk
¹/₂ teaspoon paprika

Place potatoes in a saucepan; add water to cover and ¹/₂ teaspoon salt. Bring to a boil; cover. Reduce heat to medium and simmer 25 minutes or until potatoes are tender. Drain. Peel potatoes; place in a large mixing bowl and mash with a potato masher. Add 2 tablespoons butter, sour cream, cream cheese, milk, and remaining ³/₄ teaspoon salt, mixing until all ingredients are blended.

Spoon mixture into a lightly greased 12x8x2-inch baking dish. Brush top of mixture with remaining tablespoon melted butter; sprinkle with paprika. Bake immediately, or cover and refrigerate. If refrigerated, let stand at room temperature 30 minutes before baking. Bake at 350°, uncovered, 30 minutes or until hot. Yields 6–8 servings.

Serving Our Best

Sweet Potato Casserole

A favorite dish on the Thanksgiving table.

While the terms are used interchangeably, especially in the South, yams and sweet potatoes are not the same. Yams (the tuber of a tropical vine) are not widely grown or available in the U.S. Sweet potatoes are the roots of a vine in the morning glory family. If it is called a yam at the grocery store, it is most likely really a sweet potato. But whichever you get, rest easy, they are interchangeable in recipes.

3 cups cooked sweet potatoes (fresh or canned)
¹/₂ cup brown sugar
2 eggs, beaten
¹/₂ teaspoon salt
¹/₂ stick margarine, melted
¹/₂ cup evaporated milk
1¹/₂ teaspoons vanilla

TOPPING:
¹/₂ cup brown sugar
¹/₃ cup plain flour
1 cup chopped pecans
¹/₃ stick margarine, melted

Mash cooked sweet potatoes. Add sugar, eggs, salt, margarine, milk, and vanilla. Put mixture into casserole dish.

Mix Topping ingredients and spread over sweet potato mixture. Bake at 325° for 30 minutes. Serves 6.

Sample West Kentucky

Candied Yams

That's what I like about the South.

2 large sweet potatoes
¹/₂ stick butter
¹/₂ cup sugar or brown sugar
1 teaspoon vanilla
1 teaspoon lemon juice
1 tablespoon water
Dashes of cinnamon, nutmeg (optional)

Parboil potatoes till barely tender; peel and slice in ³/₄-inch slices or wedges. Melt butter in heavy skillet; add potato slices (a 29-ounce can of sweet potatoes is good, too). In small saucepan, boil sugar, vanilla, lemon juice, water and spices (if desired); pour over potatoes in skillet. Bubble-boil till syrup is thickened, about 15 minutes (or bake in 350° oven 20–25 minutes). Serves 4 sweetly.

Gwen McKee

Pineapple Soufflé

Terrific with ham or pork.

4 slices white bread, crust trimmed
2 teaspoons flour
Pinch of salt
¹/₂ cup sugar
3 eggs, beaten
1 (14-ounce) can crushed pineapple
1 stick margarine

Break up bread into greased 1¹/₂-quart casserole. Add flour, salt, sugar, eggs, and pineapple. Mix well. Dot with margarine and bake at 350° for 45 minutes. Easy. Do ahead. Serves 6.

Culinary Classics

Pan-Fried June Apples

After long winters, my family yearned for fresh fruit. Mother fried the fresh June apples and served them with hot biscuits, freshly churned butter, and milk. Yum!

2 tablespoons bacon drippings
4 cups sliced apples, peeled (or unpeeled)
1¹/₂ cups sugar
¹/₂ teaspoon cinnamon
¹/₂ teaspoon salt

Heat bacon drippings in skillet and add apples. Stir in sugar, cinnamon, and salt, then cover and cook for about 5 minutes, or until the sugar liquefies. Remove lid and fry, stirring occasionally, until apples are tender, and the liquid is cooked away. Good served with fresh butter and hot biscuits. Serves 4–6.

More than Moonshine: Appalachian Recipes and Recollections

Macaroni Pie

¾ pound uncooked macaroni

¼ pound margarine (1 stick)

3 eggs

1 pound Cheddar cheese, grated

1½ cups milk

Salt and pepper to taste

Boil macaroni in salted water until tender. Drain and add margarine; stir till melted. Add eggs and cheese, reserving enough cheese to garnish top; stir. Add milk and season to taste; stir well and pour into buttered casserole dish. Sprinkle with reserved cheese. Bake in 350° oven for 20–25 minutes or until bubbly.

The Sandlapper Cookbook

> Everyone looked forward to Uncle Dan's macaroni pie—it was sooo much better than *just* macaroni and cheese. He believed in lots of butter and lots of cheese. Superb!
> —*Barbara*

Summer Pasta

A favorite use-the-garden-tomatoes veggie meal.

4 fresh tomatoes, peeled, seeded, and chopped

1 pound mozzarella cheese, diced

¼ cup freshly minced basil, or 2 tablespoons dry basil

1–2 cloves garlic, crushed

1 cup olive oil

Salt and pepper to taste

1 pound spaghetti, cooked

Grated Parmesan cheese

Combine all ingredients except spaghetti and Parmesan. Let stand at room temperature for about an hour. Toss with hot cooked spaghetti. Serve immediately with grated Parmesan cheese. Serves 4–6.

Puttin' on the Peachtree

Editor's Extra: Many southerners prefer the taste of regular or light olive oil over the stronger-flavored extra virgin variety.

Red Rice

So flavorful, so southern . . .

4 strips bacon
2 medium onions, chopped
2 medium bell peppers, chopped
1 (14 1/2-ounce) can tomatoes, diced
1 cup tomato sauce or ketchup
1/2 teaspoon Tabasco sauce
2 cups rice, cooked
Salt and pepper to taste
1 teaspoon Parmesan cheese

Fry bacon crisp, remove, and drain on paper towels. Sauté onions and bell peppers in drippings. Add tomatoes, sauce, Tabasco, rice, seasoning, and crumbled bacon. Pour in greased casserole, sprinkle top with Parmesan cheese, and bake at 325° for 30 minutes or until rice is dry enough to separate.

Variation: For shrimp rice, and other meat casseroles, add 1 pound of cooked deveined shrimp to red rice recipe or 1 cup cooked sausage, pork, or ham.

Famous Recipes from Mrs. Wilkes' Boarding House

Glamour Mushroom Rice

1 small onion, chopped
1/3 cup butter or margarine
1 (7-ounce) can sliced mushrooms, drained
1 cup uncooked long-grain rice
1 (10 1/2-ounce) can beef consommé
3/4 cup water
1/2 teaspoon salt
1/4 teaspoon pepper

Sauté onion in melted butter or margarine. Add mushrooms, rice, consommé, water, salt, and pepper. Pour into a greased 2-quart Pyrex dish. Cover and bake 1 hour at 350°.

Note: This is very good served with chopped minute steaks smothered in brown gravy. Corn bread goes well with this, too.

Prairie Harvest

Broccoli Rice Quiche

This makes a nice luncheon dish with a salad.

1½ cups cooked rice

1 egg, beaten

**¾ cup (3 ounces)
shredded cheese, divided**

**1 (10-ounce) package
frozen chopped broccoli**

2 teaspoons minced onion

⅓ cup milk

2 eggs, beaten

¼ teaspoon pepper

**1 (4-ounce) jar sliced
mushrooms, drained**

Combine rice, one egg and ½ cup cheese, mixing well. Press mixture into a greased 9-inch pie plate; set aside. Cook broccoli according to package directions; drain well. Add ¼ cup cheese and remaining ingredients to broccoli; mix well. Pour broccoli mixture into rice-lined pie plate. Bake at 375° for about 50 minutes, or until done. Yields 1 (9-inch) quiche.

Olivia's Favorite Menus and Recipes

Quiche Lorraine

This classic recipe has been served for many a southern brunch. Serve with fresh fruit and warm muffins.

6–8 slices bacon

**1 (8-inch) pastry shell,
preferably puff pastry**

**1 cup (4 ounces) Gruyère
or Swiss cheese, sliced**

3 large eggs

1¼–1½ cups heavy cream

¼ teaspoon salt

**Pinch of pepper and
nutmeg**

1–2 tablespoons butter

Cut bacon into ¼-inch piece, brown and drain. Partially cook pastry shell (about 6 minutes in preheated 450° oven). Spread bacon bits on bottom of pastry shell alternately with cheese. Beat eggs, cream, and seasonings well and pour into shell. Dot with butter. Bake at 375° in upper third of oven 25–30 minutes until puffed and browned. Serve warm or cold.

The Country Mouse

Corn Quiche

Cinnamon and brown sugar add a spicy taste to corn.

1 (9-inch) deep-dish pie shell

1 (12-ounce) can whole-kernel white corn, drained

4 ounces Swiss cheese, shredded

3 eggs, beaten

1 cup half-and-half

1/2 teaspoon salt

1/8 teaspoon white pepper

1/8 teaspoon nutmeg

1 1/2 tablespoons butter, melted

1 1/2 tablespoons brown sugar

1/4 teaspoon cinnamon

Preheat oven to 425°. Bake pie shell for 5 minutes. Reduce oven temperature to 350°. Place corn in pastry shell and sprinkle with cheese. Combine eggs, half-and-half, salt, pepper, and nutmeg, and pour over corn and cheese. Bake for 30 minutes. Drizzle melted butter over top of quiche and sprinkle combined brown sugar and cinnamon on top. Return to oven for 5 minutes or until center is firm.

Quiche can be made ahead and frozen by omitting topping and the last 5 minutes of baking time. Defrost and bring quiche to room temperature, add topping, and bake in preheated 350° oven for 15 minutes. Delicious alternative to sweet potatoes, or can be sliced into small wedges and served instead of bread with a meal. Serves 6.

Magic

Gone Fishin'

Fish & Seafood

Catfish is one of the finest eating fishes in the world.

—Willard Scott

Mississippi Catfish Fillets

The BEST!

¾ cup yellow cornmeal
¼ cup self-rising flour
½ teaspoon salt
½ teaspoon black pepper
1 teaspoon garlic salt
½ teaspoon cayenne red
   pepper
2 pounds catfish fillets
Oil for frying

Mix meal, flour, salt, pepper, garlic salt, and cayenne. Roll fish in mixture until coated good. Heat oil in skillet, about 400°. Add fish in single layer. Fry until golden brown, to your desire. Drain on paper towels or brown bag. Serve hot. Also good cold or warmed in microwave.

Mississippi Stars Cookbook

Carolyn's Pan-Fried Catfish

Soft on the inside and firm on the outside . . . delicious all the way through.

4 catfish fillets
Seasoning suggestions:
   salt and paprika;
   salt and lemon pepper;
   seasoned salt; salt,
   pepper, and garlic
   powder
¼ cup lemon juice

A nonstick skillet is a must for this dish. Heat skillet on medium-high heat; add seasoned fish and sauté, uncovered, for 6–8 minutes. Turn over and cook other side 6–8 minutes. The fish will be crisp and sometimes blackened, depending on the seasoning used. Remove fish from skillet and place on serving plate. Lower heat and add lemon juice. Stir to make sauce, then strain over fish. Serves 4.

Family Secrets...the Best of the Delta

Delta Baked Catfish

2 cups dry bread crumbs
³/₄ cup grated Parmesan cheese
¹/₄ cup chopped parsley
¹/₂ teaspoon oregano
1 teaspoon paprika
¹/₄ teaspoon basil
2 teaspoons salt
¹/₂ teaspoon black pepper
6 whole catfish fillets
³/₄ cup margarine, melted
Lemon wedges

Grease a 9x13x2-inch baking dish well. Combine bread crumbs, cheese, herbs, and seasonings. Dip catfish in melted margarine and roll in crumb mixture. Arrange fish in baking dish. Bake in a preheated oven at 375° for 25 minutes or until fish flakes easily. Garnish with lemon wedges. Yields 6 servings.

With Special Distinction

Editor's Extra: Don't hesitate to use fillets; bake only 15–20 minutes, depending on size.

Billy's Baked Bass

This gives you time to tell tall tales.

¹/₂ cup butter
²/₃ cup crushed crackers
¹/₄ cup Parmesan cheese
¹/₂ teaspoon basil
¹/₂ teaspoon oregano
¹/₂ teaspoon salt
¹/₄ teaspoon garlic powder
8 bass fillets

Melt butter in 9x13-inch baking dish. Mix together next 6 ingredients. Dip fish in cracker batter, breading both sides. Place in baking dish and sprinkle extra crumbs over fish. Bake at 350° for 15–20 minutes. To test for doneness, flake with fork. Yields 4–6 servings.

To Market, To Market

Easy Flounder Fillets

2 pounds flounder (or other fish) fillets, fresh or frozen, skinned
2 tablespoons grated onion
1½ teaspoons salt
⅛ teaspoon pepper
2 large tomatoes, peeled, cut into small pieces
¼ cup butter or margarine, melted
1 cup shredded Swiss cheese

Thaw fillets if frozen. Place fillets in a single layer on a well-greased bake-and-serve platter. Sprinkle fish with onion, salt, and pepper. Cover fillets with tomatoes. Pour butter over tomatoes. Broil about 4 inches from source of heat for 10–12 minutes or until fish flakes easily when tested with a fork. Remove from heat; sprinkle with cheese. Broil 2–3 minutes longer, or until cheese melts. Yields 6 servings.

Southern Seafood Classics

Trout Almandine

An all-time classic.

SAUCE:
½ cup butter
Juice of ½ lemon
2 tablespoons Worcestershire
2 tablespoon chopped parsley
¼ cup browned, blanched, chopped almonds

Melt butter in small saucepan. Add lemon juice and Worcestershire; cook, stirring for 2 minutes. Add parsley and almonds.

FISH:
2 egg yolks
½ cup milk
Trout fillets
Flour
Oil for frying

Beat egg yolks and add milk slowly in shallow dish, mixing well. Dip fillets in this mixture and roll in flour. Heat oil and cook fish 3–5 minutes or until brown on both sides. Pour Sauce over Fish and serve.

Recipe Jubilee!

Avery Island Trout

8–12 trout fillets (allow ⅓ pound per person)

Milk to cover (flavored with 1 teaspoon salt and 6 drops Tabasco)

Salt

¾ cup flour

2 sticks butter, divided

½ teaspoon Tabasco

½ cup finely chopped green onions

½ cup finely chopped green pepper

⅔ cup dry white wine

Soak fillets one hour in flavored milk to cover. Dry fish well and salt generously on both sides. Dredge in flour and shake off excess. Put one stick butter and Tabasco in baking dish (not aluminum) large enough to hold fillets without crowding. Place pan on middle shelf in broiler and let butter start to bubble. Remove from oven and sprinkle green onions and green pepper in bottom of pan, laying fillets on top. Use remaining butter to dot tops, and return to broiler. Cook 15–20 minutes (depending on size of fillets), basting twice.

When fish is done and browned on top, remove them with a spatula to a heated serving platter, and keep warm. Add wine to pan juices and place pan over a medium flame on top of range. Allow sauce to bubble rapidly, stirring constantly for 3–4 minutes. Spoon some sauce over trout and serve the rest in a heated sauceboat.

The Plantation Cookbook

Snapper in Foil

Soft and succulent . . . the flavor is locked in.

1 (4½-pound) snapper, filleted

Seasoned salt

Pepper

Fresh lemon juice

2 thick onion slices

1½ tablespoons butter

2 green peppers, quartered

Place each fillet on a separate piece of heavy-duty foil. Sprinkle each with seasoned salt, pepper, and lemon juice to taste. Top with onion slices, butter, and green pepper; seal foil leaving some room for expansion. Place each package on a baking sheet and bake at 375° for 45 minutes. Slit foil at the table being careful not to let the juices escape. This may be prepared ahead of time and refrigerated until baking. Serves 4.

Bay Leaves

125

Pecan Crusted Redfish

1 cup flour
½ teaspoon salt
¼ teaspoon pepper
½ teaspoon Creole
  seasoning
1 stick butter
8 (6- to 7-ounce) redfish
  fillets

Preheat oven to 325°. Combine flour with seasonings. Melt butter in large skillet over medium-high heat. Lightly dust fillets in seasoned flour and place in skillet. Lightly brown both sides, then place on a baking sheet. Spread Pecan Butter over the top surface of each fillet. Bake 15 minutes. Yields 8 servings.

PECAN BUTTER:
2 sticks butter, softened
2 cups chopped pecans
½ cup diced onion
1½ tablespoons lemon
  juice
2 teaspoons hot sauce
1 tablespoon minced garlic

Place ingredients in a food processor and purée until well incorporated. Butter may be made in advance and stored in refrigerator. Allow butter to soften before preparing fish.

Deep South Staples

"Can you get the hook out, Dad?"
"Here it comes. He's still kickin'. Wanna throw him back?"

Shrimp Étouffée

No wonder it's a classic.

1 bunch green onions, chopped

1 onion, chopped

¹/₂ bell pepper, chopped

¹/₂ cup chopped celery

2 tablespoons olive oil

¹/₂ stick margarine

2 pounds shrimp, peeled and deveined

1 cup chicken broth

2 tablespoons cornstarch, dissolved in ¹/₂ cup cold water

1 tablespoon Worcestershire sauce

1 teaspoon tomato paste

1 cup raw rice, cooked as directed

In large skillet, cook green onions, onion, bell pepper, and celery till soft in olive oil and margarine. Add shrimp; cook 10 minutes. Add chicken broth, and thicken with cornstarch in water. Add Worcestershire and tomato paste. Cook 5 minutes. Serve over cooked rice. Serves 6.

A Pinch of Rose & A Cup of Charm

Shrimp Tetrazzini

2 tablespoons butter

1 medium onion, minced

8 ounces shrimp, peeled and deveined

8 ounces fresh mushrooms, sliced

¹/₄ cup all-purpose flour

¹/₄ cup mayonnaise

2 cups milk

¹/₄ cup sherry

¹/₂ (8-ounce) package thin spaghetti, cooked and drained

Parmesan cheese

Sauté onion in butter until tender. Add shrimp and mushrooms. Cook 5 minutes, stirring often; remove from skillet. Add flour and mayonnaise to skillet. Blend well. Add liquids; cook until thickened. Toss with shrimp mixture and spaghetti. Pour into a greased 1¹/₂-quart casserole. Top generously with cheese. Bake in 350° oven for 30 minutes. Yields 4 servings.

Once Upon a Stove

Shrimp and Rice Casserole

1½ cups chopped onion

¾ cup chopped green
    pepper

1½ sticks margarine

3 pounds shrimp, peeled
    and cooked

2 (4-ounce) cans
    mushrooms with juice

2–3 tablespoons
    Worcestershire sauce

6 cups cooked rice

2 (10¾-ounce) cans cream
    of mushroom soup

A few shakes of Tabasco

Sauté onion and pepper in margarine until soft. Add all ingredients and mix. Place in buttered baking dish and bake at 300° until thoroughly hot. Add another can of soup if it bakes too dry.

Seasoned with Light

Shrimp-Chicken Jambalaya

2 medium onions, chopped

2 cloves garlic, minced

2 ribs celery, chopped

1 large green pepper,
    chopped

⅔ cup uncooked regular
    rice

2 cups chicken broth

8 ounces chicken breasts,
    cooked and cubed

1 (16-ounce) can stewed
    tomatoes

8 ounces shrimp, deveined
    and rinsed

½ teaspoon hot sauce

¼ teaspoon pepper

Coat a large skillet with cooking spray; place over medium heat until hot. Add onions, garlic, celery, and green pepper; sauté until tender. Add remaining ingredients. Bring to a boil, cover, reduce heat, and simmer 25 minutes or until rice is done, stirring occasionally. Yields 4 servings.

Per serving: Cal 311; Chol 129mg; Sat Fat 1g; Fat 3g; Sod 650mg; Pro 36g; Cho 35g. Exchanges: 4 meat, 1 bread, 3 vegetable.

Southern BUT Lite

The South's Best Shrimp and Grits

A proven favorite that will make grits lovers out of all who try it.

CHEESE GRITS:

6 cups water

1½ cups quick grits

2 teaspoons salt

½ stick butter

1 (6-ounce) roll Kraft Garlic Cheese, chunked

1 cup grated cheese

¼ teaspoon cayenne

In large saucepan, bring water to a boil; stir in grits and salt. Lower heat and stir occasionally till thickened. Add remaining ingredients and stir till smooth. Pour into greased casserole and bake 20 minutes at 350° while preparing Shrimp Sauce.

SHRIMP SAUCE:

2–3 pounds shrimp, peeled, deveined

3 tablespoons olive oil or bacon drippings

1 stick butter or margarine

8 ounces sliced mushrooms

1 bunch (8) green onions, chopped

1–2 cloves garlic, minced

½ cup chopped parsley

2 tablespoons lemon juice

Sprinklings of cayenne, basil, thyme, oregano, paprika

Salt and pepper to taste

Have Shrimp Sauce ingredients ready. In a large skillet, sauté shrimp in oil and butter for just a few minutes. Immediately add remaining ingredients. Stir well and heat on medium high another few minutes. Do not simmer longer than 10 minutes.

Serve over a scoop of Cheese Grits. Add a salad and French bread, and you will serve 8 lucky people a marvelous meal.

Gwen McKee

Shrimp Creole

1/4 cup flour

1/4 cup oil

2 cups chopped onions

1/2 cup chopped green onions and tops

2 buds garlic, minced

1 cup chopped green pepper

1 cup chopped celery with leaves

2 bay leaves

3 teaspoons salt

1/2 teaspoon pepper

1 (6-ounce) can tomato paste

1 (16-ounce) can diced tomatoes

1 (8-ounce) can tomato sauce

1 cup water

5 pounds raw shrimp, peeled and deveined

Dash of Tabasco

1/2 cup chopped parsley

Juice of 1/2 lemon

In a Dutch oven or large heavy pot, make a roux of flour and oil. Add onions, green onions, garlic, green pepper, celery, bay leaves, salt and pepper. Sauté, uncovered, over medium heat until onions are transparent and soft. Add tomato paste and sauté 3 minutes. Add tomatoes, tomato sauce, and water. Simmer for 45 minutes to 1 hour, stirring occasionally. Add shrimp and cook until shrimp are just done, about 5 minutes. Add Tabasco, parsley, and lemon juice. Stir, cover, and remove from heat.

This is best prepared several hours before serving. Let stand so seasonings and flavors can blend. Heat, but do not boil, and serve over rice. Serves 10.

The Gulf Gourmet

Golden Fried Shrimp Batter

Perfect!

1 egg, separated
1/2 cup milk, divided
2 tablespoons melted
   butter or margarine
1/2 cup self-rising flour
Salt and pepper to taste
Nature's Seasons Seasoning
   Blend, to taste
Peeled and deveined
   shrimp
Extra flour to roll shrimp

Put egg yolk in small mixing bowl, and egg white in separate bowl. Beat yolk, 1/4 cup milk, and melted butter in mixing bowl. Add flour, seasonings, and remaining milk and beat well. Beat egg white until stiff, and fold into batter. Dip shrimp in batter, then roll in flour. Fry in hot grease until golden.

This batter can also be used for fried onion rings. If you like spicy shrimp, add a teaspoon of liquid crab boil to grease.

The Gulf Gourmet

Fried Shrimp

1 cup all-purpose flour
1/2 teaspoon sugar
1/2 teaspoon salt
1 cup ice water (leave 1 or
   2 cubes in)
1 egg, slightly beaten
2 tablespoons oil
2 pounds fresh, frozen,
   shrimp, unpeeled

Combine ingredients, except shrimp; stir until smooth, then set in refrigerator or freezer to chill. Peel shells from shrimp, leaving tail intact; "butterfly" shrimp by cutting lengthwise to tail. Dry shrimp, dip into batter, and fry in deep hot fat (350°–400°) till floating and golden brown, 3–5 minutes. Serve immediately.

Note: Also good for frying soft-and hard-shelled crabs, eggplants, onions, etc.

Cajun Cooking

Baked Shrimp, New Orleans Style

Often called "Barbecue Shrimp," this is outstanding!

2 pounds large shrimp,
  unpeeled, with heads on

¹/₂ pound (2 sticks)
  margarine

4 cloves garlic, chopped

¹/₂ teaspoon Italian
  seasoning

2 tablespoons paprika

2 teaspoons coarse-ground
  black pepper

¹/₈ teaspoon cayenne
  pepper

¹/₂ teaspoon salt

2 tablespoons fresh lemon
  juice

Preheat oven to 450°. Put the shrimp in a large baking pan and spread evenly. Heat remaining ingredients in a small saucepan and mix well. Pour mixture over the shrimp and bake for about 10–12 minutes, stirring a few times during the cooking time. (Shrimp is done when the shell separates from the shrimp at the tail section.) Serve with lots of hot French bread to "sop up" the butter and juices. Makes 4–6 servings.

Cajun Cooking for Beginners

Editor's Extra: Okay, of course, to use headless shrimp. Either way, have lots of napkins handy.

New Orleans Shrimp Rémoulade

¹/₂ pound shrimp per
  person for an entrée; ¹/₄
  pound for first course

Cook the shrimp your favorite way and serve with Rémoulade Sauce.

RÉMOULADE SAUCE:

1 medium onion, grated

1 pint Hellmann's
  mayonnaise

4 tablespoons finely
  chopped parsley

4 tablespoons finely
  chopped Kosher dill
  pickles

1 hard-boiled egg, finely
  chopped

Juice of 1 lemon

3 tablespoons dry mustard

Garlic salt to taste

Pepper to taste

Grate onion on a paper towel and let it stand until moisture is absorbed. Add it to mayonnaise with remaining ingredients. If it is too thick, add a little juice from the dill pickles. Serve cold with shrimp (or your favorite seafood).

Hors D'Oeuvres Everybody Loves

Editor's Extra: This is so good, it makes your nose tingle. You may want to start with a little less dry mustard.

Shrimp Boil Dinner

With a salad, this is a complete meal for a fun supper party.

2 packages crab boil
6 lemons, halved
1 tablespoon Tabasco
  sauce
2–3 tablespoons ice cream
  salt or kosher salt
20 new potatoes
15 onions
10 ears of corn, shucked
  and halved
6 pounds fresh unpeeled
  shrimp

In a large roaster filled half full with water, bring the crab boil, lemon halves, Tabasco, and salt to a boil. Add the new potatoes and onions and boil until the potatoes are tender. Add corn. When corn is tender, add the shrimp. The shrimp are ready when they turn pink. This will take only a few minutes after the water has come to a full boil again. Drain and serve. Yields 10 servings.

Encore! Nashville

Shrimp Stuffed Peppers

6 bell peppers
2 cups cooked, cleaned
  shrimp
1 cup bread crumbs
2 eggs, beaten
1/2 cup milk
3 tablespoons butter or
  margarine
1 tablespoon chopped
  onion
3 tablespoons chopped
  celery
1 teaspoon salt
1/8 teaspoon pepper
1 tablespoon
  Worcestershire sauce
Butter for tops
  (2 tablespoons)

Cut off tops and remove seeds from peppers. Cook pepper shells in boiling water for 5 minutes, then plunge into cold water. Chop shrimp slightly. Combine bread crumbs, eggs, and milk.

Melt butter in skillet; cook onion and celery for about 3 minutes, then add to shrimp with remaining ingredients, except butter. Stuff mixture into peppers. Dot tops with butter. Bake in a moderate (350°) oven 30 minutes. Makes 6 servings.

Historic Kentucky Recipes

Stuffed Shrimp

$^{1}/_{4}$ cup chopped parsley

1$^{1}/_{2}$ teaspoons hot sauce

1$^{1}/_{2}$ teaspoons salt

2 eggs and 3 yolks

$^{3}/_{4}$ cup mayonnaise

$^{1}/_{2}$ cup sour cream

$^{1}/_{4}$ cup Dijon mustard

2 tablespoons cider vinegar

1$^{1}/_{2}$ teaspoons Old Bay
Seasoning

1 tablespoon dried dill

1 (10-ounce) package
frozen spinach, thawed
and squeezed dry

$^{1}/_{2}$ cup bread crumbs,
coarse

1$^{1}/_{2}$ pounds crabmeat

10 saltine crackers,
crushed into crumbs

$^{1}/_{4}$ cup olive oil

32 shrimp, peeled and
butterflied

Preheat oven to 350°. Mix together all ingredients except crab, cracker crumbs, oil, and shrimp. Add crab and gently fold in. Add cracker crumbs; fold in until just incorporated. Oil a 3-quart baking dish. Top each shrimp with 1$^{1}/_{2}$ tablespoons of crab mixture. Arrange shrimp in baking dish. Bake 20 minutes. Remove from oven and serve. Yields 8 servings.

Deep South Staples

Boiled crawfish, crabs, shrimp, corn, potatoes . . . it all gets dumped right in the middle of the table. Laissez le bon temps rouler—let the good times roll!

Creole Crawfish Casserole

2 large onions, chopped
3 stalks celery, chopped
1 green bell pepper, chopped
1/2 cup margarine
1 pound cooked, peeled crawfish tails
1 egg
1 tablespoon minced parsley
3 cups cooked rice
1 (10³/₄-ounce) can cream of mushroom soup
1¹/₂ cups (6 ounces) grated mozzarella cheese, Cheddar cheese, or pasteurized processed cheese spread
Cajun seasoning salt or salt and black pepper to taste
Bread crumbs

Sauté onions, celery, and bell pepper in margarine in large saucepan until vegetables are softened. Add crawfish and cook for several minutes. Stir in egg, parsley, and rice, mixing well. Add soup and cheese. Season with seasoning salt or salt and black pepper. Spread crawfish mixture in a greased 2-quart casserole and sprinkle with bread crumbs. Bake at 375° for 25 minutes. Serves 6.

Cane River's Louisiana Living

Creamy Crawfish Fettuccini

12 ounces fettuccini noodles
1 large onion, chopped
1 cup chopped bell pepper
1 cup chopped celery
1¹/₂ sticks butter
2 (12-ounce) packages frozen crawfish tails
1 (6-ounce) roll jalapeño cheese
1 (6-ounce) roll garlic cheese
1¹/₂ cups sour cream
1/2 cup grated Swiss cheese

Cook noodles. In very large skillet, sauté vegetables in butter. Add crawfish, cheese rolls, and sour cream. When totally melted and mixed, stir in drained noodles. Put in greased casserole dish. Sprinkle Swiss cheese over top. Bake in 350° oven till cheese is melted. Serves 8.

Gwen McKee

Oyster Po-Boys

Oysters (about 1 per inch
  of bread)

Corn flour, salt, pepper

Po-boy bread or French
  mini-loaves

Mayonnaise, salad
  dressing, or tartar sauce

Tomato slices

Shredded lettuce

Dill pickle slices (optional)

Salt and pepper to taste

Dip drained oysters in seasoned corn flour and fry quickly in very hot oil (350°); drain on paper towels. Heat French bread in oven just long enough to get hot—do not toast. Split and spread generously with mayonnaise. Cover with hot oysters, tomato slices, lettuce, and a few pickles. Put the top half on and give it one good mash with the palm of your hand . . . and chomp in! Have the ketchup handy . . . and the Tabasco.

Note: Fried shrimp, roast beef and gravy, ham and cheese, softshell crab and crawfish are other popular choices. Your po-boy is "dressed" when you put on the lettuce and tomatoes.

The Little New Orleans Cookbook

Editor's Extra: The secret to frying oysters is to not fry too many at a time since that lowers the oil temperature and you'll end up with soggy oysters. As soon as they float to the top of the oil, they're done Crispy is the key.

Crab Cakes à la Mobile Bay

These are WOW!

1 egg

1 tablespoon prepared
  mustard

1 tablespoon baking
  powder

1 tablespoon minced
  parsley

1/2 teaspoon Old Bay
  Seasoning or salt

2 tablespoons mayonnaise

1 pound crabmeat

1 cup bread crumbs

Mix all but crabmeat and bread crumbs to form a paste. Add crabmeat and enough bread crumbs to hold mixture together. Shape into flat cakes about 2 1/2 inches in diameter. Refrigerate about 2 hours.

Fry in iron skillet with 1/4 inch medium-hot oil until brown on both sides. Serve with beer, slaw, and crackers. Allow 2 per person. Serves 4–6.

Heavenly Hostess

Boiled Crabs in a Chest

4 dozen live crabs

Water

1 ice chest big enough to hold 4 dozen crabs

Tony's Creole Seasoning, or 1 box salt mixed with 1 (4-ounce) bottle red pepper

Plunge crabs in boiling water; boil for 11 minutes. Remove and immediately place (while hot) 1 layer crabs in bottom of ice chest. Sprinkle generously with seasoning, then place another layer of crabs. Season and repeat process until all crabs are placed and covered with seasoning. Cover with newspaper and close top securely. Heat will steam crabs and melt seasoning for flavor. After one hour, take out and eat. Crabs will keep hot for 5–6 hours. Serves 8.

Note: You can do this with crawfish or shrimp the same way. Use a styrofoam chest—it will not warp.

Tony Chachere's Cajun Country Cookbook

Almond Crab Supreme

The delicate taste of crabmeat is amplified in this outstanding recipe.

2 tablespoons butter

2 tablespoons flour

1/2 teaspoon paprika

1/2 teaspoon salt

1/8 teaspoon pepper

1 cup whipping cream

1 tablespoon minced onion

1 beaten egg yolk

1–2 tablespoons sherry

1/2 cup sour cream

1 pound lump crabmeat

2 tablespoons lemon juice

1/2 cup chopped almonds, divided

1 package Pepperidge Farm Patty Shells

Melt butter over low heat and stir in flour, paprika, salt, pepper, cream, and onion. Cook, stirring constantly, until sauce comes to a boil. Remove from heat. Stir in beaten egg yolk, sherry, and sour cream. Gently stir in crabmeat and heat through. Stir in lemon juice and half the almonds. Serve over baked patty shells and garnish with remaining almonds. Serves 4–6.

Frederica Fare

Tartar Sauce

1 cup mayonnaise
2 tablespoons dill pickle
   relish
2–3 tablespoons grated
   onion
1 tablespoon horseradish
Salt and hot pepper sauce
   to taste

Combine all ingredients; let stand at least 30 minutes before serving. Serve with fried seafood.

Cajun Cuisine

Editor's Extra: Sweet pickle relish instead of dill is good, too. Great on Oyster Po-Boys (page 136).

Kum-Back Sauce

Great served with shrimp, fish, or as a salad dressing. This originated in a Mississippi restaurant in the 1950s and is still popular today.

¼ cup salad oil
2 garlic cloves, chopped
   fine
1 cup mayonnaise
¼ cup chili sauce
¼ cup catsup
1 teaspoon Worcestershire
   sauce
1 teaspoon black pepper
Dash Tabasco sauce
Dash paprika
Juice of grated onion
2 tablespoons water
1 teaspoon prepared
   mustard

Put all ingredients in quart jar and shake well. Keep in refrigerator. Makes a full pint.

Best of Bayou Cuisine

What's for Supper?

Meat & Poultry Main Dishes

HAM AND EGGS—A day's work for a chicken;
A lifetime commitment for a pig.

—Anonymous

Chicken Fried Steak and Cream Gravy

2 pounds boneless round steak
1 cup all-purpose flour
1 teaspoon salt
1 teaspoon pepper
1/2 teaspoon garlic salt
2 eggs
1/4 cup milk
Vegetable oil

Trim excess fat from steak; pound steak to 1/4-inch thickness, using a meat mallet. Cut into serving-size pieces. Combine flour, salt, pepper, and garlic salt. Combine eggs and milk; beat well. Dredge steak in flour mixture, dip in egg mixture, then dredge in flour mixture again. Lightly pound steak. Heat 1 inch of oil in a skillet to 375°. Fry steak in hot oil until browned, turning steak once. Drain steak on paper towels. Reserve 1/4 cup pan drippings for gravy. Serve steak with Cream Gravy. Yields 6–8 servings.

CREAM GRAVY:
1/4 cup all-purpose flour
1/4 cup pan drippings
2–3 cups milk
1/2 teaspoon salt
1/4 teaspoon pepper

Add flour to pan drippings; cook over medium heat until bubbly, stirring constantly. Gradually add milk till desired consistency is reached; cook until thickened and bubbly, stirring constantly. Stir in salt and pepper.

Golden Moments

Deviled Swiss Steak

1 tablespoon dry mustard
1/2 cup flour
1 1/2 pounds top round steak
Salt and pepper to taste
1 cup sliced onion
1 carrot, diced
1 1/2 cups diced tomatoes
2 tablespoons Worcestershire sauce
1 tablespoon brown sugar

Mix dry mustard with flour; pound into 1-inch thick pieces of steak. Season with salt and pepper. Brown on both sides in a little fat. Place in small roaster. Add sliced onion, carrot, tomatoes, Worcestershire sauce, and brown sugar. Cover and bake at 325° for 1–1 1/2 hours. Serves 6.

Dutch Pantry Cookin'

Delicious Beef Roast

1 (1³/₈-ounce) package dry
  onion soup mix
1 (5- to 6-pound) chuck,
  sirloin, or shoulder roast
1 (10³/₄-ounce) can cream
  of mushroom soup
1¹/₃ cups water
¹/₂ teaspoon pepper
5 medium potatoes, cut in
  chunks
5 carrots, cut in 2-inch
  pieces

Sprinkle dry soup mix in bottom of Dutch oven. Add roast, cream of mushroom soup, water, and pepper. Bring to a boil; cover and simmer 2 hours. Add potatoes and carrots and cook 45 minutes or until tender. Serves 10–12.

Third Wednesday Homemakers

24-Hour Crockpot Barbecue

Takes the fat out . . . leaves the taste in. Superb!

3 medium onions, sliced,
  divided
1 (4- to 5-pound) Boston
  butt pork roast
2 cups water
6 whole cloves
1 (16-ounce) bottle hickory
  smoked barbecue sauce
10 drops Tabasco sauce

The night before serving, put 1 sliced onion in crockpot. Add meat, water, and cloves. Top with another sliced onion. Cover and cook on LOW 10–12 hours, or until meat falls off bone. Drain contents of crockpot in colander. Remove bone and fat from meat. Discard onions and cloves. Return meat to crockpot. Add remaining chopped onion, barbecue sauce, and Tabasco sauce. Cover and cook remainder of day on LOW, or 1–3 hours on HIGH. Serve on warm buns. Yields 6–8 servings.

Note: Leftovers will freeze. Good with coleslaw and corn on the cob.

Prescriptions for Good Eating

Slow Cooker Barbecued Pot Roast

Easy and good!

1 (2- to 3-pound) beef
    chuck roast
2 tablespoons oil
$^1/_2$ cup barbecue sauce
1 large onion, sliced

Brown meat in hot oil in skillet, then transfer to slow cooker. Add sauce and onion; cover. Cook at high heat 4–5 hours, or until tender. Slice and serve with sauce. Serves 6–8.

Favorite Recipes

Barbecued Brisket

3 ounces liquid smoke
Garlic salt to taste
Onion salt to taste
Celery salt to taste
1 (5- to 6-pound) beef
    brisket
5 tablespoons
    Worcestershire sauce
Salt and pepper to taste
6 ounces barbecue sauce
2 tablespoons all-purpose
    flour
$^1/_2$ cup water

Sprinkle liquid smoke and salts over brisket placed in a baking dish sprayed with nonstick cooking spray, and refrigerate overnight.

When ready to bake, sprinkle with Worcestershire sauce, salt and pepper; place foil loosely on top. Cook at 250° for 5 hours; uncover and pour barbecue sauce over meat. Cook without foil for another hour. Remove to platter and let cool before slicing. Remove fat from sauce remaining in dish. Add flour and water to sauce and stir. Cook until sauce thickens. Serve sauce hot with meat. Serves 10.

Temptations

Railroad Special

This corn bread pie is a tasty all-in-one-pan meal.

1 pound ground beef
1 large onion, chopped
1 can tomato soup
2 cups water
1 teaspoon salt
$^3/_4$ teaspoon pepper
1 tablespoon chili powder
1 cup whole-kernel corn, drained
$^1/_2$ cup chopped green pepper

Brown beef and onion in skillet; add soup, water, seasonings, corn, and green pepper. Mix well. Let simmer 15 minutes. Fill casserole or 11x7x2-inch pan, leaving room for Topping.

TOPPING:
$^3/_4$ cup cornmeal
1 tablespoon sugar
1 tablespoon flour
$^1/_2$ teaspoon salt
$1^1/_2$ teaspoons baking powder
1 egg
$^1/_2$ cup milk

Sift together cornmeal, sugar, flour, salt, and baking powder. Stir together with egg and milk. Top meat mixture; bake at 350° for 45 minutes or until done.

The Way Pocahontas County Cooks

Children of all ages are fascinated by trains. How much fun is the zoo choo-choo! All aboard!

143

Meat Balls and Spaghetti

A very old Italian recipe.

My mother loved to simmer her meat balls and spaghetti till the tomato sauce was more brown than red. The tempting smell lured us in from play. When she finally ladled this divine sauce thickly over our spaghetti and served it up with crusty buttered French bread, and creamy tiny English peas, we all declared it was our favorite meal. There was never any left. I cook it this way to this day.

—Gwen

$1^1/2$ pounds ground chuck
1 cup Italian grated cheese
8 small crackers (soaked in water and squeezed)
3 large eggs
2 teaspoons salt
1 teaspoon pepper
2 dashes Tabasco
1 large bunch green onions, sliced
$1/2$ cup olive oil
2 (8-ounce) cans tomato purée
1 quart water
2 large cloves garlic, minced
1 cup finely chopped parsley
1 teaspoon salt
$1/2$ teaspoon red pepper
1 teaspoon oregano

Combine first 7 ingredients. Make into small meat balls—about $1^1/2$ inches in diameter. In a very large pot, brown meat balls and onions in olive oil. Remove meat; add tomato purée and water. Add garlic, parsley, and seasonings to taste. Cook one hour or until reduced to about one half. Add meat balls. Simmer one hour.

Serve over cooked, drained, buttered spaghetti. Pass additional cheese.

A Cook's Tour of Shreveport

Lucy's Spaghetti Meat Sauce

None better . . . great for company . . . makes a lot . . . freeze some.

3 large onions, chopped

2 cloves garlic, minced

¼ stick butter

¼ cup oil

3 pounds ground chuck

1 pound fresh mushrooms, sliced (use stems, too)

2 (28-ounce) cans Italian tomatoes

1 (12-ounce) can tomato paste

1 tablespoon chili powder

1 tablespoon sugar

¼ teaspoon each: marjoram, oregano, basil, and thyme

3 bay leaves

Salt and pepper to taste

Cook onions and garlic in butter and oil until clear. Add meat and brown. Stir in sliced mushrooms. Combine tomatoes, tomato paste and all seasonings; add to meat mixture. Simmer, uncovered, until thick; at least 3 hours. When cool, put in refrigerator. Before reheating to serve, or freezing, skim off fat. Serve over very thin spaghetti. Serves 10–12.

Cook and Deal

It's cotton pickin' time down South.

Blue Ribbon Chili

2 pounds chili ground meat

1 large onion, chopped

1 large bell pepper, chopped

3 ribs celery, chopped

1 (10½-ounce) can diced Ro-Tel tomatoes

3 heaping tablespoons chili powder

1 heaping tablespoon paprika

2 teaspoons Ac'cent (optional)

1 (8-ounce) can tomato sauce

1 sauce can water or more

1 teaspoon cayenne pepper

1 teaspoon salt

3 (16-ounce) cans cream-style red kidney beans

Brown meat just to get the red out, then cook all but beans together with meat for about 45 minutes. Add kidney beans and cook another 15 minutes.

A Shower of Roses

Editor's Extra: If you can't find cream-style red kidney beans, use regular, but drain 2 of the cans and cook a little longer.

The Moseleys use this 1926 Model T Ford to let people know about their Christmas tree farm. With a Christmas tree in the back, and grandkids throwing candy to the bystanders, it's a fun "float" in the Christmas parade. "Oo-gah! Oo-gah!"

146

Chunky Venison Chili with Dumplings

2 cups venison, cut into
  $\frac{1}{2}$-inch cubes

1 cup water

1 (15-ounce) can tomato
  sauce

1 ($1\frac{3}{4}$-ounce) package
  chili seasoning mix

1 (15-ounce) can black
  beans, undrained

1 (8-ounce) can kidney
  beans, undrained

1 (8-ounce) can whole-
  kernel corn, undrained

Quick Dumplings

Tabasco sauce to taste

Salt and pepper to taste

$\frac{1}{2}$ cup shredded Cheddar
  cheese

Mix venison, water, tomato sauce, and seasoning mix in a 4-quart Dutch oven. Heat to boiling; reduce heat. Cover and simmer 10 minutes, stirring constantly. Stir in beans and corn.

Prepare Quick Dumplings. Heat chili to boiling; reduce heat to low. Drop 12 spoonfuls dumplings into the hot chili. Cook uncovered 10 minutes. Cover and cook 10 minutes longer. Season to taste. Sprinkle with cheese. Cover and cook about 3 minutes or until cheese is melted. Serves 6.

QUICK DUMPLINGS:

$1\frac{1}{2}$ cups Bisquick

$\frac{1}{2}$ cup yellow cornmeal

$\frac{2}{3}$ cup whole milk

$\frac{1}{2}$ teaspoon sugar

Mix dumpling ingredients until soft dough forms. Roll out and cut into 1x2-inch rectangles.

The Complete Venison Cookbook

Pizza Pop Up

Everybody loves this!

1 pound ground beef

1 onion, chopped

1 (16-ounce) jar spaghetti
sauce

$^1/_2$ pound fresh
mushrooms, sliced and
sautéed in 1 tablespoon
butter

$^1/_4$ teaspoon oregano

Salt to taste

1 (6-ounce) package
mozzarella cheese, sliced

Sauté beef and onion; drain. Add to spaghetti sauce; add sautéed mushrooms. Blend in seasonings. Pour into a 9x13-inch casserole dish. Top with mozzarella cheese. Bake at 400° for 10 minutes. In the meantime, make pop-up batter.

POP-UP BATTER

1 cup flour

$^1/_2$ teaspoon salt

2 eggs

1 cup milk

1 tablespoon vegetable oil

$^1/_2$ cup fresh grated
Parmesan cheese for
topping

Place flour and salt in a deep bowl. Make well in center of flour. Combine eggs, milk, and oil. Pour into well of flour. Whisk thoroughly. Remove casserole from oven; pour batter over meat mixture. Sprinkle with Parmesan cheese. Bake at 400° for 30 minutes more. Serve immediately. Serves 6–8.

Fillies Flavours

Editor's Extra: Also interesting to substitute pizza sauce for spaghetti sauce.

Juicy Hamburgers

My daddy loved to grill hamburgers on his home-built cinder block grill. We usually had extra people for supper, so he deliciously "stretched" his patties a bit with crumbs and eggs, declaring that they kept their big size better. They were always "the best."

—Gwen

2 pounds ground beef
2 teaspoons garlic salt
1 cup fine bread crumbs
1/2 cup tomato catsup
1/2 teaspoon salt
2 teaspoons Worcestershire sauce
2 teaspoons onion salt
2 eggs
1 teaspoon pepper

Combine all ingredients; form into patties and broil 4 minutes on each side. Yields 12 servings.

Historic Kentucky Recipes

Editor's Extra: If you like crusty buns, place the inside halves on the grill or griddle for a half minute or so . . . and have the plates and fixin's ready!

Hamburger Potato Bake

2 pounds ground chuck
2 eggs, beaten
2 cups bread crumbs
2 tablespoons catsup
4 teaspoons salt
4 teaspoons pepper

TOPPING:
8 medium potatoes
1 carton sour cream
1 stick butter, softened
3 ounces cream cheese, softened
Garlic salt to taste
Salt and pepper to taste
8 ounces grated sharp Cheddar cheese

Combine meat, eggs, bread crumbs, catsup, salt, and pepper. Mix well, adding more crumbs if needed to make mixture firm. Put in an ungreased oblong glass baking dish and bake at 350° for 20–30 minutes or until brown.

Peel and cube potatoes; cook in water to cover until done. Mash, adding sour cream, butter, cream cheese, garlic salt, salt and pepper. Whip. Spread over meat mixture. Sprinkle with Cheddar cheese. Return to oven and bake until cheese melts and is slightly browned. Serves 8–10.

Jarrett House Potpourri

Beef Stuffed Peppers

3 large green peppers
3 tablespoons minced
   onion
2 tablespoons butter
1 pound ground beef
½ cup instant rice, cooked
½ teaspoon salt
2 (8-ounce) cans tomato
   sauce, divided
½ cup water
½ cup sherry (or water)
1 cup sour cream
4 ounces sharp Cheddar
   cheese, grated

Split green peppers into halves lengthwise. Remove seeds and stems. Wash peppers; drop into a large pot of boiling, salted water. Turn off heat; let stand 5 minutes. Drain; arrange peppers in baking dish.

Sauté onion in butter for 5 minutes. Drain and mix onion with raw ground beef, rice, salt, and 1 can tomato sauce. Fill peppers with meat mixture. Combine 1 can tomato sauce, water, sherry, and sour cream; pour over stuffed peppers. Bake at 350° for 40 minutes. Sprinkle with cheese and bake for 20 minutes longer. Yields 6 servings.

Kitchen Sampler

Editor's Extra: My mother-in-law used half ground beef and half finely diced ham—a very special taste I'll always remember.

Stuffed Green Peppers

An easy microwave method.

1 pound lean ground beef
⅔ cup Italian bread
   crumbs
1 egg
½ cup tomato sauce
2 tablespoons water
¾ teaspoon salt
½ teaspoon cayenne
   pepper
¼ cup chopped green
   pepper
4 medium green peppers,
   washed and halved
½ (8-ounce) can tomato
   sauce
1 (15½-ounce) jar Ragu
   spaghetti sauce

In medium mixing bowl, mix beef, bread crumbs, egg, tomato sauce, water, salt, pepper, and chopped green pepper. Fill pepper halves with beef mixture. Place in 7x11-inch glass oblong casserole dish.

Combine tomato sauce and spaghetti sauce. Pour over peppers. Cover with plastic wrap. Micro on 70% Power for 25 minutes. Let stand 10 minutes. Serves 8.

Southern Spice à al Microwave

Editor's Extra: This is so easy! (If you like really soft peppers, parboil a few minutes before stuffing.)

Eggplant Parmigiana Barbara

This recipe may be altered for a meatless meal by eliminating ground beef and doubling or tripling the amount of mozzarella.

1/2 cup chopped onion

1 clove garlic, minced

1 pound ground beef

2 tablespoons butter or margarine

1 (16-ounce) can tomatoes

1 (6-ounce) can tomato paste

2 teaspoons dried oregano

1 teaspoon basil

1 1/2 teaspoons salt

1/4 teaspoon pepper

1/2 cup plus 1 tablespoon water, divided

1 tablespoon brown sugar

1 large eggplant

2 eggs, beaten slightly

1/2 cup dry bread crumbs

1/4 cup salad oil

1 1/4 cups grated Parmesan cheese, divided

6–8 ounces mozzarella, shredded, divided

In large skillet, sauté onion, garlic, and ground beef in butter until meat is no longer red. Add tomatoes, tomato paste, oregano, basil, salt, and pepper. Stir well. Add 1/2 cup water and brown sugar. Bring all ingredients in skillet to a boil. Simmer uncovered 20 minutes.

Heat oven to 350°. Peel eggplant and cut into 1/2-inch slices. Combine eggs and remaining 1 tablespoon water in shallow bowl; mix well. Dip eggplant in egg wash; coat well. Dip in crumbs and coat well.

In skillet, sauté eggplant in hot oil until brown, and arrange half of them in bottom of sprayed baking dish; sprinkle with half Parmesan, cover with half of tomato sauce, and top with half of mozzarella cheese. Repeat except for mozzarella. Bake uncovered 20 minutes. Arrange remaining mozzarella cheese over top and bake 20 minutes longer or until mozzarella is melted and slightly brown. Yields 6 servings.

Pass the Plate

The World's Last Meatloaf

Search no further—this is as good as it gets.

1 tablespoon bacon grease
(or canola oil)
1 cup minced onion
³/₄ cup minced celery
³/₄ cup minced bell pepper
1 teaspoon minced garlic
¹/₈ teaspoon dried thyme
¹/₄ teaspoon dried oregano
2 teaspoons steak
seasoning or seasoned
salt
1 tablespoon salt
1 cup milk
3 eggs
1 tablespoon
Worcestershire sauce
¹/₂ cup ketchup
2 pounds ground beef
1 cup coarse bread crumbs

Preheat oven to 325°. Heat bacon grease in a large skillet over medium heat. Sauté vegetables with seasonings until tender. Allow to cool.

Combine milk, eggs, Worcestershire, and ketchup and mix well. Place ground beef, cooled vegetables, and egg mixture into a large mixing bowl. Using your hands, squish meat until you have mixed everything together and all is well incorporated. Fold in the bread crumbs last.

Shape meat mixture into the form of a loaf on a baking sheet. Using your hand, make an indention down the center of the loaf (this is where the Glaze will go). Bake 50 minutes.

While meatloaf is cooking, make the Tomato Glaze. Yields 8–10 servings.

TOMATO GLAZE:
1 teaspoon bacon grease
(or canola oil)
1 tablespoon minced onion
1 teaspoon minced garlic
¹/₄ cup brown sugar
2 tablespoons yellow
mustard
1 tablespoon
Worcestershire sauce
1 cup ketchup

For Tomato Glaze, heat bacon grease over low heat. Cook onion and garlic 2–3 minutes. Add brown sugar and stir until dissolved. Stir in remaining ingredients.

Remove loaf from oven and spoon Glaze down center of the meatloaf and spread over the sides. Return meatloaf to oven, lower heat to 300° and bake 30 minutes more. Allow meatloaf to rest 15 minutes before serving.

Deep South Staples

152

Beef Tips Over Rice

A favorite southern "rice and gravy" dish.

1 pound sirloin steak, cubed (sprinkled with unseasoned tenderizer, if desired)

1 medium onion, chopped

2 cloves garlic, minced

2 tablespoons olive oil

1 (4-ounce) can mushrooms, or 8–10 fresh mushrooms

$1/2$ cup white wine

2 teaspoons beef bouillon

Salt and freshly ground black pepper to taste

1 tablespoon parsley flakes

1 tablespoon cornstarch

$1/2$ cup cold water

Hot cooked rice

Brown cubed steak, onion, and garlic in olive oil in a large heavy skillet. Add mushrooms, wine, beef bouillon, salt, pepper, and parsley. Let simmer 15 or 20 minutes until meat is done, then add the dissolved cornstarch-water mixture and let thicken. Takes just a few minutes.

Serve over hot cooked rice. Baked squash and fresh spinach salad complete this meal. Yields 3–4 servings.

Betty is Still "Winking" at Cooking

Editor's Extra: When I have leftover wine, I freeze it—sometimes in a Ziploc bag. It will be "slushy" ready for the next recipe that calls for wine. Water or broth will substitute quite well.

Venison Roast

1 large venison roast

1 medium onion, chopped

1 clove garlic, chopped

$1/2$ stick butter

Pepper to taste

Cayenne pepper to taste

Worcestershire sauce to taste

Bay leaves (optional)

1 stalk celery, chopped

2 large potatoes, chopped

2 carrots, chopped

1 green bell pepper, chopped

Salt and pepper to taste

Place roast in crockpot with water to cover top of roast. Add onion, garlic, butter, peppers, and Worcestershire sauce to taste. Add bay leaves, if desired. Cook on LOW overnight.

Remove and place in large baking dish. Add all vegetables, small amount of juices from roast, and salt and pepper to taste. Cover and bake at 325° until vegetables are tender (about 50 minutes). Uncover and brown slightly.

Around the Bend

Southern Shredded Pork

Served in buns, this is a great item for a teen party.

3$^1/_2$ pounds fresh pork
2 tablespoons margarine
$^2/_3$ cup chopped onion
$^1/_4$ cup vinegar
2 tablespoons brown sugar
1 cup catsup
$^1/_4$ cup water
3 tablespoons
  Worcestershire sauce
1 teaspoon prepared
  mustard
2 teaspoons salt

Place pork in a large pot and cover with water. Bring to a boil. Reduce to simmer and cook until tender and easy to shred (approximately 1–1$^1/_2$ hours). Remove from water and pull meat apart, discarding all fat.

To prepare sauce, melt the margarine in a saucepan. Add onion and brown slightly. Add other ingredients and simmer until blended. Add shredded pork, then simmer 15–20 minutes. Serve on buns or as a main course over rice. Serves 6–8.

Note: Beef may be used instead of pork. Substitute 3$^1/_2$ pounds stew beef (or chuck roast) and treat in same manner.

Palm Beach Entertains

Sticky Bones

1 cup vinegar
$^1/_2$ cup ketchup
$^1/_2$ cup honey
2 tablespoons
  Worcestershire sauce
1 teaspoon salt
1 teaspoon ground mustard
1 teaspoon paprika
1 clove garlic, minced
$^1/_4$ teaspoon pepper
4 pounds bone-in beef
  short ribs

In a saucepan, combine vinegar, ketchup, honey, Worcestershire sauce, salt, mustard, paprika, garlic, and pepper. Bring to a boil. Reduce heat; cover and simmer for 15 minutes. Set aside one cup for basting. Place ribs in a greased roasting pan; pour marinade in saucepan over ribs. Cover and refrigerate for at least 2 hours.

Drain and discard marinade. Bake, uncovered, at 325° for one hour or until meat is tender, basting frequently with reserved cup of marinade. Makes 4 servings.

Simply Southern

North Carolina Barbecue Sauce

In North Carolina the most traditional barbecue sauce is a straight-forward mix of vinegar and red pepper. To my taste, it is a classic, hardly interfering with a smoky roast, and just setting it off. Ketchup and mustard sauces make a thick, sticky coating. The vinegar sauce gives the roast a crisp coat and cuts the fat.

The word "barbecue" (barbeque, Bar-B-Q, B-B-Q) comes from the cooking method used by Indians in the Caribbean, called "barbacoa" by early Spanish explorers. Over time the word came to mean the method of preparation, and often the event where it is served.

1 cup apple cider vinegar
1/2–3/4 cup water
2/3 cup minced onion
1 garlic clove, crushed
1/2 teaspoon salt
1 teaspoon ground black pepper
1–2 teaspoons red pepper flakes
1 teaspoon sugar
1 bay leaf
2/3 teaspoon thyme
3 tablespoons peanut oil
2–3 teaspoons dry mustard
4–6 teaspoons cold water

Combine all the ingredients except the last 2 in a small stainless steel or enamel or coated saucepan. Bring to a rapid boil, then simmer 5 minutes. Remove from heat. Dissolve mustard in cold water, then thin it out with some of the hot vinegar sauce. Stir this wet mustard into the sauce. Let cool, bottle, and store in the refrigerator. Yields about 2 cups.

Bill Neal's Southern Cooking

Barbecue Ribs

4–5 pounds beef ribs
Salt and pepper
1 teaspoon liquid smoke

Cut ribs into serving pieces, place on a rack in broiler pan. Salt and pepper. Place under broiler and brown on both sides. (This takes away a lot of grease.) When ribs are nice and brown, sprinkle with liquid smoke, place in a crockpot and pour Barbecue Sauce over them. Set dial of crockpot at LOW and cook for 12 hours.

BARBECUE SAUCE:
1½ cups tomato catsup
½ cup vinegar
1 large onion, chopped
2 tablespoons brown sugar
Dash Tabasco sauce
1 teaspoon mustard
½ teaspoon salt
¼ teaspoon black pepper

Mix all sauce ingredients and cook for about 7 minutes. This sauce may also be used for barbecue chicken by adding ½ cup butter or oil.

My Old Kentucky Homes Cookbook

Barbequed Country Style Pork Ribs

2 tablespoons butter
½ cup chopped onion
1 tablespoon paprika
½ teaspoon pepper
4 tablespoons sugar
1 teaspoon prepared
    mustard
2 teaspoons Tabasco sauce
¼ cup catsup
3 tablespoons vinegar
5 pounds country-style
    pork ribs

Melt butter; add chopped onion and cook until clear. Add rest of sauce ingredients and simmer 5 minutes. Pour over ribs and bake at 350° for one hour. Test for doneness. Sauce is also good to make barbequed chicken.

Jarrett House Potpourri

Pork Chops and Cheesy Potatoes

A simple meat-and-potato dish, but oh, so good.

8 medium potatoes, sliced
1 onion, chopped
6 slices Cheddar cheese
2 (10³/4-ounce) cans cream
   of mushroom soup
1 soup can milk
Salt and pepper to taste
6 pork chops, browned

In a 3-quart buttered dish, place alternate layers of potatoes, onion, and cheese. Combine soup, milk, and seasonings; pour over all—do not stir. Top with browned pork chops, cover and bake at 350° for 1¹/₂ hours. Serves 6.

Holiday Treats

Rose Davidson's Pork Chops

If you haven't eaten Rose Davidson's pork chops, then you have really missed something good. She was delighted to give me her recipe. I only wish it were possible to give you her recipe for the hospitality that always abounds in her kitchen!

Salt and pepper to taste
6 pork chops
¹/₂ cup flour, divided
3–4 tablespoons oil
1 (10³/4-ounce) can cream
   of mushroom soup
1 soup can water
2 tablespoons
   Worcestershire sauce

Preheat oven to 350°. Salt and pepper pork chops; dredge in flour. Fry in medium amount of oil until meat is golden brown. Remove pork chops from skillet and set aside. Add several teaspoons flour to drippings in skillet and brown lightly. Add mushroom soup, water, and Worcestershire sauce, and simmer for a few minutes. Return pork chops to skillet. Place in preheated oven for about 30 minutes.

Hearthside at Christmas

Sweet 'n Sour Chops

A hands-down favorite.

6 butterfly (boneless) pork chops

1 (10^1/$_2$-ounce) can beef consommé

^{1}/$_2$ cup drained pineapple chunks

^{1}/$_4$ cup chopped green pepper

^{1}/$_4$ cup ketchup

2 tablespoons wine vinegar

1 tablespoon brown sugar

1 teaspoon soy sauce

^{1}/$_2$ teaspoon dry mustard

Brown chops in fry pan; pour off excess fat. Arrange chops in 9x13x2-inch casserole. Combine consommé, pineapple, chopped pepper, ketchup, wine vinegar, brown sugar, soy sauce, and dry mustard. Pour over chops and bake uncovered in 400° oven for 45 minutes. Serves 6.

Southern Secrets

Pork Chops with Apples, Onions, and Raisins

Salt and pepper to taste

4 pork chops, center cuts (1^1/$_2$ inches thick)

1 tablespoon cooking oil

^{1}/$_3$ stick butter

1 large yellow onion, sliced

^{1}/$_4$ cup raisins

1 large sweet apple, peeled, wedged

1 ounce port wine

Use a 10- or 12-inch skillet that can be covered. Salt and pepper pork chops. Place oil and butter in skillet and brown chops well on both sides. Place sliced onion over chops and cover skillet. Cook slowly for 15 minutes. Remove cover. Place pork chops over onions. Sprinkle raisins around pan bottom. Place wedged apple around chops; add wine; cover and simmer 15 minutes. Turn apple wedges during cooking to assure even cooking. Remove skillet lid and simmer additional 5 minutes to thicken sauce. Serve chops with apples, onions, raisins, and sauce for garnish. Serves 4.

Paul Naquin's French Collection II—Meats & Poultry

Picnic Shoulder Ham

Let your crockpot do the cookin'.

½ glass (about 6 ounces) sweetened tea

1 tablespoon Worcestershire sauce

1 tablespoon barbecue sauce

2–3 tablespoons ketchup

1 picnic shoulder ham (small enough to fit into your crockpot)

Mix all ingredients except ham. Put ham in crockpot (skin-side-up) and cover with tea mixture. Cook on HIGH for one hour, then cook on LOW all night. Ham will be so tender you can pull it apart with a fork.

Munchin' with the Methodists

Pawleys Island Ham

1 (12- to 14-pound) smoked ham (processed, precooked variety)

¾ cup bourbon, divided

2 cups dark brown sugar

1 tablespoon dry mustard

Whole cloves

Preheat oven to 325°. Place ham fat-side-up on a rack set in a shallow roasting pan. Bake without basting for 20–25 minutes per pound or until done. When ham is cool enough to handle, cut away rind. Score ham by cutting deeply through the fat until you reach the meat, making incisions ½-inch apart lengthwise and crosswise. Brush ham on all sides with ½ cup bourbon. Then combine sugar, mustard, and remaining bourbon. Pat this mixture firmly into scored fat. Stud fat at each intersection or in center of each diamond with a whole clove.

Baste ham lightly with drippings on bottom of pan and bake undisturbed in 450° oven for 15–20 minutes, or until sugar has melted and formed a brilliant glaze. Garnish with pineapple slices, cherries, apricots, or mandarin orange slices. Save the bone for soup! Serves 28.

The Enlightened Gourmet

Atlanta Baked Ham

Easy, can prepare ahead, can freeze.

1 (7-pound) half or whole ham
2 tablespoons prepared mustard
¹/₃ cup firmly packed brown sugar
2 tablespoons peanut butter
1 teaspoon horseradish
18–20 whole cloves
¹/₂ cup Coca-Cola

Preheat oven to 325°. Bake ham 25 minutes per pound for a half ham, or slightly less for a whole ham. Combine mustard, brown sugar, peanut butter, and horseradish, mixing well. Set aside. When about 45 minutes baking time remains, remove ham from oven. Trim off rind and fat; pour excess fat from pan. Spread top of ham with mustard sauce, then pierce with cloves. Pour Coca-Cola in pan and return to oven, basting ham several times with pan juices. Serves 8–10.

Atlanta Cooknotes

Red Beans and Rice

2 pounds red kidney beans
2 cups chopped onions
¹/₂ cup chopped green pepper
1¹/₂ cloves garlic, mashed
2 tablespoons parsley
1 pound cured ham, cubed
1 pound smoked sausage, sliced
1 ham bone (optional)
1 tablespoon salt
¹/₂ teaspoon pepper
¹/₄ teaspoon cayenne
2 bay leaves
¹/₂ teaspoon thyme
2 quarts water
2 cups raw rice, cooked

Soak washed beans overnight in water (about 4 quarts). Add remaining ingredients, except rice. Cook on low heat 3 hours. Stir the mixture only once every half hour. Serve over fluffy rice.

The Pick of the Crop

Country Ham Slices

Quick, easy, superb.

**Cured ham slices, cut
    ¹/₄ inch thick**
Brown sugar
Black pepper

Sprinkle both sides of ham with brown sugar and black pepper. Brown on both sides in greased skillet. Cover 5 minutes to tenderize.

Mountain Recipe Collection

Sausage, Red Beans and Rice Casserole

Red beans and rice done a little quicker.

1 pound ground beef
1 tablespoon cooking oil
1 large onion, chopped
¹/₄ bell pepper, chopped
**1 (14¹/₂-ounce) can
    tomatoes**
1 cup water
2 teaspoons salt
1 tablespoon chili powder
Dash black pepper
1 cup raw rice
**1 (16-ounce) can kidney
    beans**
³/₄ pound smoked sausage

Brown meat in oil; add onion and green pepper. Cook until transparent, stirring constantly. Add tomatoes, water, salt, chili powder, and black pepper. Simmer 10 minutes. Remove from fire; add raw rice and beans. Pour into buttered dish. Slice half of sausage over top, cover with foil. Bake at 350° for one hour. Stir slightly. Slice remainder of sausage over top, cover, and bake ¹/₂ hour longer. Serves 6–8.

Treasured Tastes

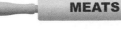
Jambalaya

An African dish, ham (jamba) and rice (paella) are the main ingredients, but like gumbo, almost anything goes—right in the pot!

Jambalaya was traditionally made outdoors in huge black iron pots used for boiling sugar cane syrup, and was stirred with boat paddles—this is still done at LSU tailgate parties. Since it can be made ahead, and with most any kind of meat, game, or seafood, it is a great dish for parties.

1 pound smoked sausage, sliced (or ground)

1 large onion, chopped

$\frac{1}{2}$ bell pepper, chopped

2 cloves garlic, minced

$\frac{1}{2}$ pound ham chunks

$\frac{1}{2}$ teaspoon each: salt, pepper, thyme, soy sauce, and Worcestershire

$\frac{1}{8}$ teaspoon red pepper or more to taste

$2\frac{1}{2}$ cups water

1 cup uncooked rice

1 tablespoon chicken or beef bouillon granules

1 (4-ounce) can mushrooms, partially drained

Brown sausage. Add onion, bell pepper, garlic, and ham, then spices. Stir till all is softened. Add water, rice, and bouillon. Bring to a boil and stir well. Cover and cook over low heat 30 minutes; add mushrooms, stir, and cover. Serves 6–8.

The Little New Orleans Cookbook

Decades ago, when football became so popular in the South that it was hard to get a parking space near the stadium, people began coming earlier and earlier, and so brought food and chairs, met their friends, and had an outdoor party without having to clean up the house! It caught on quickly—the vehicles got bigger and more accommodating, the chairs got more comfortable, the team colors appeared on everything . . . but always, the food was and is the highlight of the party. Tailgating has grown to the point that it is a vital part of what makes a football game the wonderful experience that it is.

Grillades and Garlic Cheese Grits

This delicious dish can be served for breakfast, brunch or supper. Good anytime!

1 pound round steak

1 teaspoon salt

½ teaspoon pepper

6 tablespoons flour, divided

4 tablespoons oil

2 medium onions

4 cloves garlic, chopped

1 cup chopped bell pepper (optional)

2 cups water

1 (15-ounce) can stewed tomatoes, or
2 tablespoons tomato paste

1 tablespoon parsley

¼ teaspoon thyme

Cut round steak into small pieces of your choice (medallions or strips). Mix salt, pepper, and 3 tablespoons flour together. Dredge meat pieces in flour. In a heavy skillet, heat oil and brown meat. Set meat aside.

In the same skillet, sauté onions, garlic, and bell pepper, if used. Set aside with meat. Add remaining 3 tablespoons flour to drippings in pan, and brown until a medium roux. Add water, stewed tomatoes or tomato paste, parsley, and thyme. Lower heat and add meat and vegetables; cover and simmer for 45 minutes or until meat is tender (may take longer). Serve with Garlic Cheese Grits.

GARLIC CHEESE GRITS:

1 cup uncooked grits

4 cups water, salted

½ cup (1 stick) butter

2 tablespoons minced garlic

3 eggs, beaten

1 cup (or more) shredded Cheddar cheese

Heat oven to 350°. Add grits to boiling water; reduce heat, and stir for 30 seconds. Cook as directed until thickened. Remove from heat. Add butter, garlic, eggs, and cheese. Pour into a greased casserole dish. Bake at 350° for one hour or until starting to brown slightly on top. Remove and let sit for 15 minutes. Serve with grillades or as a side dish.

Straight from the Galley Past & Present

Fried Squirrel

"Tastes like chicken." Seriously, this is good.

4 squirrels, cut into serving
   pieces
3 cups milk
1½ cups flour
Seasoned salt to taste
4 eggs, beaten
3 cups peanut oil
3 beef bouillon cubes
   (optional)

Combine squirrel and milk in a large bowl and refrigerate for 4–6 hours.

Remove squirrel from milk, reserving milk. Combine flour with seasoned salt in a bowl. Coat squirrel with this mixture, then dip into eggs and roll in flour again. Brown in 375° peanut oil in a large skillet, covered. Remove lid toward end of cooking so squirrel can brown. Drain all but 1 tablespoon of cooking oil from skillet.

Place squirrel in a pressure cooker with 1–2 inches of water and 3 beef bouillon cubes, if desired. Cook squirrel in 15 pounds pressure for 15–18 minutes, using manufacturer's directions. Remove squirrel from pressure cooker, reserving cooking liquid. Add the reserved cooking liquid to skillet. Add 1 cup reserved milk. Simmer over low heat until thickened. Serve squirrel and gravy on biscuits or toast. Makes 4–6 servings.

Note: The bouillon cubes added to the water make the best gravy!

Cooking Wild Game & Fish Southern Style

Editor's Extra: You can use chicken or fowl, rabbit, frog legs, etc. A perfect recipe.

Sunday Supper Snack

Modern-day southern moms and dads like to have quick meals the kids all love—this is one of them.

1 pound ground chuck
1 medium onion, chopped
1 clove garlic, crushed
1/2 cup barbecue sauce
1/2 teaspoon salt
1/4 teaspoon thyme
1/4 teaspoon oregano
1 (12-count) can biscuits
Several slices sharp
   processed cheese

Brown hamburger, onion, and garlic together. Add barbecue sauce and seasonings, and simmer until hamburger is cooked. Meanwhile, press biscuits into greased muffin tins, forming cups. Fill cups with hamburger mixture and top with a piece of cheese. Bake about 10 minutes in a 375° oven, until crust is done. Serves 6.

Of Pots and Pipkins

Editor's Extra: Also good to separate flaky biscuits in half for thinner cups . . . and more of them.

Ham and Chicken Casserole

A great company's-coming-with-kids casserole.

1/2 pound spaghetti,
   broken in 1-inch pieces
   and cooked until just
   tender
2–3 cups diced cooked
   chicken
1 cup diced ham
1/2 cup chopped pimento
1/2 cup chopped green
   pepper
2 (10³/₄-ounce) cans cream
   of chicken soup
1 cup chicken broth
1/4 teaspoon celery salt
1/4 teaspoon pepper
1 large onion, grated
2 cups grated cheese,
   divided

Mix all ingredients but one cup of the cheese together and pour into a greased 3-quart casserole. Add extra cup of grated cheese to top of casserole. Bake at 350° for one hour. Serves 15.

A Taste of South Carolina

Fried Chicken

1 (3-pound) whole fresh
    chicken
Salt and pepper (for
    marinade)
3 cups buttermilk
2 cups flour
2 teaspoons salt
1 tablespoon black pepper
Crisco for deep frying

Wash chicken well in cold water and cut chicken in serving pieces. Place chicken in a bowl with ice water to draw out excess blood. Pat chicken dry and sprinkle liberally with salt and pepper; marinate in buttermilk for 2 hours in the refrigerator.

Season flour with salt and pepper. Heat Crisco in a large cast-iron skillet, to 365° on a deep-fat thermometer. There should be just enough grease in the skillet to come up just around the edge (halfway) of each piece of chicken. Drain chicken thoroughly and dust with flour, shaking off all excess.

Place chicken, skin-side-down, in oil and make sure none of the chicken is touching. (Cook chicken in smaller batches if skillet is too small.) Cover skillet and cook for approximately 5–7 minutes; turn and cover for another 5–7 minutes. Uncover skillet and continue cooking for 10–15 minutes. Only turn the chicken once. Drain on a wire cake rack with a paper bag or paper towels underneath the rack to catch excess grease (draining straight to a paper bag causes the chicken to sit in the drained grease). Yields 8 pieces.

Deep South Staples

Before the rush of today's world, Sunday dinner was a family meal, with everyone at the table at the same time, and you looked very much forward to it. The good china was always used . . . fancy platters full of fried chicken, bowls of mashed potatoes and whatever vegetables were fresh from the garden, and always hot corn bread stacked on a beautiful plate. The whole table was brimming with hot delicious food, and it was passed around the table while family members and often guests (like the visiting preacher) visited. Oh, for times past, when we had time to enjoy the bounty.   —*Barbara*

Belle Grove Inn Fried Chicken

This is the way my mother fried chicken for guests when she and my father operated Belle Grove as an inn in the 1920s. The chickens were raised on the farm, the lard rendered at butchering time, and the butter churned in the kitchen. These ingredients, along with the iron skillet, wood range, careful attention and patience, were my mother's essentials.

1 (2³/₄- to 3-pound)
   chicken, cut up
Salt and pepper to taste
1¹/₄ cups flour
³/₄ cup lard or vegetable
   shortening
¹/₄ cup butter

Wipe chicken pieces lightly with a wet towel; sprinkle salt and pepper on both sides, and coat each piece carefully with flour. Place on a cookie sheet and set aside.

Heat a large heavy cast-iron or aluminum frying pan to medium high, then add lard or vegetable shortening and butter. If butter begins to brown, lower heat to medium. Add pieces of chicken, without crowding. Fat should be halfway up on each piece; add more if necessary. Cook to an even golden brown, turning pieces 2 or 3 times for 25–30 minutes cooking time. Keep fat sizzling hot. When all pieces are evenly browned, put a lid on the pan and cook 5 minutes more. Transfer chicken to drain on a cookie sheet lined with paper towels, and place in a 300° oven while making Gravy.

GRAVY:
3 tablespoons fat
4 tablespoons flour
2 cups milk, scalded
Salt and pepper to taste

Pour off all fat, leaving brown crumbs in frying pan. Measure 3 tablespoons of the fat back into the pan; stir in flour, and brown quickly. Add scalded milk, stirring vigorously to avoid lumps. When gravy thickens, season with salt and pepper. (Great over mashed potatoes, rice, or open biscuits.) Serves 4–6.

The Belle Grove Plantation Cookbook

Mississippi State Chicken-on-a-Stick

4 boneless, skinless
  chicken breasts
Salt to taste
2 medium onions
1 large bell pepper
24 dill pickles (small)
1 (15-ounce) can whole
  potatoes
2 eggs, beaten
¼ cup buttermilk
1 cup flour
1 teaspoon paprika
Red pepper to taste

Cut chicken breasts into bite-size cubes, and salt to taste. Quarter onions. Cut pepper into bite-size pieces. Place chicken, onions, bell pepper, dill pickles, and potatoes on wooden skewers. (Use proportions that suit your family—some like more vegetables, and some like loads of chicken!)

Combine eggs and buttermilk in a shallow bowl. Combine flour, paprika, and red pepper in a plate. Dredge skewer of chicken and vegetables in flour. Then, drench in egg-milk mixture. Dredge in flour again. Fry skewer in deep, hot fat until golden brown.

Variation: For more heat, place some hot sauce in egg-milk mixture and increase red pepper in flour. Also, for a real kick, add some whole jalapeño peppers to the skewers.

Offerings for Your Plate

Southern Pecan Chicken

Just as good as it sounds.

1 cup buttermilk
1 egg, lightly beaten
1 cup flour
1 cup ground pecans
¼ cup sesame seeds
1 tablespoon paprika
2 teaspoons salt
Pepper to taste
1 (3- to 3½-pound)
  chicken, cut up, washed,
  drained
½ cup butter, melted

Mix buttermilk and egg; place in shallow dish. In medium bowl, combine flour, ground pecans, sesame seeds, paprika, salt, and pepper. Dip chicken in buttermilk mixture, then in flour mixture. Place chicken in roasting pan, skin-side-up. Drizzle melted butter evenly over chicken. Bake at 350° for about one hour, or until chicken is golden brown. Serves 8.

Grits 'n Greens and Mississippi Things

Chicken Key West

Tangy and terrific.

¹/₄ pound butter or margarine
1 broiler-fryer chicken, cut in parts and skinned
1 teaspoon salt
1 teaspoon freshly-ground pepper
¹/₄ teaspoon paprika
1 large onion, thinly sliced
3–4 cloves garlic, crushed
¹/₄ cup Key lime juice

Melt butter over medium heat in large frying pan with cover. Add chicken and cook until light brown on all sides. Sprinkle with salt, pepper, and paprika. Add onion and garlic. Cook, stirring occasionally, 5 minutes. Pour lime juice over chicken. Cover and simmer 25 minutes or until fork can be inserted with ease. Remove cover and cook a few minutes until chicken is a golden color.

Margaritaville Cookbook

Parmesan Chicken

1 cup bread crumbs
¹/₂ cup Parmesan cheese
¹/₂ cup finely cut almonds
2 teaspoons minced parsley
1 teaspoon salt
¹/₂ teaspoon dried thyme
¹/₂ teaspoon pepper
¹/₂ cup margarine
1 clove garlic, minced
6 pieces chicken

Combine dry ingredients. Melt margarine with garlic in shallow baking pan. Dip chicken pieces in margarine, then in dry crumb mix. Place in same baking pan and bake in a 400° oven for 45 minutes to 1 hour. Baste occasionally with drippings. Do not turn chicken.

Easy Livin'

Editor's Extra: This is one of our favorite ways to fix chicken. I like to use chicken breast tenders so each bite can get lots of this fantastic crunch! Bake these little guys only about 25 minutes.

Baked Chicken Breasts

2 cups seasoned bread
  crumbs
3 tablespoons sesame seeds
1/2 cup grated Parmesan
  cheese
3–4 chicken breasts, halved
1/2 cup butter, melted

Mix bread crumbs, sesame seeds, and Parmesan cheese. Dip pieces of chicken breast into melted butter, then into crumb mixture. (Can freeze or refrigerate until ready to cook.) Bring to room temperature to cook. Place in shallow pan, dot with butter, and bake 1 hour at 350°. Serve with Cumberland Sauce.

CUMBERLAND SAUCE:
1 cup red currant jelly
1 (6-ounce) can frozen
  orange juice
4 tablespoons dry sherry
1 teaspoon dry mustard
1/4 teaspoon ground ginger
1/4 teaspoon hot pepper
  sauce

Combine in saucepan Cumberland Sauce ingredients and simmer until smooth.

More Fiddling with Food

Editor's Extra: Cumberland Sauce is an English sauce for game, duck and venison, often enjoyed at the feast after the hunt. It goes well on chicken and pork and meatballs . . . and can even enhance a block of cream cheese for a tangy hors d'oeuvre on a cracker.

Elegant Chicken

A family favorite.

4 whole boned chicken
  breasts
8 slices bacon
4 ounces chipped beef
1 (10³/₄-ounce) can cream
  of mushroom soup
1/2 pint (1 cup) sour cream
Almond slivers

Halve chicken breasts (to make 8) and wrap each half in a slice of bacon. Cover the bottom of a greased 8x12-inch baking dish with chipped beef. (If beef is too salty, scald beef with boiling water and drain well.) Arrange chicken on top of this. Blend soup and sour cream, and pour over chicken breasts. Sprinkle with almond slivers. Refrigerate at this point, if desired.

Bake, uncovered, at 275° for 3 hours. The gravy is delicious over rice.

The Stuffed Griffin

170

Lemon Chicken for the Grill

2 chickens, cut in pieces
1 cup vegetable oil
1 tablespoon salt
2 teaspoons onion powder
$^{1}/_{2}$ teaspoon thyme
$^{1}/_{2}$ cup lemon juice
1 teaspoon paprika
2 teaspoons crushed basil
$^{1}/_{2}$ teaspoon garlic powder

Place chicken in 9x13-inch glass dish. Combine remaining ingredients, blending well. Pour over meat and cover tightly. Chill 6 hours, turning chicken occasionally. Remove from refrigerator one hour before grilling. Cook 20–25 minutes on medium heat on grill, basting often and turning for 20 minutes more.

Pulaski Heights Baptist Church Cookbook

Charcoal Grilled Chicken

Simple and delicious.

$^{1}/_{2}$ cup butter, melted
$^{1}/_{2}$ cup cooking oil
$^{1}/_{3}$ cup lemon juice
$^{1}/_{2}$ cup soy sauce
1 clove garlic, minced
1 teaspoon oregano
$^{1}/_{2}$ teaspoon salt
$^{1}/_{2}$ teaspoon pepper
2–2$^{1}/_{2}$ pounds ready-to-cook broiler/fryer, halved, quartered or disjointed

To make barbecue sauce, mix melted butter, oil, lemon juice, soy sauce, minced garlic, oregano, salt and pepper. Refrigerate chicken marinated in sauce for one hour.

Remove from sauce and place on grill over hot coals and cook until tender, about 30–45 minutes, turning with tongs and brushing occasionally with sauce.

Note: For a barbecue sauce shortcut, add 2 packages of herb-seasoned or garlic salad dressing mix to $^{1}/_{2}$ cup of melted butter and $^{1}/_{2}$ cup cooking oil.

Pigging Out with the Cotton Patch Cooks

Chicken Pie

I used to watch my grandmother toss this together effortlessly. She had about 12 inches of counter space to work with, and she'd be covered with flour when she was finished.

1 (3-pound) chicken
1 quart water
1 quart vegetables
2 potatoes, cut up
2 hard-boiled eggs, chopped
3 tablespoons flour
10 biscuits, or a pie crust

Boil chicken in water until done; debone and cook the broth down to 2 cups. Cook up some vegetables (green beans, peas, corn, carrots . . . whatever you have) along with potatoes. Combine vegetables, chicken, hard-boiled eggs, the broth, and flour dissolved in a little cold water. Place in a greased baking dish and top with biscuits or a vented pastry crust. Bake at 400° about 20–25 minutes, until bubbly and browned. Put it on the table after everyone's seated.

Take Two & Butter 'Em While They're Hot!

Chicken Puffs

2 cups cooked, cubed chicken
$\frac{1}{2}$ teaspoon salt
$\frac{1}{8}$ teaspoon pepper
1 (3-ounce) package cream cheese, softened
2 tablespoons milk
1 tablespoon minced onion
1 tablespoon pimiento
1 (8-ounce) can crescent dinner rolls
1 tablespoon butter, melted
$\frac{3}{4}$ cup Parmesan cheese or crushed seasoned croutons
$\frac{1}{2}$ ($10\frac{3}{4}$-ounce) can cream of chicken or celery soup

Blend first 7 ingredients. Separate rolls into 4 rectangles and seal perforations. Spoon $\frac{1}{2}$ cup chicken mixture into center of each rectangle. Pull up corners and seal. Brush tops with melted butter. Dip in croutons or sprinkle with Parmesan cheese. Bake at 350° on ungreased cookie sheet 20–25 minutes, or until golden brown. Heat soup, undiluted, or thinned with a little milk, and spoon over top of each puff. Serves 4.

Note: Easy to double and can be made in advance. You may substitute crabmeat, shrimp, tuna, or your favorite ground beef mixture for the chicken. You may also substitute a cream sauce for the soup.

Well Seasoned

Chicken and Dumplings

CHICKEN AND STOCK:

1 frying chicken, cut into pieces (or equivalent breasts and thighs)

2 quarts (or more) water to cover chicken

2 ribs celery, cut into large pieces

1 onion, quartered

3 sprigs fresh parsley

Salt and black pepper to taste

Canned chicken broth as needed

Place all ingredients, except canned broth, in a large stockpot, and bring to a boil. Reduce heat and simmer until chicken is very tender (about one hour). Allow to cool.

Remove meat from bones and discard bones. Cut deboned chicken into medium-size pieces; wrap tightly in plastic wrap, and refrigerate overnight.

Strain and reserve the stock and discard vegetables. If stock does not come to $1^3/4$ quarts, add enough canned broth to make that amount. Refrigerate stock overnight.

DUMPLINGS:

Fat from chicken broth

Vegetable shortening as needed

3 cups all-purpose flour

$3/4$ teaspoon salt

Ice water

$1/2$ cup sweet milk

$1/4$ stick butter, cut into small pieces

Skim the solidified chicken fat from the refrigerated stock and reserve. If fat does not come to $1/3$ cup, add enough vegetable shortening to make that amount. Separate fat into small pieces and place in a mixing bowl. With your hands, briefly mix fat with flour and salt until fat is the size of peas. Add ice water one tablespoon at a time, stirring gently with your hands until mixture holds together and is the consistency of flaky pie crust dough. On a lightly floured surface with a rolling pin, roll dough as thinly as possible without breaking it. Cut dough into rectangles about 1x2 inches.

Place cooked, chopped chicken into strained, de-fatted stock and bring to a gentle simmer (not a boil). Drop dumplings into simmering broth and cook about 30 minutes or until liquid begins to thicken. Turn off heat. When liquid stops simmering, add sweet milk and butter. Stir very gently until butter dissolves. Serves 6–8.

The Southern Cook's Handbook

173

Chicken à la King

4 tablespoons butter
1 cup sliced mushrooms
1 bell pepper, chopped
2 tablespoons flour
1 cup chicken broth
2 cups chopped chicken
2 eggs, beaten
1 cup sour cream
2 (4-ounce) jars chopped
  pimento, drained
Salt and pepper to taste
2 tablespoons sherry

Melt butter in skillet. Add mushrooms and bell pepper. Stir. Add flour; mix thoroughly; add chicken broth and chicken. Cook on low heat 10 minutes. Add eggs and sour cream. Add pimento. Heat—do not boil. Add salt, pepper, and sherry. Serve in pastry shells or on rice or toast. Serves 6–7.

Heavenly Hostess

Italian Chicken Delight

Tomato-y, cheese-y, garlic-y, good!

6 boned and skinned
  breast halves
1 egg, beaten
3/4 cup Italian bread
  crumbs
1/2 cup oil
1 (15-ounce) can tomato
  sauce
Salt and pepper
1 tablespoon butter
1 tablespoon basil
Generous amount garlic
  powder
3/4 cup Parmesan cheese
Mozzarella cheese

Dip boned and skinned chicken into beaten egg, coating well. Roll breasts in bread crumbs. Brown in hot oil. Drain chicken and place in casserole in single layer.

To oil in skillet, add tomato sauce, salt, pepper, butter, basil, and garlic powder. Simmer and pour over chicken in casserole. Sprinkle with Parmesan cheese. Seal top with foil. Bake at 350° for 30 minutes. Uncover and top with triangles of mozzarella cheese. Bake 10 more minutes. Serves 4–6.

Bouquet Garni

Louisiana Chicken Sauce Piquant

2 cups vegetable oil or
  shortening

2 (3-pound) chickens,
  cut into pieces

Salt to taste

Red pepper to taste

Black pepper to taste

3 pounds onions, finely
  chopped

4 cloves garlic, finely
  chopped

1 cup finely chopped celery

1 cup finely chopped green
  pepper

3 (8-ounce) cans tomato
  sauce

2 tablespoons
  Worcestershire sauce

3 cups water, more as
  needed

Heat oil in a large cast-iron pot. Season chicken with salt, red pepper and black pepper; brown in oil. Remove from pot and set aside. Pour off all but $1/2$ cup oil, and sauté finely chopped onions, garlic, celery, and green pepper slowly in remaining oil for about 10 minutes. Add browned chicken, tomato sauce, Worcestershire sauce, and water to sautéed vegetables. Lower heat and simmer slowly, stirring occasionally to prevent sticking. Cook chicken until tender. Serve over long-grain rice.

Hint: Add a small amount of Roux (see page 65), if a thicker sauce is desired.

'Tiger Bait' Recipes

Sour Cream Chicken Breasts

6 chicken breasts

1 (10^3/4-ounce) can
  mushroom soup

1 (3-ounce) can sliced
  mushrooms or $1/2$ cup
  fresh mushrooms

1 cup sour cream

$1/4$ cup sherry or white
  wine (optional)

Hot cooked rice

Place chicken breasts in baking dish, skin-side-up. Combine soup, mushrooms, sour cream, and sherry. Mix well and pour over chicken. Bake, uncovered, at 325° for $1^1/2$ hours, or until fork-tender. Serve over rice.

Victorian Sampler

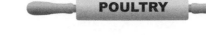

Chicken-Spaghetti Casserole

½ cup diced celery

½ cup chopped onion

¼ cup chopped bell
pepper

2 cups chicken broth

1 (14½-ounce) can diced
tomatoes

1 (10¾-ounce) can
mushroom soup

Salt and pepper to taste

2 cups diced, cooked
chicken

1 (8-ounce) package thin
spaghetti, cooked and
drained

Grated cheese for topping

In large saucepan, simmer celery, onion, and bell pepper in chicken broth until tender. Add tomatoes and soup; season to taste; bring to a boil. Remove from heat; fold in chicken and spaghetti. Pour into a greased 9x13-inch baking dish; top with cheese. Bake at 400° until cheese melts.

Celebration

Chicken Stew Cabanocey

The fricassee or stewed chicken has been the most popular poultry dish among the Cajuns and Creoles. The traditional chicken stew was always prepared on Sunday in our home and is still a family favorite today.

1 (3- to 4-pound) stewing
hen

½ cup vegetable oil

1 cup diced onions

1 cup diced celery

1 cup diced bell peppers

¼ cup minced garlic

2 cups sliced mushrooms

6 cups chicken stock

6 fresh chicken livers

1 cup sliced green onions

1 cup chopped parsley

Salt and cracked black
pepper to taste

Cut stewing hen into serving pieces. In a 2-gallon heavy-bottomed saucepot, heat oil over medium-high heat. Add flour, and whisk constantly until light brown roux is achieved. Do not scorch. Should black specks appear, discard and begin again. When browned, add onions, celery, bell peppers, garlic and mushrooms. Sauté 10–15 minutes or until vegetables are wilted. Add hen pieces and sauté for 5–10 minutes. Slowly add chicken stock, one ladle at a time, stirring constantly until all is incorporated. Bring to a rolling boil, reduce to simmer, and cook for 1 hour or until hen is tender. Add chicken stock, if necessary to retain volume of liquid. Add chicken livers, green onions, and parsley and season to taste. Cook an additional 20 minutes. Serves 6.

Chef John Folse & Company

Sunday School Chicken

Nothing fancy . . . just plain good.

1 whole fryer
1 pound fresh carrots,
  cut into large chunks
4 potatoes, unpeeled,
  quartered
4 onions, quartered
1 pound fresh mushrooms
Salt and pepper to taste

Place chicken and vegetables in large roaster; salt and pepper to taste, and cover. Add no water. Place in cold oven. Turn oven to 250° when you leave for Sunday School, and enjoy a delicious meal when you return from church (at least 3 hours). Alter proportions as needed.

Pulaski Heights Baptist Church Cookbook

In the Bible Belt, church services are often held outdoors, such as at this state park.

Turkey Dressing

Giblets from turkey

4 cups water

2 cups diced celery

³/₄ cup minced onion

¹/₂ cup butter

4 cups dry bread crumbs

4 cups crumbled corn
 bread

Salt and pepper to taste

1 tablespoon poultry
 seasoning (optional)

1 teaspoon sage (optional)

3 cups reserved turkey
 broth

2 eggs, beaten

Cook giblets in water till tender; chop and set aside; reserve broth. Cook celery and onion for 5 minutes in butter. Add to bread crumbs and add seasonings. Mix remaining ingredients, except eggs, thoroughly, then add beaten eggs. Stir lightly. If dressing seems dry, add more broth or enough water to moisten well. Stuff turkey and bake remainder in baking dish, uncovered, for 45 minutes to an hour at 400°. Serve this in spoonfuls around turkey. Serves 12.

Nell Graydon's Cook Book

Editor's Extra: You may also bake dressing in a greased 9x13-inch casserole dish. Add extra butter pats to top before baking for a golden brown crusty top. Delicious served with Great Giblet Gravy (below).

Great Giblet Gravy

Giblets from turkey or
 chicken (liver, heart,
 gizzard, and neck),
 cooked

4 cups turkey (or chicken)
 stock or broth

2 chicken bouillon cubes

2 teaspoons poultry
 seasoning

2 heaping tablespoons
 reserved uncooked
 Turkey Dressing (see
 recipe above)

3 tablespoons cornstarch

¹/₃ cup cold water

Salt and freshly ground
 pepper

1 hard-boiled egg, sliced

Chop the giblets and the meat that has been removed from the neck. Using a saucepot, bring the stock to a boil. Add the giblets, bouillon cubes, poultry seasoning, and raw stuffing to the mixture.

In a separate bowl, mix the cornstarch and water, and add to the boiling stock, stirring constantly. Reduce the heat, and continue to cook for 2–3 minutes. Add the salt and pepper to taste, then the sliced boiled egg.

Paula Deen, www.foodnetwork.com

POULTRY

Fried Turkey

A recipe concocted out of the swamps of South Louisiana. (You get a few Cajuns around a pot of hot oil and something's going to get put in it.)

1 whole turkey
1 jar Cajun injector marinade for poultry
Tony Chachere's Creole Seasoning
1½ cups mustard
4–5 gallons peanut oil

The night before you cook this bird, you want to have him thawed out sufficiently to inject the marinade, and if you like a little extra spice, you can add a little Tony Chachere's Creole Seasoning to the marinade. Inject the turkey in all its major meat areas. Take the mustard in your fingers and cover the turkey thoroughly. Then sprinkle some Tony's on the bird. Cover and leave in the refrigerator overnight.

Place enough oil in a large crawfish pot or boiler to submerge the turkey completely. Important: do not let the oil exceed 375°. Best to use cooking thermometer. Carefully lower turkey in oil. As a rule of thumb, cook the turkey for 4 minutes per pound. Most turkeys cook for approximately one hour.

Note: Sometimes the wings get overcooked because the size of the bird requires a longer cooking time. You may want to cut off the wings and add them to the oil later in the cooking process.

Cooking on the Coast

179

Baked Quail with Dressing

1 onion, diced
1/4 cup (1/2 stick) butter
4 cups bread cubes, toasted
1 (10³/4-ounce) can cream
  of mushroom soup
2 eggs, beaten
Salt and pepper to taste
8 quail, dressed
8 slices bacon

Sauté onion in hot butter in a large skillet. Add bread cubes, soup, eggs, salt and pepper, and mix well. Stuff dressing into cavity of quail. Wrap each quail with bacon. Arrange in baking dish. Add a small amount of water. Bake at 350° for one hour. Makes 8 servings.

Cooking Wild Game & Fish Southern Style

Editor's Extra: A quail (or any fowl, game, or fish) is "dressed" when it is cleaned, prepared, and ready to be cooked.

Carolina Quail

1¹/2 cups long-grain rice,
  uncooked
10 cleaned quail
1 (10³/4-ounce) can cream
  of mushroom soup
4 cups water
1 package dried onion soup
  mix
Pepper to taste

Place rice in bottom of shallow baking pan; add quail. Spoon mushroom soup over birds. Add water and sprinkle with onion soup mix. (There is no need to add salt, as mushroom and onion soup mix contain adequate seasoning.) Cover pan with aluminum foil and bake 2 hours at 350°. Uncover last 10 minutes to brown. Add pepper to taste. Serves 5.

Southern Wildfowl and Wild Game Cookbook

Mississippi Delta Duck

4 duck breasts

8 slices bacon

1 onion, sliced and
separated into rings,
divided

1 lemon

Pepper to taste

1 cup soy sauce

$^1/_2$ cup Worcestershire
sauce

Lemon pepper

Salt

Fillet meat from bone, making 8 duck breast halves. Wrap each half with a slice of bacon; secure with a toothpick. Layer the bottom of a covered container with $^1/_2$ the onion rings; place duck breasts on top. Squeeze lemon over duck; season with pepper. Combine soy sauce and Worcestershire sauce; pour over duck. Sprinkle generously with lemon pepper. Top with remaining onion rings. Marinate for 6 hours; turn duck after 3 hours.

Cook in a water smoker with the top on for 20 minutes; turn and cook for 25 additional minutes. Add salt to taste when cooked. Serves 4.

Taste of the South

Daddy's Baked Duck

3 ducks (preferably
mallards)

Salt and pepper to taste

Pepper to taste

6 slices bacon

1 large onion, chopped

1 (10$^3/_4$-ounce) can cream
of mushroom soup,
undiluted

$^1/_4$ cup water

2 (4-ounce) cans sliced
mushrooms, drained

Hot cooked rice

Preheat oven to 425°. Season ducks with salt and pepper; place in a roaster pan. Place 2 slices bacon on each duck. Bake at 425° for 20 minutes. Cover; reduce heat to 300°. Cook 1–1$^1/_2$ hours or until tender. Cool duck and debone. Reserve stock.

Skim 2 tablespoons oil from duck stock; heat in a skillet until hot. Sauté onion in hot oil until tender. Add remaining stock and cream of mushroom soup. Add $^1/_4$ cup water to soup can; add water and mushrooms to mixture. Simmer 20 minutes. Add sliced deboned duck to mixture; simmer 30 minutes. Serve over hot, fluffy rice.

Foods à la Louisiane

Duck Tenders with Mushrooms

Breast meat of 4 large
  ducks
1 cup flour
Dash salt and pepper
Dash sage
³/₄ cup (1¹/₂ sticks) butter,
  divided
1 cup chopped fresh
  mushrooms
1 cup chopped white onion
1 cup chopped celery
3 slices bacon, crisp-fried
  and crumbled
¹/₂ teaspoon thyme
¹/₄ teaspoon garlic salt
Hot cooked rice

Cut duck meat into strips. Coat with mixture of flour, salt, pepper, and sage. Brown in ¹/₂ cup hot butter in heavy skillet over medium heat. Remove meat. Add mushrooms, onion, and celery to skillet. Cook until tender, stirring occasionally. Add duck, bacon, thyme, garlic salt, and remaining ¹/₄ cup butter to skillet. Simmer 30 minutes, stirring frequently. Serve over hot cooked rice. Makes 6 servings.

Cooking Wild Game & Fish Southern Style

Just a Sliver, Please

Cakes

Somehow in rural southern culture, food is always the first thought of neighbors when there is trouble . . . "Here, I brought you some fresh eggs for breakfast. And here's a cake and some potato salad."

—W. D. Campbell

Mardi Gras King Cake

½ cup milk
½ cup sugar
1 teaspoon salt
½ cup shortening
2 packages yeast
⅓ cup warm water
3 eggs
1 teaspoon grated lemon
   rind
½ teaspoon nutmeg
4½–5 cups bread flour,
   sifted
1 tiny plastic baby, or a
   raw bean, or a pecan half
Lemon Glaze
Colored sugar

Combine milk, sugar, salt, and shortening in saucepan. Scald, then cool to lukewarm. Dissolve yeast in warm water in large bowl, then add eggs, lemon rind, nutmeg, milk mixture, and 2 cups flour; beat till smooth. Add remaining flour a cup at a time. Knead on floured board till smooth and elastic. Place in greased bowl, turn, then cover with damp cloth. Let rise in warm place about 2 hours.

Punch dough down and knead again about 5 minutes. Divide into thirds and roll each into a strip about 30 inches long. Braid strips and place on greased baking sheet, pressing ends together to form oval. Now insert baby (or bean) into dough. Cover and let rise until double, about an hour.

Bake in preheated 375° oven about 20 minutes till golden brown. Cool and frost, then immediately sprinkle sugar strips of purple, green, and yellow around the ring (easy to put ⅓ cup sugar with a little food coloring in a food processor to get even color; blend red and blue to make purple). Decorate with halved candied cherries, if desired. Freezable . . . and fun!

LEMON GLAZE:
1½ cups powdered sugar
2 tablespoons lemon juice
1 tablespoon water

Combine all and stir till smooth, adding more water if necessary to make easily spreadable so that it will slowly drip down the sides of the cake.

The Little New Orleans Cookbook

My granddaughter, Mercer Ann, and I make this every February. It's a tradition that's fun . . . and delicious! King Cakes celebrate the finding of baby Jesus on the Epiphany, January 6th, by the Three Wise Men. The lucky person who finds the baby in the cake is declared King or Queen for the day . . . and is obliged to bring a King Cake to the next seasonal celebration. Traditionally King Cakes are oval-shaped rings to show unity of all Christians, and are the Mardi Gras colors of purple, yellow, and green. Mardi Gras means Fat Tuesday and marks the beginning of Lent—and the end of King Cakes. —*Gwen*

Strawberry Shortcake

STRAWBERRIES:
2 quarts strawberries
1 cup granulated sugar

Cut strawberries into quarters and cover with sugar. Allow 2–3 hours for strawberries to bleed before using.

SHORTCAKE:
5$\frac{1}{4}$ cups Bisquick
1$\frac{1}{4}$ cups milk
6 tablespoons granulated sugar
6 tablespoons melted butter

Mix Bisquick, milk, sugar, and butter in a mixing bowl. Roll out to $\frac{1}{2}$-inch thickness; use a 4-inch biscuit cutter. Bake at 425° for 8–10 minutes.

To serve, cut each shortcake in half, place in a bowl, top with $\frac{1}{2}$ cup strawberries (with plenty of juice), then top with whipped cream. Place other $\frac{1}{2}$ of shortcake on top, then $\frac{1}{2}$ cup of strawberries (with plenty of juice), and top with whipped cream.

Fine Dining Tennessee Style

Punching down the risen King Cake dough is fun!

"I wonder where the little baby is hiding."

Mississippi Mud

2 cups plain flour

2 cups sugar

½ teaspoon salt

1 teaspoon baking soda

1 stick margarine

½ cup oil

4 tablespoons cocoa

1 cup water plus 1
  teaspoon cold water,
  divided

2 eggs, beaten

½ cup buttermilk

1 (10-ounce) bag large
  marshmallows, cut

Sift flour, sugar, salt, and soda together. Bring margarine, oil, cocoa, and one cup water to a boil. Add to flour mixture. Add eggs, one teaspoon cold water, and buttermilk. Mix well. Pour into a greased and floured 9x13-inch pan, and bake at 375° for 25–30 minutes. Top with marshmallows while warm. Pour Icing over top.

ICING:

1 stick margarine

3 tablespoons cocoa

6 tablespoons milk

1 (16-ounce) box
  confectioners' sugar

1 teaspoon vanilla
  flavoring

Combine margarine, cocoa, and milk. Bring to a boil. Add sugar and mix well. Add flavoring. Pour over hot cake as soon as it comes out of oven.

Callaway Family Favorites

Editor's Extra: Add chopped nuts to cake or icing, if desired. Also easy to use mini-marshmallows. Good any way you cut it!

A fun tradition in our family is getting to eat your own little cake in your own style on your first birthday! Gwen's grandson, Nathan Creel, definitely has his own style.

Hilbert's Turtle Cake

There won't be any leftovers.

1 (18¼-ounce) box
    German chocolate cake
    mix
1 (14-ounce) package
    caramels, peeled
½ cup evaporated milk
1 (6-ounce) package
    chocolate chips
1 cup chopped nuts

Prepare cake mix according to directions, using butter instead of oil. Bake ½ of batter in a greased 9x13-inch pan for 15 minutes. In a pan, melt caramels and evaporated milk. Pour over cake; add chocolate chips and nuts. Cover with remaining cake batter. Bake 350° for 20–25 minutes.

Entertaining the Louisville Way, Volume II

Pecan Pie Cake

The taste of the South.

3 eggs, divided
1 (18¼-ounce) box yellow
    cake mix
½ cup butter, softened
1 (1-pound) box powdered
    sugar
1 (8-ounce) package cream
    cheese, softened
1 teaspoon vanilla
1 cup (or more) coarsely
    chopped pecans

Mix one egg, cake mix, and butter together. Pat in bottom of a greased 9x13-inch baking pan. Mix 2 eggs, powdered sugar, cream cheese, vanilla, and pecans together, and cover the cake mixture completely. Bake 1 hour 15 minutes at 350°. Cut into squares. Serve hot or cold.

Note: Keep a check on the color. When it starts turning brown, it is done.

From the Firehouse to Your House

Red Velvet Cake

Although red velvet cake may not have originated in the South, it is served so often and has become a part of so many southern traditions that we have declared it deliciously southern.

CAKE:
- **1/2 cup (1 stick) butter, softened**
- **1 1/2 cups granulated sugar**
- **2 large eggs**
- **2 teaspoons red food coloring**
- **1 teaspoon pure vanilla extract**
- **1/4 cup cocoa powder**
- **2 cups all-purpose flour**
- **1 teaspoon baking soda**
- **1/2 teaspoon salt**
- **1 cup buttermilk**

Preheat oven to 350°. Grease and flour 3 (8-inch) round cake pans, tapping out any excess flour; set aside.

In a large mixing bowl, cream butter and sugar together with an electric mixer until smooth. Add eggs one at a time, beating well after each addition. Add food coloring and vanilla; beat until well blended.

In a medium-size mixing bowl, combine cocoa, flour, baking soda, and salt. Add dry ingredients alternately with buttermilk to creamed mixture, beating well after each addition and ending with dry ingredients. Scrape batter evenly into 3 prepared pans, and bake until a cake tester or straw inserted in center comes out clean, about 25 minutes. Let cakes cool in pans for about 10 minutes, then turn them out onto a wire rack and let cool completely.

ICING:
- **1 (8-ounce) package cream cheese, softened**
- **1 stick unsalted butter, softened**
- **1 pound confectioners' sugar, sifted**

In a small bowl with an electric mixer, blend cream cheese and butter until light. Gradually add confectioners' sugar, a couple of tablespoons at a time, beating well after each addition, until fluffy and light.

To assemble cake, place 1 layer on a cake plate and spread 1/3 of frosting over top. Repeat with 2 remaining layers and remaining frosting; do not frost sides of cake. Makes 1 (3-layer, 8-inch) cake and serves 10–12.

The Southern Cook's Handbook

Editor's Extra: If you want it really red, it's okay to use as much as 1/4 cup of red food coloring. Pretty!

This recipe calls for pure vanilla. My mother wouldn't use any other kind. Grammy was a wonderful baker and would wrinkle her nose at the mere mention of *artificial* vanilla!

—*Gwen*

Elvis Presley Cake

Rumor has it this cake was made for Elvis by his personal cook, Mary Jenkins.

Elvis Aaron Presley was born in a small two-room house in Tupelo, Mississippi, at 4:35 a.m. on January 8, 1935, during the Great Depression. Times were especially hard in the rural South where the average annual salary was $1,368 and unemployment was over 25%. Milk was 14¢ a quart and bread 9¢ a loaf. Despite his humble beginnings, Elvis moved on to great stardom as the King of Rock and Roll.

1 (18¼-ounce) box yellow cake mix
1 (3-ounce) box vanilla pudding (not instant)
4 eggs
½ cup oil
1 cup milk
1 (16-ounce) can crushed pineapple, undrained
1 cup sugar

Mix cake mix, pudding, eggs, oil, and milk. Beat until smooth. Bake in greased 9x13-inch pan in 350° preheated oven for 45–60 minutes (or until center springs back). While cake is baking, boil pineapple and sugar on top of stove until sugar has melted. While cake is still hot, punch holes in cake and pour hot pineapple over cake. Let cool. (More pineapple may be added, if desired.)

FROSTING:
1 (8-ounce) package cream cheese, softened
1 stick butter or margarine, softened
3 cups confectioners' sugar
½ cup chopped pecans (optional)

Beat cream cheese and butter until smooth. Add confectioners' sugar gradually and beat until creamy. Add pecans, if desired, and mix well. Frost cake.

Cooking with Gilmore

Praline Cake

1 (18¼-ounce) yellow cake
mix

Prepare cake mix as directed on package. Pour batter into 2 greased and floured 9x13x2-inch pans. Bake at 350° for about 30 minutes, or until done. Remove from oven and cool.

PRALINE TOPPING:
½ cup butter
1 (1-pound) package light
brown sugar
2 tablespoons flour
2 eggs, beaten
1 teaspoon vanilla
1½ cups coarsely chopped
pecans

In skillet, melt butter. Mix in light brown sugar, flour, and eggs, and cook for 3 minutes over low heat. Remove from heat and stir in vanilla and pecans. Spread evenly over surface of cooled cakes.

Bake for about 8 minutes at 400° to set the frosting. Cool and cut into 1½-inch strips. Makes 60 bite-sized servings.

Pirate's Pantry

Rotten Cake

Only southerners would dare to call a cake this good "rotten."

1 (18½-ounce) box yellow
cake mix

Mix cake according to directions on box for 2-layer cake. Cool and slice each layer in half to make 4 thin layers.

FROSTING:
1 cup sugar
1 pint sour cream, divided
1 teaspoon vanilla
2 large (12-ounce)
packages frozen coconut,
divided
1 (8-ounce) carton frozen
whipped topping, thawed

Combine sugar, 1 cup sour cream, vanilla, and 2/3 of the coconut. Spread between all layers. Combine remaining 1 cup sour cream and whipped topping. Spread on top and sides of cake. Sprinkle with remaining ⅓ coconut. Refrigerate in tightly covered container for 3 days.

Boarding House Reach

Hummingbird Cake

3 cups all-purpose flour
2 cups white sugar
1 teaspoon salt
1 teaspoon baking soda
1 teaspoon ground
  cinnamon
3 eggs, beaten
1/2 cup oil
1 1/2 teaspoons vanilla
1 (8-ounce) can crushed
  pineapple, undrained
1 cup chopped pecans or
  black walnuts
1 cup chopped bananas

Preheat oven to 350°. Combine flour, sugar, salt, baking soda, and cinnamon in a large mixing bowl. Mix well until all ingredients are thoroughly mixed.

Add eggs, oil, and vanilla. Stir until dry ingredients are moistened. DO NOT BEAT.

Stir in pineapple, nuts, and bananas. Mix thoroughly, but do not beat batter. Spoon into 3 well-greased and floured 9-inch cake pans. Bake for 25–30 minutes or until cake tests done. Cool 10 minutes and remove from pan. Cool completely and frost.

FROSTING:
2 (8-ounce) packages
  cream cheese, softened
1 cup butter, softened
2 (16-ounce) boxes
  powdered sugar
1 tablespoon cocoa
2 teaspoons vanilla
1 cup chopped nuts
  (optional)

Combine cream cheese and butter until smooth. Add sifted powdered sugar and cocoa, and beat until fluffy. Stir in vanilla. Sprinkle chopped nuts between layers and on top of frosting, if desired. Makes enough for 3-layer cake. This cake must be refrigerated.

Sweet Surrender with Advice à la Carte

During WWII when some things were rationed, my mother saved up enough sugar to make a cake for my daddy's birthday. She was so proud to present that cake! But, oh my, when we tasted it, it was awful! What on earth happened? She was so distraught that she went to the kitchen cabinet to try to find out what went wrong, and suddenly we heard her scream. She had discovered the problem, all right. Her liquid iron supplement was in a round bottle just like the vanilla! Poor Mother had wasted her precious sugar and ruined Papa's birthday cake. Thank goodness they at least got some enjoyment out of the telling and laughing afterward.

—*Barbara*

French Chocolate Cake

Unbelievably delicious!

**6 ounces semisweet
chocolate**
2 egg yolks, well beaten
1 cup buttermilk
¹/₂ cup butter, softened
2 cups sifted brown sugar
3 cups all-purpose flour
1¹/₂ teaspoons salt
1¹/₂ teaspoons baking soda
1 cup very strong coffee
2 teaspoons vanilla

Preheat oven to 350°. Grease 2 (9-inch) pans, then line with waxed paper and flour pans. Melt semisweet chocolate in double boiler. Add egg yolks. Slowly stir in buttermilk. Mix well. Cook until thick. Cool.

With mixer, cream together butter and brown sugar. Sift flour with salt and soda. Add this to butter mixture alternately with the coffee. Add chocolate mixture and vanilla. Pour into prepared pans and bake about 30 minutes.

RUM GLAZE:
¹/₄ cup butter, softened
²/₃ cup sugar
¹/₂ cup rum

Mix ingredients in small saucepan. Cook over low heat until sugar is dissolved. Pour evenly over warm cakes. Let stand in pans until cool.

CREAM FILLING:
**1 (6-ounce) package
semisweet chocolate
chips**
4 ounces evaporated milk
1 egg, beaten

Mix chocolate chips and evaporated milk. Stir over low heat until smooth. Do not boil. Add beaten egg. Mix well and chill. (If sauce is too thin, add a beaten egg yolk.)

TOPPING:
2 cups whipping cream
Shaved chocolate

Whip the cream to ice the entire cake.

To assemble, remove cakes from pans and generously spread a layer of Cream Filling between layers and on top. Ice cake with Topping and shave chocolate over top of iced cake.

Temptations

Exquisite Coconut Cake

2³/₄ cups sifted cake flour
4¹/₂ teaspoons baking
   powder
1³/₄ cups sugar
1 teaspoon salt
²/₃ cup soft shortening
1¹/₄ cups milk, divided
2 teaspoons flavoring
5 egg whites, unbeaten

Sift together dry ingredients. Add shortening, ³/₄ cup milk, and flavoring. Beat 2 minutes. Add remaining ¹/₂ cup milk and egg whites, and beat 2 more minutes. Pour into 2 (9-inch) layer pans that have been greased and floured. Bake in 350° oven for 30–35 minutes.

PINEAPPLE FILLING:
1 small can crushed
   pineapple, drain, reserve
   juice
Water
³/₄ cup sugar
¹/₄ teaspoon salt
3 tablespoons cornstarch
1 tablespoon butter

Add enough water to reserved juice to make ³/₄ cup. Gradually stir juice into sugar, salt, and cornstarch mixture. Bring to boil over direct heat, stirring constantly. Boil one minute. Remove from heat and stir in butter and crushed pineapple. Cool. Put layers together with this. Frost with Butter Icing.

BUTTER ICING:
¹/₃ cup soft butter
3 cups sifted confectioners'
   sugar
3 tablespoons cream
1¹/₂ teaspoons flavoring
Coconut (1–2 cups)

Blend butter and sugar; stir in cream and flavoring until smooth. Frost cake and cover with coconut.

Larue County Kitchens

Editor's Extra: Good with vanilla, coconut, almond, or butter flavoring—or combinations! Really.

Carrot Gold Cake

2 cups sugar
1½ cups vegetable oil
4 eggs, well beaten
2 cups flour
2 teaspoons baking powder
1½ teaspoons baking soda
1 teaspoon salt
2 teaspoons ground cinnamon
2 cups finely grated raw carrots
1 cup crushed pineapple, drained
1 cup angel flake coconut
½ cup chopped nuts

Beat sugar and oil together thoroughly. Add eggs, beating until fluffy. Sift next 5 ingredients together and blend in. Fold in remaining ingredients.

Pour into 3 greased and floured 8-inch layer pans and bake at 350° for 25–30 minutes. Or bake in a 9x13-inch pan for 45–50 minutes. Ice with Cream Cheese Frosting. (If making sheet cake, use only half recipe of frosting.)

Variation: Omit crushed pineapple and add ¾ cup chopped dates instead.

CREAM CHEESE FROSTING:
1 (8-ounce) package cream cheese, softened
½ cup soft margarine
1 teaspoon vanilla
3 cups powdered sugar
1 tablespoon milk (or more)

Combine all ingredients with one tablespoon milk or more, and mix until smooth.

Mennonite Country-Style Recipes

While traveling in rural Virginia, we came upon a fair where some Mennonite ladies were selling their jars of fruit and tasty-looking pies. We were fascinated to hear that they baked hundreds of pies to sell every Saturday. So pleasant and sweet and wonderful was this bonneted little lady we spoke with—we left with her wonderful spirit wrapped around us . . . and one of her delicious pies for the road.

Jam Cake

This frosting is like soft pralines on this yummy cake.

³/₄ cup butter
1 cup sugar
3 eggs, separated
¹/₂ cup buttermilk
1 teaspoon baking soda
1 teaspoon each: salt,
    cinnamon, allspice
2 cups flour
1 cup strawberry jam
¹/₂ cup chopped pecans

Cream butter and sugar, and add egg yolks, beating after each one. Add buttermilk. Sift soda, spices, and flour together and add to mixture, mixing well. Fold in jam and pecans. Fold in stiffly beaten egg whites. Bake in greased 9x13-inch pan at 350° for 30–40 minutes, or until top springs back when tapped. Allow to cool. Ice with Caramel Icing.

CARAMEL ICING:
3 cups sugar, divided
2 eggs
2 tablespoons butter
³/₄ cup milk
¹/₂ teaspoon salt

Melt ¹/₂ cup sugar in heavy iron skillet. In large saucepan, heat remaining 2¹/₂ cups sugar and eggs, and mix well with a long-handled wooden spoon. Add butter, milk, and salt; stir until melted. Stir browned sugar into this hot mixture. Cook slowly until it forms a soft ball in cold water, stirring all the time. Take from fire and beat (about 5 minutes) with spoon until it ribbons; spread on cake. Serves 10.

Feasts of Eden

Editor's Extra: This must have been made in the days when women spent all day in the kitchen. Though a little time-consuming, it is a delicious cake, and worth the effort. Sometimes I add chopped pecans. Licking the bowl is lovely.

Sunshine Island

A winner in the Second All-Florida Orange Dessert Contest.

$^1/_3$ cup butter

$^1/_3$ cup Crisco

$1^1/_2$ cups sugar

3 eggs

$2^1/_4$ cups sifted flour

$2^1/_2$ teaspoons baking powder

1 teaspoon salt

$^1/_2$ cup milk

$^1/_2$ cup orange juice

1 cup coconut flakes

$1^1/_2$ teaspoons grated orange rind

Cream together butter, Crisco, and sugar until fluffy. Beat eggs in thoroughly. Sift together flour, baking powder, and salt; stir in, alternating with milk and orange juice. Add coconut and rind. Bake in 2 greased and floured 9-inch pans for 25–30 minutes at 350°. Put cooled layers together with Clear Orange Filling. Frost top and sides with Orange Mountain Icing. Decorate with fresh orange sections (membranes removed) nested in coconut.

CLEAR ORANGE FILLING:

1 cup sugar

4 tablespoons cornstarch

$^1/_2$ teaspoon salt

2 tablespoons butter

1 cup orange juice

2 tablespoons grated orange rind

$1^1/_2$ tablespoons lemon juice

Mix together in saucepan; bring to rolling boil and boil one minute, stirring constantly. Cool.

ORANGE MOUNTAIN ICING:

2 egg whites

1 cup sugar

$^1/_8$ teaspoon cream of tartar

$^1/_4$ cup orange juice

Dash of salt

2 tablespoons light corn syrup

Combine all ingredients in top of double boiler. Place over boiling water, stirring occasionally, for about 2 minutes. Then with mixer on high speed, beat until mixture holds its shape.

The Gasparilla Cookbook

Tennessee Ernie Ford's Fresh Apple Nut Cake

Like his songs and hymns, this cake stands the test of time.

Tennessee Ernie Ford's deep voice was as recognizable as any of his era. He put 29 selections onto the country singles charts, and 21 onto the pop charts between 1949 and 1976. And he could really belt out a hymn—his gospel singing was second to none. Ernie Ford's most popular song was *Sixteen Tons* (1955). And he is also known for his sayings: "Bless your pea-pickin' heart"; "Nervous as a long-tailed cat in a room full of rocking chairs"; "Feels like I've been rode hard and put away wet."

2 eggs
1 cup oil
1¾ cups granulated sugar
2½ cups sifted self-rising flour
1 cup chopped nuts
3 cups pared, chopped apples
1 teaspoon cinnamon
1 teaspoon vanilla

CREAM CHEESE ICING:
2 (3-ounce) packages cream cheese, softened
¼ cup butter or margarine, softened
1 (1-pound) box powdered sugar
2 teaspoons vanilla

Grease a 9x13x2-inch baking pan. Beat eggs, oil, and sugar together thoroughly. Add flour, nuts, apples, cinnamon, and vanilla; mix well. Turn batter into prepared pan and bake at 300° for 1 hour 10 minutes. Yields 8–10 servings.

Blend icing ingredients until smooth. Frost cooled cake. Store in refrigerator.

Encore! Nashville

197

Strawberry Cream Cake

Light and refreshing . . . and so impressive.

1 (18¼-ounce) angel food
 cake mix, baked
 according to directions
1 (8-ounce) package cream
 cheese, softened
1 (14-ounce) can
 condensed milk
⅓ cup lemon juice
1 teaspoon almond extract
2 cups sliced strawberries
1 (8-ounce) carton Cool
 Whip or whipped cream
Additional strawberries

Bake cake and cool completely. Cut a 1-inch slice from the top of cake and set aside. Cut one inch from center hole and outer edge and remove center of cake, pulling with fingers. Leave one inch at bottom.

Beat cream cheese. Add sweetened condensed milk, lemon juice, and almond extract. Fold in cake pieces and strawberries. Spoon into center of cake. Top with reserved top slice. Chill 8 hours or overnight. May frost with Cool Whip and additional strawberries.

Note: Can use fat-free cream cheese and fat-free sweetened condensed milk for a very low-fat dessert. It is just as delicious. May use store-bought angel food cake.

Shared Treasures

Lemon Cake

A southern standard.

1 (3-ounce) box lemon
 Jell-O
1 cup hot water
1 (18¼-ounce) box lemon
 cake mix
¾ cup oil
4 eggs
1 cup powdered sugar
1½ teaspoons lemon juice

Dissolve Jell-O in hot water until clear. Mix cake mix, oil, and Jell-O mixture together. Add eggs, one at a time. Pour into lightly greased 9x13-inch pan. Bake in a 350° oven for 35 minutes. While still hot, prick with fork. Glaze with powdered sugar dissolved in lemon juice to make a light glaze.

Our Best Home Cooking

My husband and son and son-in-law declare this their favorite cake. When they come in from a golf game, no one is a loser when they discover this cake. It's my favorite, too, because it's so easy to do! I make it with a yellow cake mix, too.

—*Gwen*

Lemon Ice Box Cake

Delicious and beautiful.

FILLING:
2 (14-ounce) cans
   sweetened condensed
   milk
$^2/_3$ cup fresh lemon juice

Preheat oven to 350°. In a bowl, combine Filling ingredients. Place in refrigerator to thicken while preparing Cake.

CAKE:
1 (18$^1/_4$-ounce) box yellow
   cake mix
1 (8-ounce) carton sour
   cream
4 eggs
$^1/_3$ cup vegetable oil
$^1/_3$ cup sugar
$^1/_3$ cup water
1 teaspoon vanilla

Combine Cake ingredients. Pour into 4 greased and floured 8-inch round cake pans or 2 (9-inch) pans, and split layers after baking. Bake 20–22 minutes. Let cool. Set aside $^3/_4$ cup Filling mixture for Icing. Spread cake layers with remaining Filling mixture.

ICING:
$^3/_4$ cup reserved Filling
   mixture
1 (8-ounce) carton frozen
   whipped topping, thawed

Combine reserved $^3/_4$ cup Filling mixture and whipped topping. (Use wooden skewers, if necessary, to secure cake layers while icing.) Keep cake refrigerated. Makes 12 servings.

Prime Meridian

Editor's Extra: Allowing the cake to cool completely before splitting layers makes it easier to slice.

Fresh Peach Cake

1 (18¼-ounce) package yellow or white cake mix

1½ cups sugar

4 tablespoons flour

4 cups fresh chopped peaches

½ cup water

1 (8-ounce) carton sour cream

2 (½-pint) cartons whipping cream

3 tablespoons powdered sugar

Bake cake as directed on package in 2 greased and floured round cake pans, and split into layers.

Combine sugar, flour, peaches, and water in saucepan. Cook over slow heat until thick; remove from heat and cool completely. Assemble cake by placing first layer on a platter, then a layer of peach mixture (½), then the sour cream, and repeat.

Whip the cream and add powdered sugar. Frost cake and refrigerate.

The Junior Welfare League 50th Anniversary Cookbook

Pineapple Upside Down Cake

1½ sticks margarine

2 cups packed light brown sugar

8 slices pineapple

½ cup reserved pineapple juice

3 eggs, separated

1 cup sugar

1 teaspoon vanilla

1½ cups flour

2 teaspoons baking powder

¼ teaspoon salt

Maraschino cherries (optional)

Using a 9- or 10-inch iron skillet, melt margarine over low heat. Remove from heat; add brown sugar, then pineapple slices, overlapping some, if necessary. Beat egg yolks until light and smooth. Add sugar with ½ cup pineapple juice and vanilla. Beat until sugar is well dissolved. Sift flour, baking powder, and salt. Add to egg yolk mixture and mix well. Beat egg whites until stiff, then fold into flour mixture. Pour batter evenly over pineapple slices. Bake at 350° for 35–45 minutes. Let cool for 10 minutes; put plate over skillet and turn upside down. If desired, place a maraschino cherry in the center of each pineapple ring.

Gwen McKee

Rum Pound Cake

This is the best recipe for pound cake that I have ever used.

3 cups sifted flour
1/2 teaspoon baking soda
1 cup butter, softened
3 cups sugar
5 large eggs
1 cup sour cream
3 tablespoons dark rum or rum flavoring
Sifted confectioners' sugar (optional)

Sift together the flour and baking soda. Cream butter until smooth. Add sugar gradually, beating well. Add eggs, one at a time, and continue beating until light and fluffy. Add dry ingredients to creamed mixture alternately with sour cream and rum, beginning and ending with dry ingredients, stirring until well blended after each addition.

Spoon into a greased and floured 10-inch tube pan. Bake in a slow oven (300°) for 1 hour to 1 hour 15 minutes or until cake tester inserted in center comes out clean. Cool in pan for 10 minutes, then remove from pan and transfer to a wire rack, right-side-up, to finish cooling. Sprinkle with confectioners' sugar, if desired.

Apron Strings

Editor's Extra: Good with a raspberry sauce of a blended, sieved pint of raspberries plus 2 tablespoons sugar.

Mrs. Shingleton's Buttermilk Pound Cake

Want a dessert that everybody loves? This is it!

3 cups sugar
1/2 cup shortening
1 cup butter, softened
4 eggs
1 teaspoon vanilla
1/2 teaspoon baking soda
1/2 teaspoon salt
3 cups flour
1 cup buttermilk
1 cup chopped pecans

Preheat oven to 325°. Grease and flour a 10-inch tube pan. Cream together sugar, shortening, and butter until light and fluffy. Add eggs, one at a time, beating after each. Add vanilla. Sift baking soda, salt, and flour together. Add sifted dry ingredients alternately with buttermilk to creamed mixture, beating after each addition. Line greased and floured pan with chopped nuts. Pour cake batter on top of nuts. Bake for 1 1/2 hours. Cool cake in pan for 10 minutes. Remove from pan and cool on rack. Yields 10–12 servings.

Almost Heaven

Gingerbread

This recipe was handed down to Mrs. Panky by her grandmother who came to Harveyton, Kentucky in 1920 from Tennessee. Mrs. Panky has been making this gingerbread since she was eight years old, and her husband has sold it on the streets of Hazard for twenty years. Everyone calls him "The Gingerbread Man."

1¹/₂ cups sugar

2 eggs

1 stick butter, softened

1 cup molasses

1 tablespoon vanilla

4 cups plain flour

1 tablespoon baking powder

1 tablespoon baking soda

1 teaspoon each: nutmeg cinnamon, cloves, ginger,

1 cup lukewarm water

Cream sugar, eggs, and butter. Add molasses and vanilla. Sift flour, baking powder, baking soda, and spices together. Add to sugar mixture alternately with lukewarm water. Mix well until no lumps appear. Pour into greased muffin tins and bake at 350° until done.

Mountain Recipe Collection

Editor's Extra: My mother loved lemon sauce (butter, powdered sugar, lemon juice) on hers. I like whipped cream and chopped cherries on top.

Praline Cheesecake

Top with a sprig of holly for an elegant Christmas cake . . . but good anytime.

2 cups honey graham cracker crumbs

2 tablespoons sugar

6 tablespoons butter, melted

3 (8-ounce) packages cream cheese, softened

4 eggs

2 cups packed dark brown sugar

1¹/₂ teaspoons instant coffee

1 tablespoon vanilla

¹/₈ teaspoon salt

¹/₂ cup chopped pecans

12–15 pecan halves for garnish

Butter

Blend graham cracker crumbs with sugar and butter. Press into the bottom and sides of a buttered springform pan. Preheat oven to 350°.

Mix cream cheese with eggs and sugar, adding eggs one at a time and beating well after each addition. Add instant coffee, vanilla, salt, and pecans. Mix until well blended. Pour into prepared pan and bake 40–45 minutes. Cool to room temperature, then chill.

To serve, top with pecan halves that have been toasted and lightly tossed in melted butter.

Hors D'Oeuvres Everybody Loves II

Cheesecake

CRUST:

1 cup graham cracker
  crumbs

$^1/_4$ cup softened butter

$^1/_4$ cup sugar

Mix well and press into bottom of 10-inch springform pan. Bake at 325° for 8–10 minutes.

FILLING:

4 (8-ounce) packages
  cream cheese, softened

$1^3/_4$ cups sugar

4 extra large eggs

1 teaspoon vanilla extract

Beat cream cheese with electric mixer until very light and fluffy (about 5 minutes). Add sugar gradually, and beat well. Add eggs one at a time, beating well after each addition. Add vanilla and beat about 3 minutes longer, or until thick and creamy. Pour into springform pan and bake at 325° for 45–60 minutes, or until only a 3-inch circle in center will shake. Remove from oven and let cool for 20 minutes.

TOPPING:

1 (16 ounce) carton sour
  cream

3 tablespoons sugar

$1^1/_2$ teaspoons vanilla

Mix sour cream, sugar, and vanilla together and spread on top of cheesecake after it has cooled for 20 minutes. Bake at 325° for 15 minutes. Remove cake from oven and let it cool completely. Refrigerate cooled cake for at least 8 hours before serving.

GLAZE:

1 cup fresh strawberries

1 cup water

$1^1/_2$ tablespoons cornstarch

$^1/_2$ cup sugar

Crush strawberries in blender. Place in medium saucepan and add water. Cook for 2 minutes. Mix cornstarch and sugar together and stir into hot berry mixture. Bring to a boil, stirring constantly. Cook until thick. Cool, and add more berries, if desired. Spread Glaze over top of cooled cheesecake. Additional whole berries may be used as garnish.

Restoration Recipes

My son-in-law thinks this should be called, "The World's Greatest Cheesecake." This is his very favorite, with or without the glaze.   —*Gwen*

203

Almond Cheesecake

$^{1}/_{4}$ cup butter, divided

1 cup sugar

1 pound cream cheese, softened

$^{1}/_{2}$ cup light cream, divided

$^{1}/_{4}$ cup cake flour (sifted before measuring)

2 tablespoons honey

5 eggs, separated (whites beaten stiff, but not dry)

$^{1}/_{4}$ teaspoon almond extract

1 teaspoon vanilla extract

$^{1}/_{2}$ cup finely chopped blanched almonds (measured after chopping)

TOPPING:

$^{1}/_{4}$ cup light brown sugar

1 teaspoon cinnamon

$^{1}/_{4}$ cup finely chopped almonds

Cream butter and sugar together until well mixed. Add cream cheese and enough cream until mixture is fluffy. Blend in flour and honey, then egg yolks. Beat well after adding egg yolks. Add remaining cream and extracts; then lightly fold in beaten egg whites. Last fold in chopped almonds with a few deft strokes, distributing them through batter. Pour into a well-buttered spring-form pan; sprinkle Topping mixture; set on low rack in 325° oven for one hour. Turn off heat and allow to cool in oven one additional hour.

Grand Tour Collection

A Little Bite of Heaven

Cookies & Candies

All I can say is that there's a sweetness here, a southern sweetness, that makes sweet music. . . . If I had to tell somebody who had never been to the South, who had never heard of soul music, what it was, I'd just have to tell him that it's music from the heart, from the pulse, from the innermost feeling. . . . —Al Green

Pecan Crispies

¹/₂ cup shortening
¹/₂ cup butter, softened
1 cup sugar
1¹/₂ cups brown sugar
2 eggs, beaten
2¹/₂ cups flour
¹/₄ teaspoon salt
¹/₂ teaspoon baking soda
1 cup chopped nuts

Cream shortening, butter, and sugars; add eggs and beat well. Add sifted dry ingredients and nut meats. Drop from teaspoon about 2 inches apart onto greased baking sheet. Bake in moderate (350°) oven for 12–15 minutes. Makes 5 dozen cookies.

The South Carolina Cook Book

When Nannie and Granddaddy visited Aunt Vesta on the Coast, they always brought home some of her yummy sand tarts that were crunchy and delicious. I always wondered how she made them . . . now I know. Some people call these pecan cocoons.
—*Barbara*

Sand Tarts

2 sticks butter, softened
4 tablespoons sugar
2¹/₂ cups flour
1 teaspoon vanilla
1 cup chopped pecans
Powdered sugar

Cream butter and add sugar slowly. Then add flour while still stirring. Add vanilla and pecans. Shape into crescents on a large cookie sheet. Bake in a slow oven until light brown (250° for about 45 minutes). After cookies cool, roll in powdered sugar.

The Gulf Gourmet

Praline Cookies

A wonderfully sweet confection.

2 cups well-packed brown sugar
3 cups whole pecans
2 teaspoons vanilla
2 egg whites, beaten frothy

Add sugar, nuts, and vanilla to frothy (not quite dry) egg whites. Drop by small spoonfuls on greased, foil-covered cookie sheet. Preheat oven to 400°. Place cookies in oven. Cut off heat and leave for 8 minutes (or more). Remove from oven and allow to cool. Yields 4–6 dozen meringues.

The Pilgrimage Garden Club Antiques Forum Cookbook

"Frothy" means beaten just till heavily bubbly. This produces a flat, dense, yummy cookie that is chewy in the middle and crusty on the edges. Stiffly-beaten egg whites work just as well and produce more mounded cookies, but drier, like meringues. Either way, these sweet confections are so much easier than making praline candies, and tastes like them . . . the texture is the difference.

Authentic Southern Soft Teacakes

These are soft; just like Granny used to make.

1 cup shortening
1³/₄ cups sugar
2 eggs
¹/₂ cup milk
¹/₂ teaspoon vanilla extract
¹/₄ teaspoon almond extract
3 cups self-rising flour

In a mixing bowl, cream together shortening and sugar; beat in eggs; add milk and extracts; stir in flour. Drop by teaspoons about 2¹/₂ inches apart onto greased cookie sheets. Bake 15–20 minutes at 350°. Makes about 3 dozen.

Family Traditions

Butter Cookies

Very thin, quick to make, fun with kids . . . and yummy!

1 3/4 cups all-purpose flour

1/2 teaspoon baking powder

2/3 cup soft butter

1/2 cup sugar

1 small egg, well beaten

1/2 teaspoon vanilla

3/4 (2-ounce) square chocolate (optional)

Sift flour; measure and resift with baking powder. Cream butter thoroughly; add sugar and continue creaming until well mixed. Stir in the well-beaten egg. Add vanilla. Mix in sifted dry ingredients in 2 or 3 portions until dough is just smooth. If some chocolate cookies are desired, add chocolate (which has been melted and cooled) to half the dough. Roll out 1/8-inch-thick on a floured cloth or board and cut into desired shapes.

A finish or topping may be used on cookies before baking by using 1 beaten egg white and 1 teaspoon water; brush the tops of cookies with this mixture; sprinkle with sugar, bits of nuts, blanched almonds, candied fruit, chocolate sprinkles, etc. Bake on ungreased cookie sheet in a 400° oven for 6–8 minutes or until delicately browned on the edges. Cool on cake racks. Makes 3–4 dozen cookies.

Note: May add 1/2 teaspoon lemon extract and 1/4 teaspoon mace in place of vanilla flavoring.

Stirrin' the Pots on Daufuskie

PHOTO BY MILTON McLIN

Gwen (middle) and her sisters, Barbara Ann and Janet, loved to dress their baby dolls. These dolls had porcelain faces, arms and legs, with soft, stuffed bodies. Like true southern girls, they loved to have tea parties.

Oatmeal Cookies

A classic cookie for generations.

1 cup butter, softened
1 cup packed brown sugar
1 cup white sugar
2 eggs
1 teaspoon vanilla
2 cups flour
1 teaspoon baking soda
1 teaspoon baking powder
$^{1}/_{4}$ teaspoon salt
2 cups oatmeal
1 cup chopped nuts

Cream butter and sugars. Add eggs one at a time, beating well. Add other ingredients and beat until well blended. Bake for 10 minutes at 350°.

Note: You may add $^{1}/_{2}$ cup raisins, 1 cup chopped gum drops or 1 cup coconut for variation.

Country Cupboard Cookbook

Benne Cookies

Savannah's signature cookie.

1$^{1}/_{2}$ cups firmly packed
    light brown sugar
$^{1}/_{4}$ cup vegetable shortening
$^{1}/_{4}$ cup creamy peanut
    butter
1 tablespoon vegetable oil
3 eggs
$^{1}/_{4}$ cup water
2 cups all-purpose flour
$^{1}/_{2}$ teaspoon salt
1 teaspoon baking soda
1 cup sesame (benne)
    seeds*

Preheat oven to 350°. Throw everything into the bowl of an electric mixer and beat until smooth. With cookie press, pipe quarter-sized dots through $^{1}/_{2}$-inch tip onto parchment-lined (or very well greased and floured) cookie sheets. Bake one sheet at a time for 8–10 minutes; remove from sheet with metal spatula and cool on wire racks. Makes about 300 little cookies. Store in an airtight container.

Note: Rather than buying several small jars of sesame seeds at the grocery store to equal a cup of seeds, try buying them in bulk at a health food store.

Gottlieb's Bakery 100 Years of Recipes

Editor's Extra: If you don't have a cookie press, you can flatten small dots with your fingers.

Mother's Old-Fashioned Sugar Cookies

1 cup butter, room
  temperature
2 cups (scant) sugar
3 eggs, room temperature
1 teaspoon vanilla
3 cups flour
2 teaspoons (scant) baking
  powder
¼ teaspoon salt
Granulated sugar
  (for sprinkling)

Cream butter and sugar. Add eggs, one at a time, and mix well. Add vanilla. Sift together dry ingredients. Gradually add to creamed mixture, mixing well after each addition. Cover, and refrigerate 1–2 hours.

On floured board, and using floured rolling pin, roll to ⅛-inch thickness. At all times, keep rolling pin free from pieces of sticking dough. Using floured cutters, cut into desired shapes. With spatula, carefully transfer to well-greased baking sheet, spacing 2 inches apart.

Bake in preheated 375° oven for 8–10 minutes. Immediately, on removing from oven, sprinkle with sugar. Remove to rack, and cool to room temperature. Store in tightly covered container, or freezer. Yields 6–8 dozen.

Shape Variation: These cookies may also be formed into walnut-size balls, placed on well-greased baking sheet 2 inches apart, flattened and baked at 375° for 12–15 minutes.

The Cookie Connection

Editor's Extra: For added color and sweetness, add one drop of food coloring to a small amount of sugar in a small plastic bag and shake well (add more color, if desired). Sprinkle on flattened dough balls before baking, or on freshly baked cookies.

Dishpan Cookies

So good with a mid-morning cup of coffee or an afternoon glass of milk. Makes a lot, and that's a good thing.

2 cups light brown sugar
2 cups white sugar
2 teaspoons vanilla
2 cups oil
4 eggs
4 cups flour
2 teaspoons baking soda
1 teaspoon salt
1½ cups quick-cooking oats
4 cups cornflakes

In a very large bowl or "dishpan," cream first 5 ingredients together well. Add flour, soda, and salt. Fold in oats and cornflakes. Drop from spoon onto cookie sheet, and bake at 350° for 7–8 minutes. Do not overbake; these are better soft.

These are not only delicious soft, but equally good a little more crisp, accomplished by leaving in the oven for about 10 minutes. Allow them to sit on the baking pan another 5 minutes or so. Try some both ways. I also like to add milk chocolate chunks to part of the batter.

The Farmer's Daughters

Bell-Ringer Molasses Cookies

2 cups brown sugar
1 egg
1 cup shortening
1 cup molasses
4 cups flour
1 teaspoon lemon flavoring
1 teaspoon cinnamon
1 teaspoon vanilla
2 teaspoons baking soda
½ teaspoon ground ginger
½ teaspoon ground cloves
Granulated sugar for sprinkling

Cream together first 4 ingredients. Add remaining ingredients, except granulated sugar. Mix well. Roll dough into balls the size of walnuts. Place on lightly greased cookie sheet.   Bake in 350° oven 10–12 minutes. Remove from oven. Sprinkle immediately with granulated sugar. Let stand on cookie sheet 2–3 minutes before removing. Cookies will crack on top. Makes 5–6 dozen cookies.

What's Cooking for the Holidays

Lemon Sour Cookies

Most southerners love lemon things.

1 cup sifted cake flour
2 tablespoons sugar
$^1/_8$ teaspoon salt
$^1/_3$ cup butter or margarine, softened
2 eggs, slightly beaten
1 cup firmly packed brown sugar
$^1/_2$ cup chopped pecans
$^1/_2$ cup grated coconut
$^1/_2$ teaspoon vanilla

Sift flour, sugar, and salt into bowl. Cut in butter until mixture resembles coarse meal. Press firmly over the bottom of greased 9-inch-square pan. Bake at 350° for 15 minutes or until pastry is lightly browned.

Meanwhile, mix eggs, brown sugar, nuts, coconut, and vanilla. Pour over partially baked pastry. Bake 30 minutes or until topping is firm. Cool 15 minutes. Spread Lemon Glaze on top. Cut into 32 small bars. Cool.

LEMON GLAZE:
$^2/_3$ cup sifted powdered sugar
1 tablespoon lemon juice
1 teaspoon grated lemon rind

Blend all ingredients until smooth and spread over bars.

Arkansas Favorites Cookbook

Lemon Bonbons

2 sticks butter, softened
$^1/_3$ cup confectioners' sugar
$^3/_4$ cup cornstarch
$1^1/_4$ cups flour
$^1/_2$ cup finely chopped pecans

Mix butter with sugar until light and fluffy. Add cornstarch and flour, mixing well. Refrigerate until easy to handle. Start oven at 350°. Shape dough in 1-inch balls. Place balls on nuts scattered on wax paper. Flatten with bottom of glass. Put cookies nut-side-up on ungreased cookie sheet. Bake 15 minutes. Frost with Bonbon Frosting. Makes 4 dozen.

BONBON FROSTING:
1 cup confectioners' sugar
1 teaspoon soft butter
2 tablespoons lemon juice

Blend sugar, butter and lemon juice until smooth. Tint with desired food coloring.

Could I Have Your Recipe?

Aunt Lula's Mud Hen Cookies

We always thought these cookies had the funniest name. But they are good!

$^1/_2$ cup butter

1 cup sugar

3 eggs (reserve 2 egg whites)

1$^1/_2$ cups flour

1 teaspoon baking powder

1 teaspoon vanilla

$^1/_2$ teaspoon salt

1 cup chopped nuts

1 cup brown sugar

Preheat oven to 350°. Mix first 7 ingredients together. Spread very thin in a greased 9x13-inch pan. Sprinkle with chopped nuts.

Beat 2 reserved egg whites stiff and add brown sugar. Spread over nuts and bake for 25–30 minutes. Cut into squares while hot. Makes 24 (2-inch) squares.

Cooking with Heart in Hand

Fruit Cake Cookies

For those who prefer to have their fruit cake in cookie form!

6 slices candied pineapple

8 ounces candied cherries

8 ounces dates

All-purpose flour for dredging

6 cups pecans

1 cup butter, softened

1 cup firmly packed brown sugar

2 eggs

2$^1/_4$ cups self-rising flour

1$^1/_2$ tablespoons milk

$^1/_2$ teaspoon baking soda

$^1/_2$ teaspoon vanilla

1 cup pineapple preserves

Preheat oven to 325°. Grease several cookie sheets. Chop pineapple, cherries, and dates; dredge with flour. Chop pecans. Cream butter and sugar together. Add eggs, flour, milk, soda, vanilla, and preserves. Mix well. Stir in floured, chopped fruit and pecans.

Drop batter by the teaspoonful onto cookie sheets and bake for 15 minutes. Remove to wire racks to cool. Yields 6 dozen.

Hints: This recipe can be doubled. Use 3 eggs when doubling. Chop fruit ahead of time—this makes the process shorter.

Even More Special

Editor's Extra: I have found the already chopped mixed fruits in the supermarket; this is a real time saver.

Chocolate Chip Pizza

A New-South delight . . . especially for kids.

1/2 cup sugar
1/2 cup firmly packed
 brown sugar
1/2 cup margarine, softened
1/2 cup peanut butter
1/2 teaspoon vanilla extract
1 egg
1 1/2 cups flour
2 cups miniature
 marshmallows
6 ounces semisweet
 chocolate chips
1/2 cup pecan halves
 (optional)

Preheat oven to 375°. In large bowl combine sugar, brown sugar, margarine, peanut butter, vanilla, and egg. Blend well. Add flour and stir until soft dough forms. Press dough evenly over bottom of 12- to 14-inch pizza pan, forming rim along edge. Bake at 375° for 10 minutes. Remove from oven. Sprinkle with marshmallows, chocolate chips, and pecans. Continue baking for 5 minutes or until marshmallows are puffy and lightly browned. Cool and cut into wedges. (May store in tightly covered container.) Serves 15–20.

Perennials

Caramel Brickle Bars

You don't have to peel caramels to have that wonderful caramel taste!

BAR BOTTOM:
1 (18 1/2-ounce) package
 yellow cake mix
5 tablespoons butter,
 softened
1 egg

Grease a 9 x 13-inch pan. Mix Bar Bottom ingredients till crumbly and press into pan.

CARAMEL TOP:
1 (14-ounce) can
 sweetened condensed
 milk
1 egg
1 teaspoon vanilla
1 cup chopped pecans
1 (8-ounce) bag Heath Milk
 Chocolate Toffee Bits

Combine milk, egg, and vanilla, mixing well. Stir in nuts and chips. Pour over Bar Bottom and spread to cover. Bake at 350° for 25–30 minutes or until browned on edges. Leave to set up a half hour or so before cutting.

Gwen McKee

Apple Squares

Especially fun to make in the fall when the apples are so fresh and plentiful.

2 eggs
1½ cups sugar
1 cup oil
3 fresh apples, peeled and sliced thin
1 teaspoon salt
1 teaspoon baking soda
2 teaspoons dry yeast granules
3 teaspoons cinnamon
1 teaspoon nutmeg
2½ cups flour
1 cup chopped pecans or walnuts
1 (6-ounce) package butterscotch morsels

Combine eggs, sugar, and oil; beat well. Add apples, salt, soda, yeast, cinnamon, nutmeg, flour, and nuts. Mix well. Place in greased 9x13x2-inch pan. Cover with butterscotch morsels. Bake in 325° oven for 45 minutes. Cut into squares and serve with ice cream.

The Crowning Recipes of Kentucky

Sinful German Chocolate Squares

1 (14-ounce) bag caramel candies, peeled
⅔ cup evaporated milk, divided
1 (18¼-ounce) package German chocolate cake mix
¾ cup butter, softened
1 cup chopped pecans
1 (6-ounce) package semisweet chocolate chips

Preheat oven to 350°. Combine caramels and ⅓ cup evaporated milk in top of double boiler. Heat, stirring constantly, until caramels are completely melted. Remove from heat and set aside. Combine cake mix, remaining ⅓ cup of evaporated milk and butter. Beat with electric mixer until mixture holds together. Stir in nuts. Press half of mixture into well-greased 9x13-inch baking pan. Bake for 6 minutes. Sprinkle chocolate chips over crust. Cover evenly with caramel mixture. Crumble remaining cake mixture on top of caramel layer. Bake 17–20 minutes. Cool. Chill for 30 minutes before cutting into small squares. Yields 5 dozen.

Uptown Down South

Editor's Extra: For thinner squares, bake in sheet cake pan a few minutes less.

Butter Crème Brownies

**1 square semisweet
  chocolate**
¹/₄ cup butter
1 egg
¹/₂ cup sugar
¹/₄ cup flour
**¹/₄ cup finely chopped
  pecans**

Melt chocolate and butter together over hot water and cool slightly. Beat egg until frothy. Stir into chocolate mixture. Add sugar. Blend well. Add flour and nuts and stir until well blended. Pour into 8x8-inch pan. Bake 13–15 minutes at 350°.   Cool and cover with Butter Crème Filling. Yields 2 dozen.

BUTTER CRÈME FILLING:
1 cup powdered sugar
**2 tablespoons butter,
  softened**
¹/₄ teaspoon vanilla extract
**1 tablespoon heavy cream
  or evaporated milk**

Cream together and spread over brownie layer. Put pan in refrigerator for 10 minutes. Remove and spread with Glaze.

GLAZE:
2 tablespoons butter
**2 squares semisweet
  chocolate**

Melt butter and chocolate together. Spread gently over filled brownie layer, being careful not to disturb filling. Chill in refrigerator until Glaze sets. Cut into small finger strips. Can be frozen.

Note: Food coloring can be added to Crème Filling for different holidays and occasions. Also crème de menthe.

Vintage Vicksburg

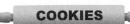

Cream Cheese Fudge Brownies

½ cup shortening

½ cup butter or
  margarine, softened

4 eggs

2 cups sugar

4 tablespoons cocoa

1 cup flour

½ teaspoon salt

1 cup flaked coconut

1 cup chopped pecans

2 teaspoons vanilla

Mix in order given. Spread ½ of batter in greased 9x13-inch pan. Spoon Cream Cheese Filling over it. Spoon remaining batter over Filling. Spread carefully. Bake at 350° for 35 minutes.

CREAM CHEESE FILLING:

2 tablespoons butter,
  softened

1 (3-ounce) package cream
  cheese, softened

¼ cup sugar

1 egg

1 tablespoon flour

½ teaspoon vanilla

Cream butter and cheese together. Add sugar, a spoonful at a time. Mix well. Add egg, flour, and vanilla. Stir until mixed well.

The Pink Lady...in the Kitchen

Praline Brownies

2 sticks margarine

1 (1-pound) package brown
  sugar

2 eggs

1½ cups flour

2 teaspoons baking powder

Dash salt

2 cups chopped pecans

2 teaspoons vanilla

Powdered sugar

Melt margarine and sugar over low heat (or in microwave). Cool mixture and add eggs. Add flour, baking powder, and salt. Stir in pecans and vanilla. Pour into greased 9x13x2-inch pan. Bake at 350° for 25–30 minutes. Dust with powdered sugar.

Fiftieth Anniversary Cookbook

Chocolate-Filled Snowballs

A chocolate lover's dream cookie.

1 cup butter, softened
½ cup sugar
1 teaspoon vanilla
2 cups sifted flour
1 cup finely chopped
   pecans
1 (5¾-ounce) package
   chocolate kisses
Confectioners' sugar

Cream butter, sugar, and vanilla until very light and fluffy. Add sifted flour and nuts, blending well. Cover bowl with plastic wrap and chill dough about one hour.

Remove foil wrappers from kisses. Preheat oven to 375°. Shape dough around kisses, using about one tablespoon of dough for each roll to make a ball. Cover completely. Bake 12 minutes until set, not brown. Remove from cookie sheet onto absorbent paper and cool slightly. While still warm, roll in confectioners' sugar. Cool completely before storing. Roll in confectioners' sugar again, if desired. Yields 5 dozen.

Bravo

Peanut Butter Sticks

Lunch box lovelies. Kids (of all ages) love these.

1 king-size loaf white thin-
   sliced bread
1 (12-ounce) jar smooth
   peanut butter
½ cup vegetable oil
1 package cornflakes,
   crumbled (3 cups
   crumbs)

Trim crust from bread. Cut slices into 5–6 strips. Place on cookie sheet and dry in oven at 200° for 3 hours. Combine peanut butter and oil in top of double boiler; heat until thoroughly blended and smooth. Remove from heat, but keep mixture over hot water.

Drop a few sticks at a time into mixture, tossing lightly until coated. Remove sticks. Toss in cornflake crumbs. Place on waxed paper to dry. Store in heavy plastic bags or airtight tins. Yields 6 dozen sticks.

Variation: Dry crusts of bread; process into bread crumbs in blender (about 3 cups of crumbs). Add cinnamon and sugar to taste. Substitute for cornflake crumbs.

Heart of the Mountains

218

Sweet Nothings

Fun to make. Even more fun to eat!

1 cup peanut butter
1/4 pound (1 stick) butter or margarine
1 (12-ounce) package semisweet chocolate chips
2 (12-ounce) boxes Rice Chex
1 (1-pound) box confectioners' sugar

Melt first 3 ingredients in double boiler. Pour over Rice Chexs in large bowl and stir to coat. Pour coated Chexs into a brown paper bag with confectioners' sugar. Shake until coated. Place on cookie sheets, one layer deep, to dry.

Hors D'Oeuvres Everybody Loves II

Cornflake Treats

What a popular munchie!

1 1/4 cups white Karo syrup
1 cup sugar
1 cup peanut butter
4 cups cornflakes
2 cups peanuts

Bring syrup and sugar to a rolling boil. Then take off heat and add peanut butter. Mix well. Pour over cornflakes and peanuts. Mix well. Then pour into a greased 9x13-inch dish. Press smooth. Cut into squares.

Recipes from Jeffersonville Woman's Club

Twisted Kisses

A pop-in-your-mouth delight! Kids love 'em.

Tiny pretzels
Hershey's Kisses
M&M's

Put 20 pretzels on a paper plate and position a kiss on top of each one. Micro-melt about one minute on HIGH, then check. Use 10-second "zaps" if necessary to soften further. Insert an M&M on top of each one when chocolate has softened enough for the M&M to stick.

Gwen McKee

Crazy Cocoa Krisps

You will make these again and again.

24 ounces almond bark
2 cups Cocoa Krispies
2 cups dry roasted peanuts

Place almond bark in microwave dish and cook one minute on HIGH. Stir and heat at 30-second intervals until melted, stirring at each interval. Stir in cereal and peanuts. Spread on jellyroll pan or cookie sheet and allow to cool. Break into pieces and store in airtight container. May be dropped by teaspoon instead. Yields 36 pieces.

Great Performances

Ambrosia Crunch

Using the holiday M&M's variety makes this a fun seasonal treat.

3 cups Rice Chex
3 cups Corn Chex
3 cups Cheerios
2 cups stick pretzels
2 cups peanuts
1 (12-ounce) bag plain M&M's
1 (12-ounce) bag peanut M&M's
1 (12-ounce) bag white chocolate morsels

Mix all ingredients, except white chocolate, in a large bowl. Melt white chocolate according to package directions. Pour white chocolate over mixture and toss well to coat. Spread on wax paper and let sit until white chocolate hardens. Store in an airtight container.

Ambrosia

Old Fashioned Butter Crunch

This candy is a favorite at my house. It's delicious. We always make it at Christmas time.

1 cup slivered almonds
1 cup butter or margarine
1¼ cups sugar
2 tablespoons light corn
  syrup
2 tablespoons water
1 (12-ounce) package
  semisweet chocolate
  pieces, melted

Spread almonds in shallow pan; toast in 350° oven, until golden (only a couple of minutes). Melt butter or margarine in large heavy saucepan; add sugar, corn syrup, and water. Cook, stirring often, to hard-crack stage. Pour quickly into greased 9x13x2-inch pan. Cool completely.

When set, turn out in one piece on wax paper. Spread half the melted chocolate over top; sprinkle with ½ cup almonds; let set. Turn candy over; spread with remaining chocolate; sprinkle with remaining almonds. Let stand until chocolate sets. Break into pieces.

Kum' Ona' Granny's Table

Peanut Brittle

1 cup sugar
½ cup white Karo syrup
1 cup dry roasted peanuts
1 tablespoon butter
1 teaspoon vanilla
1 teaspoon baking soda

Using a 4-cup Pyrex dish, combine sugar and Karo in dish. Microwave, uncovered, on HIGH 3–4 minutes. Mix with a spoon. Add peanuts. Microwave on HIGH 3 minutes. Add butter and vanilla. Microwave on HIGH 2 minutes. Take out of microwave; add baking soda, and whip quickly with spoon (it will foam). Pour quickly onto a well-greased cookie sheet (metal). Let cool. Break into pieces.

For the Love of Kids

Editor's Extra: I use my 8-cup-measure Pyrex bowl for this so that it will have plenty of room to foam.

Gold Brick Fudge

A New Orleans' original. Have the ingredients measured before you begin.

5 cups sugar
2 sticks butter
1 (12-ounce) can
  evaporated milk
1/8 teaspoon salt
3 cups chopped pecans
1 (7-ounce) jar
  marshmallow crème
160 Hershey's Kisses
  (approximately 1 1/2 bags)

Cook the sugar, butter, evaporated milk, and salt over medium-high heat, stirring constantly to a soft-ball stage, approximately 15–20 minutes. When candy reaches soft-ball stage, quickly add pecans, marshmallow crème, and Kisses.

Stir rapidly until Kisses are melted and all ingredients are well blended. Pour into a buttered 9x13-inch cake pan. The fudge should be 3/4 to 1-inch thick. When cooled and set, cut and store in a covered container. Yields about 5 pounds.

CDA Angelic Treats

Hurricane Fudge

Candy-making depends on heating the syrup to just the right temperature. It can be done to soft-ball stage by dripping a few drops from a spoon into a small amount of cool water and the drop forms a soft ball. Hard-crack stage will form a hard ball as soon as the syrup hits the water. But the best method is to use a candy thermometer—especially if you plan to make candy often. With these delicious recipes, you might as well invest in one.

3 cups sugar
2/3 cup cocoa
1/8 teaspoon salt
1 1/2 cups milk
1/4 cup butter or margarine
1 teaspoon vanilla
1/2 cup chopped pecans

Combine sugar, cocoa, salt, and milk in a large pot. Bring to a boil, stirring constantly over medium heat until it reaches soft-ball stage. Remove from heat. Add butter or margarine and cool mixture to 110° in a pan of water. Add vanilla and chopped pecans. Beat until mixture loses its gloss (about 2 minutes). Pour onto a buttered plate. Slice into squares when cool.

Tell Me More

Kentucky Bourbon Balls

2½ cups crushed vanilla
    wafers
1 cup powdered sugar
1 cup finely chopped
    pecans
2 tablespoons cocoa
3 tablespoons corn syrup
3 ounces bourbon
    (2 jiggers)
Powdered sugar

Combine first 4 ingredients. Dissolve syrup in bourbon and add to dry mixture. Form into balls, and roll them in powdered sugar. Store in tin for several days before serving. Makes about 3 dozen.

The Twelve Days of Christmas Cookbook

Creamy Pralines

Butter for saucepan
2 cups whipping cream
4 cups white or brown
    sugar
1 teaspoon vanilla
2 cups pecan halves
2 tablespoons butter

Butter a medium-large saucepan. (This will make clean-up easier.) Pour in cream and place over high heat. When it begins to boil, add sugar and stir rapidly until it dissolves. Then stir in vanilla and pecans, and continue to cook over medium heat, stirring frequently, until mixture reaches soft-ball stage (236° on a candy thermometer). Remove from heat and quickly beat in butter. This helps arrest the cooking process. The candy should lose its glossy color and become very cloudy.

Lay out a long strip of wax paper on a work surface. Moisten it with a damp towel. (Prepare paper while candy cooks, to avoid delaying this process.) When candy is ready, drop good-sized spoonfuls onto paper, stirring occasionally as you go along to keep pecans well distributed. Remove pralines from paper before they have cooled completely. (Later on, it will be hard to remove them without breaking them.) Store between layers of wax paper in tightly sealed container.

Fannye Mae's Home Made Candy

Pecan Kisses

6 egg whites
2 cups sugar
1 teaspoon cream of tartar
1 teaspoon vanilla extract
2 cups chopped pecans

Mix egg whites and sugar without beating and let stand for $^1/_2$ hour. Add cream of tartar and beat until stiff. Add vanilla and fold in pecans. Drop from tip of teaspoon onto wax-paper-lined cookie sheet. Bake at 275° for 40–45 minutes. Yields 100–125 kisses.

Nun Better

Old-Fashioned Divinity

Before air-conditioning, with windows open, usually letting in humidity even if it wasn't raining, you had to be careful when making candy, as it just simply wouldn't set up in moist air. If you are in an air-conditioned house, you can make it anytime.

Not many people have old-fashioned egg beaters any more. Nowadays, an electric mixer does the job just fine.

$^1/_2$ cup water
$2^1/_2$ cups sugar
$^1/_2$ cup white corn syrup
2 egg whites, beaten until stiff
1 cup pecan halves
Red or green cherries for garnish (optional)

Cook water, sugar, and syrup until it spins (soft-ball stage on candy thermometer). Add less than half to egg whites using old-fashioned egg beater in glass bowl. Return rest of syrup to heat, and cook to crack stage (hard-ball stage), then add to egg whites and beat until it loses its gloss. Spoon onto wax paper. Add pecan halves on top, or use red or green cherries to garnish. (May not work on rainy or humid days.)

Cooking with Friends

Did You Save Room For Dessert?

Pies & Other Desserts

When I was a child and the snow fell, my mother always rushed to the kitchen and made snow ice cream and divinity fudge. . . . It was a lark then and I always associate divinity fudge with snowstorms.
—Eudora Welty

Sweet Potato Pie

½ stick butter, softened
2 cups mashed cooked
   sweet potatoes
½ cup white sugar
¼ cup brown sugar
½ teaspoon cinnamon
½ teaspoon nutmeg
1 (5-ounce) can evaporated
   milk
3 eggs, beaten
1 (9-inch) pastry shell

Mash butter with potatoes and add sugars, cinnamon, nutmeg, milk, and well-beaten eggs. Fill pastry shell and cook in medium (350°) oven for approximately 35–40 minutes.

Best of Bayou Cuisine

Editor's Extra: If a crisp bottom is desired, prebake crust about 5 minutes before adding filling.

Southern Pecan Pie

¼ cup butter, softened
1 cup brown sugar
¼ teaspoon salt
1 cup dark Karo syrup
3 eggs, beaten
1 teaspoon vanilla
1½ cups pecan halves
1 (9-inch) unbaked pie
   shell

Cream butter and sugar together until fluffy; add next 4 ingredients. Sprinkle pecans on bottom of pie shell. Pour filling over pecans.

Bake at 450° for 10 minutes; reduce temperature to 350° and bake 35 minutes longer. Outer edges of filling should be set, center slightly soft, and knife inserted in center comes out clean.

The Crowning Recipes of Kentucky

Editor's Extra: White corn syrup is often used instead of dark . . . a slightly different taste . . . same delicious presentation.

Praline Pie

$1/3$ cup butter

$1/3$ cup firmly packed brown sugar

$1/2$ cup chopped pecans

1 (8-inch) pie crust, lightly baked (do not brown)

1 small box butterscotch pudding (not instant)

Whipped topping

Nuts for garnish

Cook and stir butter and sugar in a saucepan until sugar melts and it boils vigorously. Remove from heat. Add nuts. Pour into crust and bake for 5 minutes at 425° (it will be bubbly). Meanwhile, prepare pudding as directed; cool, stirring twice. Spoon into crust. Chill. Serve with whipped topping. Garnish with nuts.

Homemade with Love

Chocolate Chip Pecan Pie

1 (9-inch) unbaked pie shell

1 cup semisweet chocolate chips

$1^1/2$ cups broken pecans

$1/4$ cup soft butter

$1/2$ cup firmly packed brown sugar

$1/2$ cup light corn syrup

3 eggs

1 teaspoon vanilla

Preheat oven to 375°. Sprinkle chocolate chips onto pie shell, then pecans. In small bowl, combine remaining ingredients in order listed, beating well after each addition, and pour over pecans. Bake about 35 minutes till crusted on top and crust is lightly browned.

Note: This is great with a scoop of ice cream or whipped cream.

Gwen McKee

Editor's Extra: In order to try variations on the same recipe, I sometimes experiment in "condensed" ways. I love this pie, but wanted to see what it would taste like with other varieties of chips. So in one pie, I carefully placed peanut butter, butterscotch, chocolate, and brickle bits on each quarter of the pie. I cut each section, and the tastings revealed all were delicious—but chocolate was the favorite.

My Mother's Chocolate Pie

The best chocolate pie on the planet! This recipe was a favorite of Mississippi native Guy Hovis, best known for his years on The Lawrence Welk Show.

2 egg yolks
2 cups milk
1 cup sugar
$\frac{1}{3}$ cup plain flour
Pinch of salt
$\frac{1}{3}$ cup cocoa
1 teaspoon vanilla
2 tablespoons butter
1 (8-inch) pie shell, baked

Beat egg yolks and add milk. Sift dry ingredients into double boiler. Stir in just enough milk and egg mixture to moisten dry ingredients. Stir in rest of milk and egg mixture. Cook on medium heat for 20 minutes, stirring often. Remove from heat; add vanilla and butter. Pour into (cooled) baked pie shell.

Many old recipes call for double boilers. You can make one with 2 pots or a bowl on top of a pot that fits comfortably in the lower pot. Be sure it has enough room for the lower pot to boil water without touching the upper pot.

MERINGUE:
3 egg whites
$\frac{1}{4}$ teaspoon cream of tartar
$\frac{1}{2}$ teaspoon vanilla
5 tablespoons sugar

Beat egg whites with cream of tartar and vanilla until soft peaks form. Gradually add sugar. Beat until stiff, then spread over cooled filling. Bake in 350° oven until meringue peaks are golden brown. Serves 8.

Look Who Came to Dinner

Mud Pie

1 box Famous Chocolate Wafers, or 1 (15-ounce) package Oreos, crushed

²/₃ cup butter, melted

½ gallon coffee ice cream

4 squares unsweetened chocolate

2 tablespoons butter

1 cup sugar

1 (5-ounce) can evaporated milk

Whipped cream

Nuts for topping

This makes 2 pies or can be put in 1 (9x13-inch) pan. Make crust with chocolate cookies and ²/₃ cup melted butter. Press in pan. Top with coffee ice cream. Freeze hard.

Melt chocolate and 2 tablespoons butter in double boiler. Remove from heat. Mix in sugar and evaporated milk. Whisk until smooth and thickened. Cool and pour over ice cream. Freeze. Serve pie with whipped cream and nuts.

Note: You can make your own coffee ice cream: Soften ½ gallon vanilla ice cream or ice milk. Add 2–3 tablespoons powdered instant coffee dissolved in 1 tablespoon vanilla and 1–2 tablespoons rum flavoring. Mix well. Refreeze in sealed container or use to make pie.

Christmas Favorites

Cheeky's Chess Pie

This tried-and-true classic southern recipe was selected from 15 chess pies submitted. Enjoy!

1½ cups sugar

½ cup butter, melted

1 tablespoon plus 1 teaspoon cornmeal

1 tablespoon white vinegar

1 teaspoon vanilla

3 eggs, beaten

1 unbaked (8-inch) pastry shell

Combine sugar, butter, cornmeal, white vinegar, and vanilla. Add beaten eggs. Mix thoroughly. Pour into pie shell. Bake at 350° for 50 minutes.

CordonBluegrass

Weidman's Bourbon Pie

Meridian, Mississippi's famous restaurant's famous pie.

1 box Nabisco Chocolate Snaps
1/2 cup butter or margarine, melted
21 marshmallows
1 cup evaporated milk
1/2 pint whipping cream
3 tablespoons bourbon

Crush chocolate snaps; mix with melted margarine. Pat into 9-inch pie pan and bake in 325° oven until set (about 10 minutes). Cool.

Melt marshmallows in undiluted milk—do not boil. Chill. Whip cream and fold into chilled marshmallow mixture. Add bourbon, pour into cooled chocolate crumb crust, and refrigerate 4 hours or until set. If desired, top with whipped cream and chocolate crumbs.

Best of Bayou Cuisine

Tanglewood Manor House Restaurant's Tar Heel Pie

12 ounces cream cheese, softened
1/2 cup sugar
1/2 pint whipping cream
1 1/2 medium bananas
1 (9-inch) deep-dish pie shell, baked

Mix softened cream cheese with sugar. In separate bowl, whip cream until stiff peaks form. Carefully fold cream into cheese mixture and mix until thoroughly blended. Slice bananas and place in bottom and sides of pie shell. Pour cheese mixture over bananas and chill until firm.

BLUEBERRY GLAZE:
1 (16-ounce) package frozen blueberries
1/3 cup sugar
1 tablespoon cornstarch

Combine all ingredients and cook over low heat until thick. Be careful not to break up the berries. Cool to room temperature. Spoon glaze evenly over cheese mixture and chill several hours or overnight.

North Carolina's Historic Restaurants

Peanut Butter Pie

A favorite pie made even better!

1 cup powdered sugar
1/2 cup chunky peanut butter
1 (9-inch) pastry shell, baked

Blend sugar and peanut butter with fork until mixture is crumbly. Spread 1/2 mixture in bottom of baked pastry shell; reserve remainder.

FILLING:
1/4 cup cornstarch
2/3 cup sugar
3 egg yolks (reserve whites)
1/2 teaspoon vanilla
1 tablespoon peanut butter
1/4 teaspoon salt
2 cups milk

Combine cornstarch, sugar, egg yolks, vanilla, peanut butter, salt, and milk and cook in double boiler until thickened, stirring constantly. Spoon Filling over peanut butter mixture.

MERINGUE:
3 egg whites
3 tablespoons sugar
1/2 teaspoon salt

Beat egg whites, sugar, and salt until stiff, and spread over pie. Sprinkle remaining peanut butter mixture on top. Bake at 325° for 20 minutes or until Meringue is firm and brown.

More...Home Town Recipes

Summertime Pie

1 (14-ounce) can
condensed milk

1 (16-ounce) container
Cool Whip

6 tablespoons lemon juice

1 (8-ounce) can crushed
pineapple, drained

$^1/_2$–1 cup chopped pecans
(optional)

2 bananas, chopped

1 large graham cracker pie
crust

Mix together condensed milk, Cool Whip, and lemon juice. Add pineapple, pecans, and bananas. Pour into pie crust and refrigerate.

Recipes Remembered

Nostalgic Lemon Ice Box Pie

A homemade crust makes this pie extra delicious!

CRUST:

18 graham cracker squares

$^1/_2$ stick butter, melted

$^1/_4$ cup sugar

Crush graham crackers into fine crumbs. Mix with melted butter and sugar. Press into pie plate. Bake 5 minutes in 325° oven. Cool.

FILLING:

1 (14-ounce) can
condensed milk

2 egg yolks

Scant $^1/_2$ cup fresh lemon
juice

$^1/_2$ pint whipping cream,
whipped

2 tablespoons sugar

Mix condensed milk, egg yolks, and lemon juice until blended. Pour into baked pie crust and top with whipped cream that has been sweetened with sugar. Refrigerate.

For a lighter variation, fold stiffly beaten egg whites into pie mixture.

Any Time's a Party!

Lemon Chess Tarts

4 eggs, slightly beaten
1 1/2 cups sugar
6 tablespoons butter,
   melted and cooled
1/4 cup milk
1 tablespoon cornmeal
3/4 teaspoon grated lemon
   rind
1 tablespoon lemon juice
16 unbaked tart shells

In mixing bowl, combine eggs, sugar, butter, milk, cornmeal, lemon rind, and lemon juice, stirring well to distribute sugar. Place tart shells on cookie sheet and divide filling evenly among the 16 shells. Bake at 350° for 35–40 minutes or until knife inserted in center comes out clean. Cool on wire rack. Cover and chill to store.

Gran's Gems

Lemon Meringue Tarts

Put this in a regular pie crust if you want a classic lemon meringue pie.

1 1/2 cups sugar
1/3 cup cornstarch
Grated rind of 2 lemons
2 cups boiling water
4 eggs, separated
1 tablespoon butter
1/3 cup lemon juice
1/8 teaspoon salt
1/2 cup sugar
Individual pie shells

Combine sugar, cornstarch, and lemon rind. Add boiling water. Cook until it thickens. Cook slowly for 5 minutes. Beat egg yolks; add a small amount of sugar mixture to yolks. Then pour yolks into sugar mixture. Add butter, lemon juice, and salt. Cook slowly for 5 minutes. Pour into individual pie shells. Cover with meringue made by whipping 4 egg whites with 1/2 cup sugar till stiff peaks form. Bake at 325° for 15 minutes.

Inverness Cook Book

Crisp Crust Apple Pie

FILLING:

5 medium apples (Red or Golden Delicious)

1¹/₂ cups sugar

1 tablespoon flour

1 teaspoon cinnamon (or to taste)

¹/₂ cup water

Slice pared apples thin into an oblong baking dish. Mix together sugar, flour, and cinnamon; sprinkle over apples. Pour water over mixture.

CRUST:

2¹/₂ cups self-rising flour

¹/₂ teaspoon salt

²/₃ cup shortening

About ¹/₂ cup ice water

³/₄ cup sugar

1 teaspoon cinnamon

¹/₂ cup butter or margarine

Mix flour and salt; cut in shortening. Add enough water to hold dough together. Roll between sheets of wax paper to size of dish. Put on top of apple mixture. Sprinkle on sugar and cinnamon (mixed together). Dot with butter pats. Bake at 400° until Crust is browned and apples are tender.

Note: When in a rush, I have used 2 frozen pie shells for top crust and sprinkled on cinnamon and sugar.

The Apple Barn Cookbook

Clap your hands; stomp your feet. There's music inside that can't be beat.
Bring your talent, no matter where you're from. Look out, Nashville, here we come!

Fried Apple Pies

This recipe comes from the Pioneer Crafts Festival held annually in Rison. It has been a festival secret for over 70 years!

8 ounces sliced dried apples

5 cups water

1 cup sugar

1 teaspoon cinnamon

2½ tablespoons cornstarch

2 tablespoons lemon juice

Cook apples in water for 20 minutes. Combine sugar, cinnamon, and cornstarch. Add to apples. Add lemon juice. Cook until thickened. Cool.

PASTRY:

1 cup plus 2 tablespoons shortening

3 cups flour

1 egg, beaten slightly

7 tablespoons water

1 teaspoon salt

1 teaspoon vinegar

Cut shortening into flour. Combine egg, water, salt, and vinegar. Pour into flour mixture and mix.

Pinch small amount of dough and roll out on floured board. Cut out, using a saucer as a guide. Put 1 tablespoon apple mixture on dough. Wet edges of dough with iced water. Fold dough over apple mixture and seal by pressing a floured fork around edges.

Fry in 1–2 inches of oil in an electric skillet on highest setting. Cook until golden brown, turning only once. Glaze with a mixture of powdered sugar and water, if desired. Yields about 24 pies.

A Great Taste of Arkansas

Electric skillets were so popular when they first came out that many recipes specified their use. Then electric fryers came along to make frying even easier. But, of course, oil in a pot on the stove can still do the trick.

Fresh Strawberry Pie

1 cup sugar
¼ cup cornstarch
¼ cup white Karo
1½ cups hot water
1 (3-ounce) package
    strawberry Jell-O
2 pastry shells, baked
1 quart strawberries
Whipped cream for topping

Mix sugar and cornstarch. Add Karo and water. Cook, stirring constantly, until clear and thickened. Remove from heat. Add strawberry Jell-O. Cool. Line bottom of pastry shells with whole fresh strawberries and pour mixture over them. Chill. When ready to serve, add whipped cream as topping. Yields 2 (8-inch) pies.

Anniversary Collection of Delectable Dishes

Editor's Extra: Unless they are very small, we like to cut strawberries—easier to slice pie. Save a big one to fan on top of whipped cream. To fan a strawberry, hold it by its stem on a cutting board, and slice about five times with tip of knife toward stem, leaving ¼ inch of strawberry head unsliced. Gently fan slices out and perk up its leaves. Beautiful!

Light and Easy Blueberry Pie

A recipe that is made over and over . . . simply because it's so good and takes so little effort to make.

1 (8-ounce) package light
    cream cheese, softened
½ cup sugar
1 teaspoon vanilla
1 (12-ounce) carton light
    whipped topping, divided
1 graham cracker crust
1 (21-ounce) can blueberry
    pie filling

Beat cream cheese, sugar, and vanilla together till smooth. Add two thirds of whipped topping (or real whipped cream) and mix well. Spread mixture evenly into crust. Spread blueberry pie filling over top. Dollop with remaining whipped topping.

Note: This works well with any fruit pie filling . . . strawberry, cherry, lemon or pineapple. You can use a chocolate crust with cherry pie filling for a variation.

Gwen McKee

No Crust Coconut Pie

3 eggs
1½ cups sugar
2 tablespoons flour
1 (12-ounce) can
  evaporated milk
1 teaspoon vanilla
¾ stick butter or
  margarine, melted
1 (3½-ounce) can flaked
  coconut

Beat eggs slightly. Add sugar and flour. Mix well and add milk, vanilla, margarine, and coconut. Pour into a well-greased and floured deep dish-pie pan. Bake in a 375° oven for 30–35 minutes.

Note: Peach, pineapple, or other drained fruit may be substituted for coconut.

Cooking on the Go

Coconut Cream Pie

¼ cup sugar
½ cup yellow cake mix
3 egg yolks
1½ cups milk, divided
¼ stick butter
¾ cup coconut
1 pie shell, baked

Mix sugar, cake mix, and egg yolks in saucepan. Blend in enough milk to mix well. Add remaining milk; cook until thick. Add butter, then coconut. Cool slightly, then pour into baked crust. Refrigerate.

Evening Shade

Chocolate Mousse Pie

A delicious and impressive dessert. Absolutely luscious!

CRUST:

3 cups chocolate wafer crumbs

½ cup unsweetened butter, melted

Combine crumbs and butter. Press on bottom and sides of a 10-inch springform pan. Refrigerate for 30 minutes or chill in freezer.

FILLING:

1 pound semisweet dark chocolate

2 whole eggs

4 eggs, separated

2 cups whipping cream

6 tablespoons powdered sugar

Soften chocolate in top of double boiler (or in bowl over simmering water). Whisk in 2 whole eggs and mix well; then add 4 egg yolks and mix until thoroughly blended. Let cool until lukewarm. Whip cream with powdered sugar until soft peaks form. Beat egg whites until stiff but not dry. Stir a little of the cream and egg white into chocolate mixture to lighten; then fold in remaining cream and egg whites until thoroughly mixed. Pour into Crust and chill at least 6 hours, or preferably overnight.

CHOCOLATE LEAVES:

4 ounces (approximately) semisweet chocolate

1 teaspoon vegetable shortening

Camelia or other waxy leaves

Melt chocolate and shortening in top of a double boiler. Using a spoon, generously coat underside of 10–12 clean leaves. Place on wax paper and chill until firm.

TOPPING:

2 cups whipping cream

2 tablespoons powdered sugar

Whip 2 cups cream with sugar until quite stiff. Loosen Crust on all sides of pie, using sharp knife. Remove springform. Spread whipped cream over top of mousse. Peel leaves away from chocolate, starting at stem end of leaf, and decorate top of mousse.

Cut pie into wedges with a thin, sharp knife. Serves 12–15.

Note: This dessert can be prepared ahead and frozen. Thaw overnight in the refrigerator.

Suncoast Seasons

Coffee Toffee Pie

CRUST:
1½ cups finely crushed Nabisco Chocolate Wafers
¼ cup butter, melted

Preheat oven to 325°. Combine crumbs and butter with fork and press gently into 10-inch pie plate. Bake for 10 minutes and cool.

FILLING:
¾ cup butter, softened
1 cup sugar
1½ ounces unsweetened chocolate
1 tablespoon instant coffee
1 tablespoon boiling water
3 eggs

Beat butter until creamy. Gradually add sugar, beating until light and lemon-colored. Melt chocolate over hot water; cool slightly and add to butter mixture. Add instant coffee to boiling water and stir into mixture. Add eggs one at a time, beating well after each addition. Pour Filling into cooled pie shell and refrigerate overnight, covered.

TOPPING:
2 cups whipping cream
½ cup confectioners' sugar
2 tablespoons instant coffee
2 tablespoons coffee liqueur
Chocolate curls for garnish

Beat cream until stiff. Add confectioners' sugar, coffee, and coffee liqueur. Spread over Filling and garnish with chocolate curls. Refrigerate at least 2 hours before serving. Yields 8 servings.

Some Like it South!

The first time I attempted to make chocolate curls, they didn't look like "curls," but more like shavings. My mistake was using baking chocolate that was hard. The secret is that the chocolate has to be soft enough for a vegetable peeler to shave across easily. A big block (8 ounces) is your best bet for getting nice big curls, and you would need to get this at a chocolate shop or bakery. But you can use chocolate squares or even bars you find in the grocery; the curls will just not be as big. I put the chocolate on a plate on top of the refrigerator (it's usually a little warmer there than room temperature) for about an hour. Then hold it in one hand and run a vegetable peeler evenly across a side, letting the curls fall gently on wax paper. It surely can dress up a dessert!
—Gwen

Toffee Ice Cream Pie

PIE:

12 (³/₄-ounce) Heath bars

1¼ cups chocolate wafer crumbs

¼ cup butter, melted

½ gallon vanilla ice cream

Put heath bars in freezer to harden. Mix crumbs and butter. Line 9x13-inch pan. Press mixture evenly. Put into refrigerator to harden. Crush Heath bars and mix with softened ice cream. Put in crust and freeze overnight.

SAUCE:

1 stick butter

1 (12-ounce) package chocolate chips

2 cups powdered sugar

1 (13-ounce) can evaporated milk

2 teaspoons vanilla

Melt butter and chocolate chips. Add sugar and milk. Cook about 8 minutes or until thick, stirring constantly. Add vanilla. Serve warm over pie. The Sauce can be made early in day and heated at last minute. Serves 8–10.

Note: Oreos may be substituted for chocolate wafers if the filling is scraped off.

Tea-Time at the Masters©

Crème de Menthe Pie

So simple . . . so refreshing . . .

½ gallon vanilla ice cream

8 tablespoons crème de menthe

Chocolate syrup

Let ice cream soften until soft enough to mix. Add crème de menthe; stir well. Pour into Chocolate Crust. Freeze. Serve with chocolate syrup drizzled on plate and top of pie slice.

CHOCOLATE CRUST:

2 cups crumbled chocolate Oreo cookies

⅓ cup margarine, melted

Mix cookies and margarine together. Press onto bottom and sides of a 9-inch pie pan. Freeze.

Hallmark's Collection of Home Tested Recipes

Editor's Extra: Pretty with a dollop of whipped cream, some chocolate shavings, and a mint leaf on individual slices, or a fanned strawberry.

Chocolate Turtle Cheesecake Pie

1 (7-ounce) package caramels, peeled
1/4 cup evaporated milk
3/4 cup chopped pecans, divided
1 (9-inch) chocolate-crumb pie crust
2 (3-ounce) packages cream cheese, softened
1/2 cup sour cream
1 1/4 cups milk
1 (3.9-ounce) package chocolate instant pudding mix
1/2 cup fudge topping

Place caramels and evaporated milk in a heavy saucepan. Heat over medium-low heat, stirring continually, until smooth, about 5 minutes. Stir in 1/2 cup chopped pecans. Pour into pie crust. Combine cream cheese, sour cream, and milk in blender. Process until smooth. Add pudding mix; process for about 30 seconds longer. Pour pudding mixture over caramel layer, covering evenly.

Chill, loosely covered, until set, about 15 minutes. Drizzle fudge topping over pudding layer in a decorative pattern. Sprinkle top of cheesecake with remaining pecans. Chill, loosely covered, until serving time.

Dutch Pantry Simply Sweets

Beautiful Raspberry Peach Melba Pie

1 (10-ounce) package frozen raspberries, partially thawed
1 (3-ounce) package raspberry gelatin
1 cup boiling water
1 tablespoon lemon juice
1/2 pint whipping cream
2 tablespoons sugar
1 (16-ounce) can sliced peaches, drained and chopped
1 (9-inch) chocolate pie crust

Purée raspberries with their liquid in food processor or blender and set aside. Dissolve gelatin in boiling water, then stir in raspberries and lemon juice; chill till partially set. Whip cream till frothy; gradually add sugar and beat till stiff. Reserving 1/2 cup peaches for garnish, fold remaining peaches into whipped cream (whipped topping okay); spoon half this mixture onto crust. Carefully spoon half the raspberry mixture over this and chill about 20 minutes. Put remaining whipped cream/peach mixture on top, reserving a dollop or two for garnish, then remaining raspberry mixture. Garnish and refrigerate before serving. Beautiful!

Gwen McKee

Apple Cobbler

7 full cups sliced apples
$^1/_8$ teaspoon salt
$^1/_4$ teaspoon cinnamon
$^3/_4$ cup sugar
$^1/_4$ teaspoon nutmeg
1 tablespoon lemon juice
$^1/_2$ teaspoon grated lemon rind
2 tablespoons butter
1 (9-inch) pie crust

Place apples in 9-inch pie pan. Sprinkle them with mixture of all ingredients except butter. Dot with butter. Top with vented pie crust and bake at 350° for one hour.

Historic Kentucky Recipes

Super Blackberry Cobbler

4 cups blackberries
1 cup sugar
$^1/_4$ cup quick tapioca
1$^1/_3$ cups water
2 tablespoons butter
$^1/_4$ teaspoon lemon extract

Combine berries, sugar, tapioca, water, and butter, and let stand while making Crust.

Add lemon extract to berries and pour into buttered 9x13-inch baking dish. Place Crust rounds over berries and bake at 425° for 30 minutes.

CRUST:
2 cups flour
2 teaspoons sugar
5 teaspoons baking powder
$^1/_4$ teaspoon salt
6 tablespoons shortening
$^2/_3$ cup milk
Sugar for sprinkling

Sift flour, sugar, baking powder, and salt together. Cut in shortening. Add milk all at once. Stir to dampen. Roll out. Cut into 8 (2$^1/_2$-inch) rounds. Sprinkle with sugar.

A Taste from Back Home

Peach Cobbler

Houmas House had many visitors back in the mid 1800s, and often they would write of their experiences at the plantation. One such visitor wrote about the wonderful peas that were grown in the garden and eaten day after day. He mentioned the mint juleps served before breakfast and the fabulous peach cobbler that ended every meal. Here is a rendition of that dish.

FRUIT MIXTURE:
6 cups peeled sliced peaches
1³/4 cups sugar, divided
¹/4 cup water
3 tablespoons flour
Pinch of salt
Pinch of cinnamon
Pinch of nutmeg
Pinch of allspice

Preheat oven to 400°. In a heavy-bottomed saucepan, combine peaches, 1¹/2 cups sugar, and water. Bring to a rolling boil, reduce to simmer, and allow fruit to cook until softened. In a measuring cup, blend flour, remaining ¹/4 cup sugar, salt, cinnamon, nutmeg, and allspice. Pour into the peach mixture, stirring constantly, until mixture thickens. Remove from heat and pour the mixture into a 9-inch black iron skillet or cobbler pan, and allow to cool slightly.

CRUST BATTER:
1 cup all-purpose flour
¹/2 cup sugar
2 teaspoons baking powder
³/4 cup milk
¹/2 teaspoon salt

In a mixing bowl, whisk together flour, sugar, baking powder, and milk until well blended. Season with salt. Pour the batter in an irregular shape over the center of the cobbler and bake for approximately 45 minutes or until golden brown.

Note: You may wish to garnish the cobbler with fresh sliced peaches, powdered sugar, and a sprig of mint. Serves 8.

Plantation Celebrations

243

Fresh Peach Crisp

1 cup flour
$^{1}/_{2}$ cup sugar
$^{1}/_{2}$ cup firmly packed light brown sugar
$^{1}/_{4}$ teaspoon salt
$^{1}/_{2}$ teaspoon cinnamon
$^{1}/_{2}$ cup margarine
4 cups peeled sliced fresh peaches
$^{1}/_{4}$ teaspoon almond extract
2 tablespoons water
$^{1}/_{4}$ teaspoon ground nutmeg
Whipping cream

Combine first 5 ingredients. Cut in margarine with a pastry blender until mixture resembles coarse cornmeal. Set aside.

Combine peaches, almond extract, and water. Spoon into a greased 9-inch-square baking dish. Sprinkle flour mixture over peaches. Sprinkle nutmeg on top. Bake covered in a 350° oven for 15 minutes. Remove cover and bake 35–45 minutes longer or until the topping is brown. Serve warm with whipped cream. Serves 6–8.

Revel

Quick and Easy Apple Dumplings

Cinnamon-sugar is so nice to have on hand. You can buy it mixed, but it's so easy to make yourself. I mix about 2–3 tablespoons cinnamon in 1 cup sugar and put in a large shaker container. The kids love to sprinkle it on toast, and I like to have it for my fried apples and Skillet Popover (page 49) and lots of other dishes.

—Gwen

2 medium-size Granny Smith apples
2 (10-count) cans Butter-Me-Not Biscuits
Cinnamon sugar
2 cups Sprite
2 cups sugar
2 sticks margarine

Peel and core apples and cut into 40 wedges. Pat out biscuits and wrap 2 pieces of apple in each one. Place in a greased, 9x13-inch baking pan and sprinkle with cinnamon sugar. Mix Sprite, sugar, and margarine in saucepan and bring to a boil. Pour over the dumplings and sprinkle lightly with additional cinnamon sugar. Bake at 400° for about 12–15 minutes or until biscuits are a golden brown.

Munchin' with the Methodists

Peach Buckle

Some say this recipe should be called "Peach Unbuckle," since that's what a lot of it could do to your waist-line. Apples or blueberries are also good in this recipe.

2 pounds peaches (about 6 medium), or to taste
1 tablespoon lemon juice
³/₄ cup sugar, divided
4 tablespoons butter or margarine, softened
1 teaspoon vanilla extract
1 egg, lightly beaten
1 cup flour
¹/₄ teaspoon salt
1 teaspoon baking powder
¹/₃ cup milk

Preheat oven to 375°. Slice peeled peaches thinly, and toss with lemon juice and ¹/₄ cup sugar. Set aside.

Cream butter or margarine with remaining sugar, and add vanilla and egg. Blend well. Sift together flour, salt, and baking powder. Add dry ingredients alternately with milk to the creamed mixture, beating well after each addition. Pour batter into greased 10-inch baking dish. Spoon peaches over batter.

CRUMB TOPPING:
¹/₃ cup sugar
¹/₃ cup flour
¹/₄ cup butter or margarine

Combine Crumb Topping ingredients to form coarse crumbs, and sprinkle over fruit. Bake about 40–50 minutes, or until top is golden brown. Serve warm, with sweetened whipped cream or ice cream, as desired. Yields 8–10 servings.

Georgia Entertains

Creole Bread Pudding

6 slices bread, cubed

3½ cups milk, divided

4 eggs, separated

½ cup sugar, divided

**1 tablespoon vanilla
extract**

Pinch of salt

**¼ cup butter or
margarine, melted**

½ cup raisins

Combine bread cubes and 1 cup milk; set aside. Beat egg yolks, 6 tablespoons sugar, and remaining 2½ cups milk. Stir in vanilla, salt, butter, and raisins. Pour mixture over bread and mix well. Pour into shallow 2-quart baking dish. Place dish in a pan of hot water. Bake at 300° about 50 minutes or until knife inserted in center comes out clean. Beat egg whites until stiff; gradually beat in remaining 2 tablespoons sugar. Spread meringue over pudding; bake at 350° for 10 minutes or until golden. Serve with Rum Sauce. Yields 6–8 servings.

RUM SAUCE:

½ cup sugar

¼ cup water

**2 tablespoons butter or
margarine**

**1 tablespoon rum (or
bourbon)**

Combine sugar, water, and butter in a small saucepan; bring to a boil and boil one minute. Remove from heat; stir in rum (or bourbon). Serve warm. Yields about ½ cup.

Auburn Entertains

Often when taking lunch to the field for my daddy and other workers, Mamean made something a little special for them. One day she brought bread pudding, and after tasting it, one of the workers called her over to the side and sheepishly said, "Miss Jean, I believe you left out the sugar." Aghast, but refusing to have her precious pudding wasted, she quickly went back to the house and brought some raw sugar to sprinkle on top. Not only was the bread pudding saved, but heartily enjoyed.
                                                                                    —Barbara

Floating Isle

Puffs of meringue float in soft pudding . . .

My Aunt Yolande was so proudly "New Orleans," and her French cooking reflected it. I was quite small the first time I saw her Floating Isle, and I was intrigued with the presentation and its name. Its taste lived up to the hoopla and I have enjoyed it ever since. —*Gwen*

3 eggs, separated
3/4 cup plus 1 tablespoon sugar, divided
1 (12-ounce) can evaporated milk
1 can water
Pinch of salt
2 teaspoons vanilla extract
3 tablespoons cornstarch

Combine egg yolks and 3/4 cup sugar. Add milk, water, salt, vanilla, and cornstarch, and cook until mixture begins to thicken. Beat egg whites and one tablespoon of sugar until stiff. Pour custard mixture over egg whites mixture and gently streak it through. Cool before serving. Serves 4–6.

Recipes and Reminiscences of New Orleans I

Toasted Almond Bread Pudding

So tasty, it doesn't need a sauce.

3 eggs
1/2 cup sugar
2 cups half-and-half
2 teaspoons almond extract
6 bakery croissants, cubed
3/4 cup sliced almonds

Preheat oven to 350°. Mix eggs, sugar, half-and-half, and almond extract in large bowl. Add croissant cubes and mix lightly; let sit about 10 minutes. Toast almonds by spreading in baking pan and broil about 4 inches from heat for only a minute or so, watching carefully, till they are just browned. Cool slightly and fold into bread mixture. Pour into greased baking dish and bake about 30–40 minutes till golden brown.

Fine Dining Tennessee Style

Editor's Extra: A dollop of whipped cream with a few mini chocolate chips on top makes an awesome dessert, or a trail of warmed fudge sauce on the plate is nice, but it surely is a recipe that stands alone quite tastefully.

Banana Pudding with Meringue

Simply the best!

PUDDING:

¾ **cup sugar**

⅓ **cup all-purpose flour**

Dash of salt

4 egg yolks

2 cups milk

1 teaspoon vanilla extract

6–8 ripe bananas, sliced

About 3 dozen vanilla wafers

In a double boiler over simmering water, mix sugar, flour, and salt. Beat egg yolks and combine with milk. Add yolks and milk to sugar mixture, stirring constantly to blend well. Cook uncovered, stirring frequently, for 10–15 minutes until mixture thickens. Remove from heat and stir in vanilla.

In a loaf pan, make a layer of the cooked custard, then a layer of bananas, then a layer of vanilla wafers. Continue for 3 layers of each, or more if ingredients permit.

MERINGUE:

4 egg whites

¼ **teaspoon cream of tartar**

6 tablespoons sugar

½ **teaspoon vanilla extract**

Preheat oven to 350°. In a mixing bowl, beat egg whites until frothy with an electric mixer, then add the cream of tartar. Beat again until whites stand in soft peaks that fall over when the beater is removed. Then beat in sugar one tablespoon at a time. After all sugar is used, beat in vanilla.

Spread Meringue over Pudding, covering entire surface and edges of pan. Bake for about 15 minutes or until Meringue is slightly browned. Refrigerate until ready to serve. Serves 8.

The Southern Cook's Handbook

Editor's Extra: This can be done in a pretty casserole dish or deep colorful pie plate for a beautiful dessert presentation.

Great Grandmother's Chocolate Mousse

This recipe is over 100 years old.

¹/₂ pound sweet chocolate
2 tablespoons sugar
3 tablespoons water
4 eggs, separated
2¹/₂ dozen lady fingers
Whipped cream
Sherry
Vanilla

Melt chocolate in a double boiler; add sugar and water. Add slightly beaten egg yolks. Stir while thickening. Remove from heat to cool.

Beat egg whites until stiff and gently fold into chocolate mixture. Put wax paper or foil in bottom of cake pan or springform pan. Line bottom of pan with some of the split lady fingers. Pour some chocolate filling over them and continue layers of lady fingers and chocolate until pan is filled. Chill until set. Unmold, remove paper, and garnish with whipped cream flavored with sherry and vanilla. Yields 6–8 servings.

Cooking with Tradition

The Mansion Almond Chocolate Mousse

A delicious chocolate cloud of a dessert.

2 cups whipping cream
3 ounces butter (³/₄ of a stick)
1 pound semisweet chocolate
3 eggs, separated
¹/₂ cup powdered sugar
¹/₄ cup hot coffee
¹/₄ cup amaretto liqueur
Sliced almonds, toasted

Whip cream until stiff; chill. In a double boiler over hot water, melt butter with chocolate. In a small bowl, beat egg yolks with sugar until thick and lemon colored. Add hot coffee to melted chocolate; beat yolk-sugar mixture and amaretto into mixture and chill to slightly below room temperature.

Beat egg whites until stiff. Fold whipped cream into chocolate, then fold in beaten egg whites. Chill at least 2 hours before serving. Garnish with almonds. Serves 8.

Dining in Historic Kentucky

Easy-Do Fresh Strawberry Mousse

1 pint (about 1½ cups
   mashed) ripe
   strawberries, hulled,
   cleaned, and dried
1 (3-ounce) package
   strawberry-flavored
   gelatin
1 cup boiling water
½ tablespoon lemon juice
¼ cup sugar
Pinch salt
¼ cup strawberry liqueur
   or brandy (optional)
1 cup heavy cream
Sweetened whipped cream,
   strawberries, and fresh
   mint sprigs for garnish

Slice strawberries, then coarsely mash with a potato masher; set aside. In a small bowl, dissolve gelatin in boiling water. In a large bowl, combine strawberries, lemon juice, sugar, and salt. Add dissolved gelatin and strawberry liqueur, if desired, mixing well. Chill in the refrigerator until mixture is the consistency of unbeaten egg whites.

In a chilled, small, heavy bowl, beat cream with chilled beaters until stiff peaks are formed. Fold whipped cream into chilled gelatin mixture. Spoon mousse into individual sherbet glasses or dishes or a 1-quart mold; chill in the refrigerator for several hours until mousse is set. Garnish each serving with additional whipped cream, a whole strawberry, and a fresh mint sprig, if desired.

Variation: One pint fresh raspberries may be substituted. Purée and strain berries. Raspberry liqueur may be used. Yields 4 servings.

More Richmond Receipts

Milk Chocolate Crème Brûlée

2 cups milk
2 cups heavy cream
3 ounces sugar (¹/₃ cup)
¹/₂ cup rum, boiled and reduced by half
¹/₄ teaspoon mace (nutmeg spice)
¹/₄ teaspoon cinnamon
10 egg yolks
3 bananas
5 ounces milk chocolate, chopped
Granulated sugar

Combine milk, cream, and sugar and bring to a boil. Reduce rum in separate pan; add mace and cinnamon. Add spiced rum reduction to cream mixture. Whisk until blended. Temper in egg yolks. Slice bananas and place in bottom of ramekins or custard cups. Put chocolate over bananas. Pour custard over bananas. Bake in a water bath at 275° for about 25 minutes or until set in center. After custard is complete, chill for approximately 3 hours.

Sprinkle top of custards with granulated sugar and burn with blow torch, or put under broiler for approximately 15 seconds. Serve immediately.

Note: This custard is best served the day it is made so the bananas do not brown from exposure.

Fine Dining Tennessee Style

Charlotte Russe

2 envelopes Knox gelatin
¹/₂ cup cold water
2 cups milk
6 egg yolks
1 cup sugar
1 teaspoon vanilla
2 cups cream, whipped

Soften gelatin in cold water. Scald milk and stir into it egg yolks and sugar beaten together. Cook in double boiler until it thickens. Before removing from heat, add gelatin and dissolve. Add vanilla. Cool and fold in whipped cream.

Note: This is good flavored with whiskey and may be poured into molds lined with ladyfingers. For chocolate charlotte, add 2 squares melted chocolate.

DAR Recipe Book

Bananas Nourries

A dramatic flamed banana dessert (similar to Bananas Foster), this is surprisingly simple to make.

4 bananas
8 tablespoons butter
³/₄ cup light brown sugar
¹/₂ cup banana liqueur
¹/₄ cup rum
1 pint vanilla ice cream
¹/₂ cup chopped roasted hazelnuts

Slice bananas lengthwise. Heat butter in 1 large or 2 small skillets. Add brown sugar, and stir over medium-high heat until sugar dissolves and a caramel glaze is formed. Stir in banana liqueur. Lay bananas in the caramel glaze; cook, turning occasionally (carefully), for 2 minutes. Add rum and flame. Serve each person 2 banana halves over 2 scoops of ice cream. Sprinkle with nuts.

The Abbey Cookbook

Cherries Jubilee

A fanfare dessert!

Cherries Jubilee is a dessert that was created by Chef Auguste Escoffier in honor of Queen Victoria's Diamond Jubilee in England. It consists of cherries flamed tableside with sugar and Kirsch (cherry brandy) spooned over vanilla ice cream. Southern restaurants adopted it for its delicious taste and presentation.
Do try this at home . . . but be careful.

1 tablespoon cornstarch
1 teaspoon cold water
2 tablespoons sugar
1 (16-ounce) can dark cherries, drained (reserve liquid)
¹/₂ cup brandy
Vanilla ice cream

Dissolve cornstarch in water in saucepan. Add sugar and liquid drained from cherries. Cook, stirring, until thick and transparent. Pour over cherries in flameproof dish. Add brandy and light with a match. Stir as flame burns. Pour over individual servings of ice cream. Serves 4–6.

The Twelve Days of Christmas Cookbook

Pecan Tassies

1 (3-ounce) package
   cream cheese, softened
1/2 cup (1 stick) plus
   1 tablespoon butter,
   softened
1 cup all-purpose flour
1 large egg
1 cup firmly packed light
   brown sugar
1 teaspoon pure vanilla
   extract
1/8 teaspoon salt
3/4 cup coarsely chopped
   pecans

In a medium-size mixing bowl, cream cream cheese and 1/2 cup butter together with an electric mixer. Add flour a little at a time, and mix well to form a firm, smooth dough. Cover with plastic wrap and chill one hour.

Preheat oven to 325°. Remove chilled dough from refrigerator and roll into 24 (1-inch) balls. Place balls in 24 ungreased mini-muffin tins and press dough against sides and bottoms of each tin.

In a mixing bowl, combine egg, brown sugar, remaining tablespoon of butter, vanilla, and salt. Beat until smooth. Sprinkle about half the pecans into bottoms of prepared tins, fill each with an equal amount of egg mixture, and sprinkle remaining nuts over the tops. Bake until filling is just set, about 25 minutes. Let cool completely before removing from tins. Makes 24.

The Southern Cook's Handbook

Chocolate-Dipped Strawberries

These first-to-disappear delicacies tell your guests they're special.

2 pints fresh strawberries
1 (6-ounce) package
   semisweet chocolate chip
   morsels
1 tablespoon shortening

Wash and "dry" strawberries on paper towels. Melt chocolate and shortening over hot water or in microwave. Cool. Dip strawberries in chocolate and place on wax paper (or wire rack) to cool. Refrigerate until serving time. Recipe doubles easily and can be made up to 8 hours ahead.

Heather Creel

French Banana Éclair

This dessert is something to look at as well as delicious.

1 cup water
½ cup butter
½ teaspoon salt
1 cup flour
4 tablespoons sugar
4 eggs

Bring water, butter, and salt to a boil in large saucepan over medium heat. Combine flour with sugar and add all at once, stirring vigorously with spoon until dough forms ball and leaves sides of pan. Remove from heat. Beat in eggs, one at a time, and continue beating until dough is stiff and glossy. Set aside about ⅓ of dough for top. On greased 15x10x1-inch jellyroll pan, form remaining ⅔ of dough into one long oblong, about 7 inches wide. Spoon reserved dough into mounds along the top of oblong. Bake at 400° for 30 minutes. Remove from oven. With a sharp knife, make slits along sides of éclair 2 inches apart to let steam escape. Return to oven and continue baking 10 minutes longer. Remove to cooling rack. Slice off top of éclair. Remove any soft dough inside. Cool thoroughly and fill.

FILLING:
4 cups whipping cream
4 tablespoons sugar
6–8 bananas
4 tablespoons crème de cocoa

Whip cream in mixing bowl until soft peaks form. Gradually add sugar, whipping until stiff. Mash enough bananas to make about 2 cups. Add crème de cocoa to mashed bananas and fold into whipped cream. Fill éclair shell with half of whipped cream and banana mixture. Slice remaining bananas over whipped cream. Cover sliced bananas with remaining whipped cream. Replace top of éclair and drizzle with Glaze.

GLAZE:
½ cup powdered sugar
2 tablespoons cocoa
2 tablespoons butter, melted
1 teaspoon vanilla
6–8 tablespoons boiling water (or less)
½ cup chopped pecans

Combine powdered sugar, cocoa, melted butter, and vanilla in small bowl. Stir in enough boiling water to make a thin Glaze. Drizzle over filled éclair. Sprinkle with chopped pecans. Chill until serving time. Slice crosswise to serve; each slice may be cut in half. Yields 16–20 servings.

From a Louisiana Kitchen

Cream Puffs or Éclairs

1 stick butter
1 cup water
1 cup flour
4 eggs

Bring butter and water to a boil in medium saucepan. Add flour all at once. Stir vigorously until ball forms in center of pan. Remove from heat. Add eggs one at a time, beating after each egg. Shape on a slightly greased cookie sheet with spoon or pastry bag, forming an oval for éclairs or a round for cream puffs. Bake at 375° for one hour or until bubbles of moisture disappear. Cut off tops when cool. Spoon out soft center, if present. Fill with Vanilla Filling and ice with Glossy Chocolate Icing, or fill with vanilla ice cream and top with chocolate syrup and garnish with nuts.

VANILLA FILLING:
2 cups milk, divided
$^1/_3$ cup flour
$^2/_3$ cup sugar
$^1/_4$ teaspoon salt
3 egg yolks, beaten
2 tablespoons butter
$^1/_2$ teaspoon vanilla

Scald $1^1/_2$ cups milk. Mix together flour, sugar, salt, and remaining $^1/_2$ cup milk. Gradually add mixture to scalded milk. Stir constantly in top of double boiler or directly over low heat. Add a little mixture to well-beaten egg yolks, then add with butter. Cook until thick. Add vanilla. Cool.

GLOSSY CHOCOLATE ICING:
3 tablespoons butter or margarine
9 tablespoons cocoa
2 cups powdered sugar
5 tablespoons milk
3 teaspoons vanilla

Melt butter and cocoa together. Mix powdered sugar and milk together and add to cocoa mixture. Add vanilla.

Somebody's Cookbook

Louisiana Swamp

Enter at your own risk!

CAKE:
1 (18¼-ounce) German
   chocolate cake mix
3 large eggs
¾ cup water
½ cup liquid coffee
⅓ cup vegetable oil

Preheat oven to 325°. Mix all Cake ingredients well and pour into a greased 11x15-inch pan. Bake 20 minutes or until Cake just begins to leave sides of pan.

FILLING:
3 (7-ounce) jars
   marshmallow crème
1 cup broken pecans

Spoon small dollops of crème all over hot Cake, but be careful not to spread around, as it will pick up the top of the Cake. Sprinkle pecans over marshmallow crème.

SWAMP TOPPING:
1 (12-ounce) package
   chocolate chips
1 tablespoon butter
1 can milk chocolate
   frosting
⅓ cup liquid coffee
1 teaspoon almond extract

Micro-melt chips in 8-cup measure 2 minutes on HIGH. Stir, then stir in butter, frosting, coffee, and almond flavoring till ribbony smooth. Pour over filling unevenly—this is a swamp, so just dollop so you can still see the nuts and marshmallows. Now you can let it sit for a while, but as soon as your resistance gives out . . . wade in!

Gwen McKee

Editor's Extra: You can make this in a 9x13-inch pan if you don't have a bigger one, but make 6 cupcakes out of some of the batter, as you don't want the cake part to be too thick.

Simply Sensational Frozen Strawberry Trifle

1 small angel food cake

6 tablespoons amaretto (or Triple Sec), divided

1 (8-ounce) can crushed pineapple, drained

1 (10-ounce) package frozen strawberries, thawed

1/2 cup sliced almonds (optional)

3 pints vanilla ice cream, softened

1 (12-ounce) carton whipped topping, divided

Break cake into chunks in large container. Pour 5 tablespoons amaretto over cake. Stir pineapple, strawberries, and almonds, if desired, into softened ice cream; fold in 2/3 of whipped topping. Mix gently with cake chunks. Stir 1 tablespoon amaretto into remaining whipped topping and spread on top of mixture. Freeze.

Serve in stemmed glasses with a strawberry or mint leaf on top. Serves 8–12.

Note: This is always ready to serve because the liqueur keeps the cake from freezing hard.

Gwen McKee

Pink House Trifle

A very old recipe . . . still as delicious as ever.

1 1/2 quarts milk

1 1/2 cups sugar

2 tablespoons cornstarch

6 eggs

1/2 cup sherry

2 cups heavy cream, whipped

1 1/2 pounds pound cake, sliced

Raspberry or strawberry preserves

Pour milk into top of a double boiler. In a mixing bowl, beat together sugar, cornstarch, and eggs until smooth. Add to milk and heat until mixture is thickened, stirring constantly. Set aside to cool. Add sherry to cooled custard. Whip cream and set aside.

Arrange cake slices in a 9x13x2-inch baking pan. Spread with preserves, then top with a layer of custard and a layer of whipped cream. Repeat until all the ingredients are used. Chill and serve. Serves 6–8.

Recipes from the Olde Pink House

Vanilla Sunshine Ice Cream

For old-fashioned fun, make homemade ice cream. This is our family's favorite—unbeatable!

When a recipe calls for raw eggs, it is an easy process to "home pasteurize" them by coddling them. Simply place the whole egg on a spoon and dip it into boiling water for 40 seconds, then immediately put it into cold water to stop the cooking process.

5 eggs
2 cups sugar
1½ pints light cream
1 (13-ounce) can
    evaporated milk
5 cups milk
3 tablespoons vanilla

Mix eggs and sugar thoroughly. Add cream and evaporated milk. Mix well. Add milk and vanilla and stir. Pour into freezer and churn (or plug in). Makes 1 gallon.

Variation: To make peach ice cream, add 2–3 cups peaches which have been put in blender for 45 seconds.

Sweet Surrender with
Advice à la Carte

Peach Buttermilk Ice Cream

1 tablespoon unflavored
    gelatin (1 envelope)
1¼ cups sugar, divided
2 cups buttermilk
1 egg, beaten
¼ teaspoon salt
4 cups whipping cream
1 tablespoon vanilla extract
2 cups fresh peaches,
    mashed

In saucepan, combine gelatin, one cup sugar, and buttermilk. Dissolve gelatin mixture over low heat, stirring occasionally. Gradually add hot mixture to egg, stirring constantly. Stir in salt, cream, and vanilla. Combine mashed peaches and ¼ cup sugar; add to mixture. Chill and churn-freeze. Yields approximately 3 quarts.

Note: If fresh peaches are not available, mashed, canned freestone peaches may be used, but do not add sugar to peaches. Regular milk may be substituted for buttermilk in the recipe.

Giant Houseparty Cookbook

Buttermilk Ice Cream

This delicious recipe was served by a now-closed Pensacola ice cream parlor.

1 quart buttermilk
1/2 pint heavy cream
1 (14-ounce) can
  condensed milk
1 (12-ounce) can
  evaporated milk
1 teaspoon vanilla
1/2 cup lemon juice
1/2 cup sugar

Combine buttermilk, cream, milks, vanilla, lemon juice, and sugar. Place in ice cream freezer can and freeze according to directions.

Variation: You can replace part or all the lemon juice with 1 cup crushed pineapple.

Gourmet Cooking II

Double Chocolate Peanut Butter Ice Cream

6 (1-ounce) squares
  semisweet chocolate
2 cups milk
1 cup sugar
1/2 cup smooth peanut
  butter
2 cups whipping cream
2 teaspoons vanilla extract
2/3 cup peanut butter cups,
  chopped

Combine chocolate, milk, and sugar in 2-quart heavy saucepan. Cook over medium heat, stirring frequently, until chocolate melts. Stir in peanut butter. Cool to lukewarm. Stir in whipping cream and vanilla. Chill one hour.

Churn-freeze. After freezing, transfer ice cream to a plastic freezer container. Stir in chopped peanut butter cups. Return to freezer at least 3 hours before serving. Yields 2 quarts.

For the Love of Kids

Deep Fried Ice Cream

1 pint vanilla ice cream
1 egg white, lightly beaten
1 cup chopped toasted
   almonds
3 cups oil

Using an ice cream scoop, shape 10 (1½-inch) balls, and freeze until firm. (A muffin tin works well for this.) Quickly roll balls in egg white, then almonds, egg white again, and almonds again. Replace in freezer until ready to deep fry. Heat at least 3 inches of oil to 375°. Lower 4 fritters only into the oil, and fry for 15 seconds. Drain quickly, and serve 2 in an individual dessert dish. Top with favorite sauce. Serves 5.

Let Them Eat Ice Cream

Editor's Extra: Any flavor ice cream is fun to try. And some chocolate or caramel drizzled over the top or decorated on the plate can only make it better!

List of Contributing Cookbooks

Listed are the cookbooks that have contributed recipes to *Beyond Grits and Gravy,* along with copyright, author, publisher, city and state. The information in parentheses indicates the BEST OF THE BEST cookbook in which the recipe originally appeared.

PHOTO BY GWEN McKEE

On a hot day in Virginia, I know nothing more comforting than a fine spiced pickle, brought up trout-like from the sparkling depths of the aromatic jar below the stairs of Aunt Sally's cellar.

—Thomas Jefferson

The Abbey Cookbook ©1982 The Harvard Common Press, Inc., Hans Bertram, Boston, MA (Georgia)

The Alabama Heritage Cookbook ©1984 Heritage Publications, First Presbyterian Church, Birmingham, AL (Alabama)

Almost Heaven ©1984 Junior League of Huntington, WV (West Virginia)

Ambrosia ©1997 Junior Auxiliary of Vicksburg, Inc., Vicksburg, MS (Mississippi)

Anniversary Collection of Delectable Dishes, The Woman's Club of Jackson, AL (Alabama)

Any Time's a Party, ©1981 Quail Ridge Press, Inc., Barbara Cook, Grace Toler, and Creath Fowler, Brandon, MS

The Apple Barn Cookbook ©1983 The Apple Barn and Cider Mill, Sevierville, TN (Tennessee)

Apron Strings ©1983 The Women's Committee of the Richmond Symphony, Richmond, VA (Virginia)

Arkansas Favorites Cookbook ©1991 J and J Collections, Hot Springs, AR (Arkansas)

Around the Bend, Around the Bend Arts and Crafts Association, Marshall, AR (Arkansas)

Atlanta Cooknotes ©1982 The Junior League of Atlanta, GA, Inc. (Georgia)

Atlanta Natives' Favorite Recipes ©1975 Ladair, Inc., Roswell, GA (Georgia)

Auburn Entertains ©1983, 1986 Auburn Entertains, Helen Baggett, Jeanne Blackwell, and Lucy Littleton, Rutledge Hill Press, Nashville, TN (Alabama)

Aunt Freddie's Pantry ©1984 by Freddie Bailey, Natchez, MS

Barbara's Been Cookin', Barbara Buckley, Edwards, MS (Mississippi)

Bay Leaves ©1975 The Junior Service League of Panama City, FL, Inc. (Florida)

The Belle Grove Plantation Cookbook ©1986 Belle Grove, Inc., Middletown, VA (Virginia)

Best of Bayou Cuisine ©1997 St. Stephen's Episcopal Church, Quail Ridge Press, Brandon, MS

The Best of South Louisiana Cooking ©1983 Bootsie John Landry, Lafayette, LA (Louisiana)

Betty is Still "Winking" at Cooking, Betty J. Winkler, Little Rock, AR (Arkansas)

Betty Talmadge's Lovejoy Plantation Cookbook ©1983 by Betty Talmadge, Peachtree Publishers, Atlanta, GA (Georgia)

Bill Neal's Southern Cooking: Revised and Enlarged Edition ©1989 by William Franklin Neal, Used by permission of the University of North Carolina Press, Chapel Hill, NC (North Carolina)

Bluegrass Winners ©1985 The Garden Club of Lexington, Lexington, KY (Kentucky)

Boarding House Reach ©1981 Dot Gibson Publications, Waycross, GA (Georgia)

The Bonneville House Presents ©1990 The Bonneville House Association, Fort Smith, AR (Arkansas)

Bouquet Garni ©1983 Pascagoula-Moss Point Mississippi Junior Auxiliary, Pascagoula, MS

Bravo ©1984 The Greensboro Symphony Guild, Greensboro, NC (North Carolina)

CDA Angelic Treats, Louisiana State Catholic Daughters, Franklin, LA (Louisiana II)

Cajun Cookin': Memories, Photos, History, Recipes, Franklin Golden Age Club, Franklin, LA (Louisiana II)

Cajun Cooking, Acadian House Publishing, Layfayette, LA (Louisiana II)

Cajun Cooking for Beginners ©1996 Acadian House Publishing, Layfayete, LA (Louisiana II)

Cajun Cuisine ©1985 Beau Bayou Publishing Co., Acadian House Publishing, Lafayette, LA (Louisiana II)

Callaway Family Favorites, Callaway Family, Cleveland, TN (Mississippi)

Cane River's Louisiana Living ©1994 The Service League of Natchitoches, LA, Inc. (Louisiana II)

Canopy Roads ©1979 Tallahassee Junior Woman's Club, Tallahassee, FL (Florida)

Capital Eating in Kentucky ©1987 American Cancer Society, Kentucky Division, Louisville, KY (Kentucky)

Celebration, A Taste of Arkansas ©1985 Sevier County Cookbook Committee, Lockesburg, AR (Arkansas)

Charleston Receipts Repeats ©1989 The Junior League of Charleston, SC, Inc. (South Carolina)

Chattanooga Cook Book ©1970 by Helen McDonald Exum, Lookout Mountain, TN (Tennessee)

Christmas Favorites, Mary Ann Crouch and Jan Stedman, Charlotte, NC (North Carolina)

The Colonel's Inn Caterers'—Tallahassee Historical Cookbook ©1984 Colonel's Inn Caterers, Delia Appleyard Mickler & Carolyde Phillips O'Bryan, Tallahassee, FL (Florida)

The Complete Venison Cookbook, ©1996 by Harold W. Webster, Jr., Quail Ridge Press, Inc., Brandon, MS (Mississippi)

Cook and Deal ©1982 by D. J. Cook, Vero Beach, FL (Florida)

A Cook's Tour of Shreveport, Junior League of Shreveport, LA (Louisiana)

The Cookie Connection ©1981 Lottye Gray Van Ness, Louisville, KY (Kentucky)

Cookin' Along the Cotton Belt, Stephens Chamber of Commerce, Stephens, AR (Arkansas)

Cookin' in the Spa, Hot Springs Junior Auxiliary, Hot Springs, AR (Arkansas)

Cooking on the Coast ©1994 by Rose Annette O'Keefe, Ocean Springs, MS (Mississippi)

Cooking on the Go ©1982 NTW Enterprises, Nancy Welch, Greer, SC (South Carolina)

Cooking Wild Game & Fish Southern Style ©2000 by Billy Joe Cross, Brandon, MS (Mississippi)

Cooking with Friends, Rena Lara Volunteers, Alligator, MS (Mississippi)

Cooking with Gilmore, Gilmore Foundation, Amory, MS (Mississippi)

Cooking with Heart in Hand ©1987 by Suzanne Winningham Worsham, Clifton, VA (Virginia)

Cooking with Tradition, Woodward Academy Parents Club, College Park, GA (Georgia)

CordonBluegrass ©1988 The Junior League of Louisville, KY, Inc. (Kentucky)

Could I Have Your Recipe? ©1981 by Janice Porter, Reston, VA (Virginia)

Country Cupboard Cookbook ©1985 Central High School Athletic Boosters Club, Thomasville, GA (Georgia)

The Country Mouse ©1983 Quail Ridge Press, Inc., Sally Walton and Faye Wilkinson, Brandon, MS

The Courier-Journal Kentucky Cookbook ©1985 The Courier-Journal and Louisville Times Co., Louisville, KY (Kentucky)

Crab Chatter ©1964 Lewis and Lewis, Mildred and Gennie Lewis, Brunswick, GA (Georgia)

The Crowning Recipes of Kentucky ©1986 Madonna Smith Echols, Marathon International Book Co., Madison, IN (Kentucky)

Culinary Classics ©1981 Young Matron's Circle for Tallulah Falls School, Roswell, GA (Georgia)

The Dapper Zapper ©1981 by Carol Jean Wheeler, Alpharetta, GA (Georgia)

DAR Recipe Book ©1984 Mississippi Society Daughters of the American Revolution, Brandon, MS

Deep South Staples ©2003 by Robert St. John, Different Drummer Press, Hattiesburg, MS

Delectable Dishes from Termite Hall ©1982 by Eugene Walter, The Willoughby Institute, Inc., Mobile, AL (Alabama)

Dining in Historic Kentucky ©1985 by Marty Godbey, McClanahan Publishing House, Kuttawa, KY (Kentucky)

Dinner on the Ground ©1990 Stoke Gabriel Enterprises, Alexandria, LA (Louisiana II)

Down Memory Lane, Straight Fork Extension Homemakers, Crawford, WV (West Virginia)

Dutch Pantry Cookin', Dutch Pantry, Williamstown, WV (West Virginia)

Dutch Pantry Cookin' II, Dutch Pantry, Williamstown, WV (West Virginia)

Dutch Pantry Simply Sweets, Dutch Pantry, Williamstown, WV (West Virginia)

Easy Livin' ©1979 Tunica Institute of Learning, Tunica, MS

Encore ©1981 Walker School Association, Dot Gibson Publications, Waycross, GA (Georgia)

Encore! Nashville ©1977 Nashville Seasons, Junior League of Nashville, TN (Tennessee)

The Encyclopedia of Cajun and Creole Cuisine ©1983 The Encyclopedia Cookbook of Cajun and Creole Cuisine, John D. Folse, Cuisine Promotions, Ltd., Baton Rouge, LA (Louisiana)

The Enlightened Gourmet ©1984 CGW Enterprises, Ann Cotton, Henrietta Gaillard, and Jo Anne Willis, R.D., Charleston, SC (South Carolina)

The Enlightened Titan ©1988 Trinity Patrons Association, Trinity Episcopal Chruch, Richmond, VA (Virginia)

Entertaining the Louisville Way, Volume II ©1983 The Queens Daughters Inc. of Louisville, KY (Kentucky)

Even More Special ©1986 The Junior League of Durham and Orange Counties, Inc., Durham, NC (North Carolina)

Evening Shade ©1991 Evening Shade School Foundation, Inc., Evening Shade, AR (Arkansas)

Everything but the Entrée ©1999 The Junior League of Parkersburg, WV (West Virginia)

Family Secrets: Famous Recipes from the Homeplace ©1985 The William Henry Thomas Family, Thomas Family Memorial Association, Cartersville, GA (Alabama)

Family Secrets...the Best of the Delta ©1990 Lee Academy, Clarksdale, MS (Mississippi)

Family Traditions, Esta White Freeland, Mer Rouge, LA (Louisiana II)

Famous Recipes from Mrs. Wilkes' Boarding House ©1976 by Mrs. L.H. Wilkes, Savannah, GA (Georgia)

Fannye Mae's Home Made Candy, Fannye Mae Gibbons, Jackson, MS (Mississippi)

The Farmer's Daughters ©1987 S-M-L, Inc., Flora Sisemore, Martha Merritt and Mary Mayfield, DeWitt, AR (Arkansas)

Favorite Recipes, Nelson County Extension Homemakers, Bardstown, KY (Kentucky)

Feasts of Eden, August House Publishers, Little Rock, AR (Arkansas)

Feeding the Flock–MOPs of Westminister, (Mothers of Preschoolers), Bluefield, WV (West Virginia)

Festival ©1983 Humphreys Academy Patrons, Belzoni, MS

Fiftieth Anniversary Cookbook, Northeast Louisiana Telephone Company, Inc., Collinston, LA (Louisiana II)

Fillies Flavours ©1984 The Fillies Inc., Louisville, KY (Kentucky)

Fine Dining Tennessee Style ©2000 by John M. Bailey, Quail Ridge Press, Inc., Brandon, MS

Flatlanders Cook Book, Helen Lanier Strickland, Lakeland, GA (Georgia)

Foods à la Louisiane ©1980 Louisiana Farm Bureau Women, Baton Rouge, LA (Louisiana)

For the Love of Kids, Marshall County Day Care, Moundsville, WV (West Virginia)

Frederica Fare ©1981 The Parents Association of Frederica Academy, St. Simons Island, GA (Georgia)

From a Louisiana Kitchen ©1983 by Holly Berkowitz Clegg, Baton Rouge, LA (Louisiana)

From the Firehouse to Your House, Don and Sue Griffith, Backdraft Smokers, Inc., Jackson, MS (Mississippi)

The Gasparilla Cookbook ©1961 The Junior League of Tampa, FL, Inc. (Florida)

Gatlinburg Recipe Collection, Nancy Blanch Cooper, Gatlinburg, TN (Tennessee)

Gazebo I Christmas Cookbook ©1984 by Rex Barrington, Auburn, AL (Alabama)

Georgia Entertains ©1983, 1988 by Margaret Wayt DeBolt, Rutledge Hill Press, Nashville, TN (Georgia)

Georgia on my Menu ©1988 League Publications/Junior League of Cobb-Marietta, Inc., Marietta, GA (Georgia)

Giant Houseparty Cookbook ©1981 Chamber of Commerce, Philadelphia, MS

Golden Moments ©1996 by Arlene Giesel Koehn, Golden Moments Publishing, West Point, MS (Mississippi)

Good Cookin' ©1982 Snell Publications, Virginia B. Snell, Metter, GA (Georgia)

Gottlieb's Bakery 100 Years of Recipes ©1983 Gottlieb's Bakery, Isser Gottlieb, Savannah, GA (Georgia)

Gourmet Cooking II ©1982 by Earl Peyroux, Pensacola, FL (Florida)

Gran's Gems, Jane Rayburn Hardin, Brandon, MS (Mississippi)

Grand Tour Collection ©1981 The Tennessee Chapter, American Society of Interior Designers, Germantown, TN (Tennessee)

Great Flavors of Mississippi ©1986 Southern Flavors, Inc., Pine Bluff, AR

Great Performances ©1990 The Symphony League of Tupelo, MS (Mississippi)

A Great Taste of Arkansas ©1986 Southern Flavors, Inc., Pine Bluff, AR (Arkansas)

Grits 'n Greens and Mississippi Things ©2002 Parlance Publishing, Joe Higginbotham, Columbus, MS (Mississippi)

The Gulf Gourmet ©1978 The Gulf Gourmet, Westminster Academy, Gulfport, MS

Gypsy, West Virginia 100th Anniversary Cookbook, Gypsy Community Group & Youth Fellowship, Gypsy, WV (West Virginia)

Hallmark's Collection of Home Tested Recipes, Freeda Rogers Hallmark, Tuscaloosa, AL (Alabama)

Head Table Cooks ©1982 American Camellia Society, Inc., Fort Valley, GA (Georgia)

Heart of the Mountains ©1987 Buncombe County Extension Homemakers, Asheville, NC (North Carolina)

Hearthside at Christmas, Patricia G. Edington, Tuscumbia, AL (Alabama)

Heavenly Hostess, St. John's Episcopal Church Women, Monroeville, AL (Alabama)

Historic Kentucky Recipes, Mercer County Humane Society, Harrodsburg, KY (Kentucky)

The Holiday Hostess, Valdosta Junior Service League, Valdosta, GA (Georgia)

Holiday Treats, Theone L. Neel, Bastian, VA (Virginia)

Home for the Holidays, The University of Arkansas Press, Fayetteville, AR (Arkansas)

Homemade with Love, Beverly Elementary, Montrose, WV (West Virginia)

The Hors D'Oeuvre Tray, Valdosta Junior Service League, Valdosta, GA (Georgia)

Hors D'Oeuvres Everybody Loves ©1983 Quail Ridge Press, Inc., Mary Leigh Furrh and Jo Barksdale, Brandon, MS

Hors D'Oeuvres Everybody Loves II ©1998 Quail Ridge Press, Inc., Mary Leigh Furrh and Jo Barksdale, Brandon, MS

In Good Taste ©1983 Department of Nutrition, School of Public Health of the University of North Carolina, Chapel Hill, NC (North Carolina)

Inverness Cook Book ©1963 All Saints Episcopal Guild, Inverness, MS

Island Events Cookbook ©1986 Island Events Cookbook, Edited by Jolie Donnell, Hilton Head Island, SC (South Carolina)

The Jackson Cookbook, Symphony League of Jackson, MS

The James K. Polk Cookbook ©1978 James K. Polk Memorial Auxiliary, Columbia, TN (Tennessee)

Jarrett House Potpourri, The Jarrett House, Dillsboro, NC (North Carolina)

The Junior Welfare League 50th Anniversary Cookbook, Mayfield-Graves County Junior Welfare League Annie Gardner Foundation, Mayfield, KY (Kentucky)

Just a Spoonful ©1985 by Phyllis Harper, Tupelo, MS

The Kentucky Derby Museum Cookbook ©1986 Kentucky Derby Museum Corp., Louisville, KY (Kentucky)

Kentucky Kitchens ©1985 Telephone Pioneers of America, Kentucky Chapter #32, Louisville, KY (Kentucky)

Kitchen Sampler ©1985 The Bessemer Junior Service League, Bessemer, AL (Alabama)

Knollwood's Cooking, Knollwood Baptist Church, Winston-Salem, NC (North Carolina)

Kum' Ona' Granny's Table, Senior Citizens Retirement Facility, Montgomery, AL (Alabama)

Lagniappe: Secrets We're Ready to Share II, Patsy Switzer, Lagniappe Restaurant, Ocean Springs, MS (Mississippi)

Larue County Kitchens, Hodgenville Woman's Club, Hodgenville, KY (Kentucky)

Lasting Impressions ©1988 Saint Joseph's Hospital of Atlanta Auxiliary, Atlanta, GA (Georgia)

Let Them Eat Ice Cream, Karen Rafuse and Margaret Minster, Amity Unlimited, Inc., Cincinnati, OH (Kentucky)

The Little Gumbo Book ©1986 Quail Ridge Press, Inc., Gwen McKee, Brandon, MS

The Little New Orleans Cookbook ©1991 Quail Ridge Press, Inc., Gwen McKee, Brandon, MS

Look Mom, I Can Cook ©1987 Dot Gibson Publications, Waycross, GA (Georgia)

Look Who Came to Dinner ©2000 The Junior Auxiliary of Amory, MS, Inc. (Mississippi)

Louisiana Entertains ©1978, 1983 Rapides Symphony Guild, Alexandria, LA (Louisiana)

Louisiana Keepsake ©1982 by Lillie Petite Gallagher, Petit Press, Baton Rouge, LA (Louisiana)

Macon Sets a Fine Table ©1986 Middle Georgia Historical Society, Inc., Macon, GA (Georgia)

Magic ©1982 The Junior League of Birmingham, AL (Alabama)

Mama's Recipes ©1976 by June Thompson Medlin, Lake Junaluska, NC (North Carolina)

A Man's Taste ©1980 The Junior League of Memphis, TN, Inc. (Tennessee)

Margaritaville Cookbook ©1984 The Environmental Studies Council, Inc., Jensen Beach, FL (Florida)

The Market Place ©1986 Augusta Junior Woman's Club, Augusta, GA (Georgia)

Marion Brown's Southern Cook Book ©1980 The University of North Carolina Press, Marion Brown, Chapel Hill, NC (North Carolina)

Maurice's Tropical Fruit Cook Book ©1979 by Maurice de Verteuil, Great Outdoors Publishing Company, St. Petersburg, FL (Florida)

Mennonite Country-Style Recipes ©1987 Herald Press, Scottdale, VA (Virginia)

The Microwave Touch ©1984 The Microwave Touch, Galen N. Hill, Greensboro, NC (North Carolina)

Mississippi Stars Cookbook, South Pontotoc Attendance Center, Pontotoc, MS (Mississippi)

More than Moonshine: Appalachian Recipes and Recollections ©1983 University of Pittsburgh Press, Pittsburgh, PA (Kentucky)

More Fiddling with Food, First Baptist Church of Mobile, AL (Alabama)

More...Home Town Recipes, South Fork Volunteer Fire Dept., Brandywine, WV (West Virginia)

More Richmond Receipts ©1990 by Jan Carlton, J & B Editions, Norfolk, VA (Virginia)

Mountain Laurel Encore ©1984 Bell County Extension Homemakers, Pineville, KY (Kentucky)

Mountain Recipe Collection ©1981 Ison Collectibles, Inc., Valeria S. Ison, Hazard, KY (Kentucky)

Munchin' with the Methodists ©2001 Carolina United Methodist Women, Booneville, MS (Mississippi)

My Old Kentucky Homes Cookbook, A Taste of Kentucky, Louisville, KY (Kentucky)

Nell Graydon's Cook Book ©1969 by Nell S. Graydon, Sandlapper Publishing Co., Inc., Orangeburg, SC (South Carolina)

North Carolina's Historic Restaurants ©1990 by Dawn O'Brien, Winston-Salem, NC (North Carolina)

Nun Better ©1996 St. Cecilia School, Broussard, LA (Louisiana)

Of Pots and Pipkins ©1971 The Junior League of Roanoke Valley, Inc., Roanoke, VA (Virginia)

Offerings for Your Plate, First Baptist Church, Fulmont, MS (Mississippi)

Old Mobile Recipes–Tried and Proven ©1956 St. Paul's Episcopal Church, Mobile, AL (Alabama)

Olivia's Favorite Menus and Recipes ©1984 by Olivia H. Adams, Greenville, SC (South Carolina)

Once Upon a Stove ©1986 Birmingham Children's Theatre, Birmingham, AL (Alabama)

The Original Vidalia Onion Cookbook ©1981 Vidalia Chamber of Commerce, Vidalia, GA (Georgia)

Our Best Home Cooking, Vienna Baptist Church, Vienna, WV (West Virginia)

Out of This World ©1983 The Oak Hill School Parents' Assn., Nashville, TN (Tennessee)

Palate Pleasers, Forest Hills United Methodist Church, Brentwood, TN (Tennessee)

Palm Beach Entertains ©1976 The Junior League of the Palm Beaches, Inc., West Palm Beach, FL (Florida)

Palmetto Evenings, American Cancer Society/South Carolina Division, Columbia, SC (South Carolina)

Pass the Plate ©1984 Pass the Plate, Inc., Alice G. Underhill and Barbara S. Stewart, New Bern, NC (North Carolina)

Paul Naquin's French Collection II ©1980 by Paul Naquin, Baton Rouge, LA (Lousiana)

Perennials ©1984 The Junior Service League of Gainesville, GA, Inc. (Georgia)

Perfectly Delicious ©1990 by Cornelia Pryor Lindsey and Elinor Pryor, Little Rock, AR (Arkansas)

The Pick of the Crop ©1978 North Sunflower P.T.A, Drew, MS

Pigging Out with the Cotton Patch Cooks, Audrey Lee McCollum, Mer Rouge, LA (Louisiana II)

The Pilgrimage Garden Club Antiques Forum Cookbook ©1986 Pilgrimage Garden Club, Natchez, MS

A Pinch of Rose & A Cup of Charm ©1998 by Rose Dorchuck, Kosciusko, MS (Mississippi)

The Pink Lady...in the Kitchen, Medical Center of South Arkansas Auxiliary, El Dorado, AR (Arkansas)

Pirate's Pantry ©1976 Junior League of Lake Charles, Pelican Publishing, Lake Charles, LA (Louisiana)

Plantation Celebrations ©1994 Chef John Folse & Company, Gonzales, LA (Louisiana II)

The Plantation Cookbook ©1972 The Junior League of New Orleans, LA (Louisiana II)

Pool Bar Jim's ©1979 by James D. Lisenby, Hilton Head Island, SC (South Carolina)

Prairie Harvest ©1981 St. Peter's Episcopal Churchwomen, Hazen, AR (Arkansas)

Prescriptions for Good Eating ©1984 Greenville County Medical Society Auxiliary, Greenville, SC (South Carolina)

Prime Meridian ©2001 Lamar Foundation, Kim Waters, Meridian, MS (Mississippi)

Pulaski Heights Baptist Church Cookbook, Members and Friends of the Congregation, Little Rock, AR (Arkansas)

Puttin' on the Peachtree ©1979 The Junior League of DeKalb County, Georgia, Inc., Decatur, GA (Georgia)

Recipe Jubilee! ©1964 The Junior League of Mobile, AL, Inc. (Alabama)

Recipes and Reminiscences of New Orleans I ©1971 Parents Club of Ursuline Academy Inc., Ursuline Convent Cookbook, Metairie, LA (Louisiana)

Recipes from Jeffersonville Woman's Club, Jeffersonville Woman's Club, Tazewell, VA (Virginia)

Recipes from Miss Daisy's ©1978 Miss Daisy's Tea Room, Daisy King and Marilyn Lehew, Rutledge Hill Press, Nashville, TN (Tennessee)

Recipes from the Olde Pink House ©1981 by Herschel S. McCallar, Jr. and D. Jeffery Keith, The Olde Pink House, Savannah, GA (Georgia)

Recipes Remembered, Alzheimer's Association, Mid-Mississippi Chapter, Jackson, MS (Mississippi)

Restoration Recipes, Chapel of the Cross, Flora, MS

Revel ©1980 Junior League of Shreveport, LA, Inc. (Louisiana)

Sample West Kentucky ©1985 by Paula Cunningham, McClanahan Publishing House, Kuttawa, KY (Kentucky)

The Sandlapper Cookbook ©1974 Sandlapper Publishing Co., Inc., Orangeburg, SC (South Carolina)

Seasoned with Light, First Baptist Church - Baptist Women, Hartsville, SC (South Carolina)

Seasons of Thyme ©1979 Charity League of Paducah, KY, Inc. (Kentucky)

Second Round, Tea Time at the Masters©, Junior League of Augusta, GA, Inc. (Georgia)

Seminole Savorings ©1982 Seminole Productions, Inc., Tallahassee, FL (Florida)

Serving Our Best, Elkins Regional Convalescent Center Auxiliary, Elkins, WV (West Virginia)

Shared Treasures, First Baptist Church, Monroe, LA (Louisiana II)

A Shower of Roses ©1996 St. Therese Catholic Church, Abbeville, LA (Louisiana)

Simply Southern, Linda and Bob Brown, Picayune, MS (Mississippi)

Some Like it South! ©1984 The Junior League of Pensacola, FL, Inc. (Florida)

Somebody's Cookbook, Woods Pharmacy, Oak Hill, WV (West Virginia)

Somethin's Cookin' at LG&E ©1986 LG&E Employees Association, L G & E, Louisville, KY (Kentucky)

The South Carolina Cook Book ©1954 University of South Carolina Press, SC Extension Homemakers Council and the Clemson Extension Home Economics Staff, Columbia, SC (South Carolina)

Southern BUT Lite ©1994 Cookbook Resources, Jen Bays Avis and Kathy F. Ward, West Monroe, LA (Louisiana II)

The Southern Cook's Handbook © 2001 Quail Ridge Press, Inc., Courtney Taylor and Bonnie Carter Travis, Brandon, MS

Southern Generations ©2002 Junior Auxiliary of Starkville, MS, Inc. (Mississippi)

Southern Seafood Classics ©1988 The Southeastern Fisheries Association, Atlanta, GA (Georgia)

Southern Secrets ©1979 Episcopal Day School Mother's Club, University School of Jackson Mother's Club, Jackson, TN (Tennessee)

Southern Spice à la Microwave ©1980 by Margie Brignac, Pelican Publishing Company, Gretna, LA (Louisiana)

Southern Wildfowl and Wild Game Cookbook ©1976 Sandlapper Publishing Co., Inc., Jon Wongrey, Orangeburg, SC (South Carolina)

Standing Room Only ©1983 New Stage Theatre, Jackson, MS

Stirrin' the Pots on Daufuskie ©1985 by Billie Burn, Daufuskie Island, SC (South Carolina)

Straight from the Galley Past & Present, Ladies Auxiliary Bay Waveland Yacht Club, Waveland, MS (Mississippi)

The Stuffed Griffin ©1976 The Utility Club, Griffin, GA (Georgia)

Sugar Beach ©1984 The Junior Service League of Fort Walton Beach, FL (Florida)

Suncoast Seasons ©1984 Dunedin Youth Guild, Inc., Dunedin, FL (Florida)

Sunday Go to Eatin' Cook Book ©1988 Rock Valley Enterprises, Nita Sappington, Decatur, AL (Arkansas)

Sunny Side Up ©1980 The Junior League of Fort Lauderdale, FL, Inc. (Florida)

Sweet Surrender with Advice à la Carte ©1985 McElyea Publications, Jane Warnock McElyea and Pam McElyea Barnard, Winter Park, FL (Florida)

Take Two & Butter 'Em While They're Hot! ©1998 Native Ground Music, Inc., Barbara Swell, Asheville, NC (West Virginia)

Taste Buds ©1985 Winslow, Wolverton, Komegay, Tyner, NC (North Carolina)

A Taste from Back Home ©1983 by Barbara Wortham, Marathon International Book Company, Madison, IN (Kentucky)

A Taste of Fayette County, New River Convention & Visitors Bureau, Oak Hill, WV (West Virginia)

A Taste of South Carolina ©1983 The Palmetto Cabinet of South Carolina, Sandlapper Publishing Co., Inc., Orangeburg, SC (South Carolina)

A Taste of the Holidays, Dot Gibson Publications, Waycross, GA (Georgia)

Taste of the South ©1984 The Symphony League of Jackson, MS

Tasteful Treasures, First Baptist Church, Ridgeland, MS (Mississippi)

Tea-Time at the Masters ©1988 Junior League of Augusta, GA, Inc. (Georgia)

Tell Me More ©1993 The Junior League of Lafayette, LA (Louisiana II)

Temptations ©1986 Presbyterian Day School, Cleveland, MS

Tennessee Treasure, Pearlie B. Scott, MC Art Co., Nashville, TN (Tennessee)

Third Wednesday Homemakers Volume II, Fraziers Bottom Pliny Homemakers, Fraziers Bottom, WV (West Virginia)

'Tiger Bait' Recipes ©1976 LSU Alumni Federation, Baton Rouge, LA (Louisiana)

To Market, To Market ©1984 The Junior League of Owensboro, KY, Inc. (Kentucky)

Tony Chachere's Cajun Country Cookbook, Tony Chachere, Creole Foods of Opelousas, LA, Inc. (Louisiana)

Tout de Suite à la Microwave II ©1977 by Jean K. Durkee, Tout de Suite à la Microwave, Inc., Lafayette, LA (Louisiana)

Treasured Family Favorites, Alisa L. Pate, Cleveland, MS (Mississippi)

Treasured Tastes ©1986 Mobile College, Mobile College Auxiliary, Daphne, AL (Alabama)

The Twelve Days of Christmas Cookbook ©1978 Quail Ridge Press, Inc., Ruth Moorman and Lalla Williams, Brandon, MS

Twickenham Tables, The Twickenham Historic Preservation District Association, Inc., Weeden House Museum, Huntsville, AL (Alabama)

Upper Crust: A Slice of the South, Junior League of Johnson City, TN (Tennessee)

Uptown Down South ©1986 Greenville Junior League Publications, Greenville, SC (South Carolina)

Victorian Sampler ©1986 by Jim and Ruth Spears, Eureka Springs, AR (Arkansas)

Vintage Vicksburg ©1985 Vicksburg Junior Auxiliary, Inc., Vicksburg, MS

Viola! Lafayette Centennial Cookbook 1884-1984 ©1983 by Jean Kellner Durkee, Lafayette, LA (Louisiana)

Virginia's Historic Restaurants and Their Recipes ©1984 by Dawn O'Brien, John F. Blair, Publisher, Winston-Salem, NC (Virginia)

The Way Pocahontas County Cooks ©1996 Pocahontas Communications Cooperative Corporation, Allegheny Mountain Radio, Dunmore, WV (West Virginia)

Well Seasoned ©1982 Les Passees, Inc., Les Passees Publications, Memphis, TN (Tennessee)

What's Cooking for the Holidays ©1984 by Irene Hayes, T. I. Hayes Publishing Co., Inc., Ft. Mitchell, KY (Kentucky)

When Dinnerbells Ring ©1978 Talladega Junior Welfare League, Talladega, AL (Alabama)

Who's Your Mama, Are You Catholic, and Can You Make a Roux? ©1991 by Marcelle Bienvenu, The Times of Acadiana, Lafayette, LA (Louisiana II)

With Special Distinction ©1993 Mississippi College Cookbook, Clinton, MS (Mississippi)

The Wonderful World of Honey ©1977 by Joe M. Parkhill, Berryville, AR (Arkansas)

The Wyman Sisters Cookbook, Laura F. Tesseneer, Crescent Springs, KY (Kentucky)

Extra Help

No one who cooks, cooks alone. Even at her most solitary,
a cook in the kitchen is surrounded by generations of cooks past,
the advice of cooks present, the wisdom of cookbook writers.

—Laurie Colwin

Equivalents:

Apple: 1 medium = 1 cup chopped

Banana, mashed: 1 medium = $1/3$ cup

Berries: 1 pint = $1^3/4$ cup

Bread: 1 slice = $1/2$ cup soft crumbs = $1/4$ cup fine, dry crumbs

Broth, beef or chicken: 1 cup = 1 bouillon cube dissolved in 1 cup boiling water

Butter: 1 stick = $1/4$ pound = $1/2$ cup

Cabbage: 2 pounds = 9 cups shredded or 5 cups cooked

Cheese, grated: 1 pound = 4 cups; 8 ounces = 2 cups

Chicken: 1 large boned breast = 2 cups cooked meat

Crabmeat, fresh: 1 pound = 3 cups

Chocolate, bitter: 1 square or 1 ounce = 2 tablespoons grated

Coconut: $3^1/2$-ounce can = $1^1/3$ cups

Cool Whip: 8 ounces = 3 cups

Cornmeal: 1 pound = 3 cups

Crackers, saltine: 23 = 1 cup crushed

Crackers, graham: 15 = 1 cup crushed

Cream, heavy: 1 cup = 2–$2^1/2$ cups whipped

Cream cheese: 3 ounces = $6^2/3$ tablespoons

Eggs: 4–5 = 1 cup

Egg whites: 8–10 = 1 cup

Evaporated milk: $5^1/3$-ounce can = $2/3$ cup; 13-ounce can = $1^1/4$ cups

Flour: 1 pound = $4^1/2$ cups

Flour, self-rising: 1 cup = 1 cup all-purpose + $1^1/2$ teaspoons baking powder + $1/2$ teaspoon salt

Garlic powder: $1/8$ teaspoon = 1 average clove

Ginger root: 1 teaspoon = $3/4$ teaspoon ground

Grits: 1 cup = 4 cups cooked

Herbs, fresh: 1 tablespoon = 1 teaspoon dried

Lemon: 1 medium = 3 tablespoons juice

Marshmallows: $1/4$ pound = 16 large; 10 mini = 1 large

Mushrooms: $1/4$ pound fresh = 1 cup sliced

Mustard, dry: 1 teaspoon = 1 tablespoon prepared

Noodles: 1 pound = 7 cups cooked

Nuts, chopped: $1/4$ pound = 1 cup

Onion: 1 medium = $3/4$–1 cup chopped = 2 tablespoons dried chopped (flakes)

Orange: 3–4 medium = 1 cup juice

Pecans: 1 pound shelled = 4 cups

Potatoes: 1 pound = 3 medium

Rice: 1 cup = 3 cups cooked

Spaghetti: 1 pound uncooked = 5 cups cooked

Spinach, fresh: 2 cups chopped = 1 (10-ounce) package frozen chopped

Sugar, brown: 1 pound = $2^1/2$ cups

Sugar, powdered: 1 pound = $3^1/2$ cups

Sugar, white: 1 pound = $2^1/4$ cups

Vanilla wafers: 22 = 1 cup fine crumbs

Whole milk: 1 cup = $1/2$ cup evaporated + $1/2$ cup water

Substitutions:

1 slice cooked **bacon** = 1 tablespoon bacon bits

1 cup **buttermilk** = 1 cup plain yogurt; or 1 tablespoon lemon juice or vinegar + plain milk to make 1 cup

1 cup sifted **cake flour** = $^7/_8$ cup sifted all-purpose flour

1 ounce **unsweetened chocolate** = 3 tablespoons cocoa + 1 tablespoon butter or margarine

1 ounce **semisweet chocolate** = 3 tablespoons cocoa + 1 tablespoon butter or margarine + 3 tablespoons sugar

1 tablespoon **cornstarch** = 2 tablespoons flour (for thickening)

1 cup **heavy cream** (for cooking, not whipping) = $^1/_3$ cup butter + $^3/_4$ cup milk

1 cup **sour cream** = $^1/_3$ cup milk + $^1/_3$ cup butter; or 1 cup plain yogurt

1 cup **tartar sauce** = 6 tablespoons mayonnaise or salad dressing + 2 tablespoons pickle relish

1 cup **tomato juice** = $^1/_2$ cup tomato sauce + $^1/_2$ cup water

1 cup **vegetable oil** = $^1/_2$ pound (2 sticks) butter

1 cup **whipping cream**, whipped = 6–8 ounces Cool Whip

1 cup **whole milk** = $^1/_2$ cup evaporated milk + $^1/_2$ cup wate

Measurements:

3 teaspoons = 1 tablespoon

1 tablespoon = $^1/_2$ fluid ounce

2 tablespoons = $^1/_8$ cup

3 tablespoons = 1 jigger

4 tablespoons = $^1/_4$ cup

8 tablespoons = $^1/_2$ cup or 4 ounces

12 tablespoons = $^3/_4$ cup

16 tablespoons = 1 cup or 8 ounces

3/8 cup = $^1/_4$ cup + 2 tablespoons

5/8 cup = $^1/_2$ cup + 2 tablespoons

7/8 cup = $^3/_4$ cup + 2 tablespoons

1/2 cup = 4 fluid ounces

1 cup = $^1/_2$ pint or 8 fluid ounces

2 cups = 1 pint or 16 fluid ounces

1 pint, liquid = 2 cups or 16 fluid ounces

1 quart, liquid = 2 pints or 4 cups

1 gallon, liquid = 4 quarts or 8 pints or 16 cups

Oven-to-Crockpot Cooking Time Conversions:

15–30 minutes in the oven = $1^1/_2$–$2^1/_2$ hours on HIGH or 4–6 hours on LOW

35–45 minutes in the oven equals 2–3 hours on HIGH or 6–8 hours on LOW

50 minutes–3 hours in the oven equals 4–5 hours on HIGH or 8–18 hours on LOW

Lighten Up!

- Use low-fat and nonfat dairy products.
- Use egg whites or egg substitute rather than whole eggs.
- Use 99% fat-free cream soups.
- Use sodium-reduced canned products.
- Use nonstick cooking spray rather than fatty oils and shortenings.
- Omit or use less salt.
- Reduce sugar or use Splenda instead.
- Consider oven frying with nonstick cooking spray or butter spray rather than frying in oil.
- Use lean cuts of meat; cut away all fat; skin chicken.
- Substitute bacon bits or turkey bacon for real bacon.
- Use brown or wild rice instead of white.
- Use whole wheat bread instead of white.
- Serve smaller portions.

Pan Sizes for Baking:

4 cups will fit into
8-inch round cake pan
9-inch round pie pan
9-inch pie pan
$4 \times 8 \times 2^{3}/_{4}$ loaf pan (small)

5 cups will fit into
$7 \times 11 \times 1^{3}/_{4}$-inch pan
10-inch pie pan

6 cups will fit into
$8 \times 8 \times 2$-inch square pan
$10 \times 10 \times 2$-inch casserole
$5 \times 9 \times 3^{1}/_{4}$-inch loaf pan (large)

8 cups will fit into
$9 \times 9 \times 2^{1}/_{4}$-inch casserole
$7^{1}/_{2} \times 11^{3}/_{4} \times 2$-inch pan

12 cups will fit into
$8^{1}/_{2} \times 13^{1}/_{2} \times 2^{1}/_{2}$-inch glass dish
$9 \times 13 \times 2$-inch pan

Index

So I'll take my time; And life won't pass me by;
Cause it's right there to find; On the dirt road.

from "The Dirt Road" by Sawyer Brown

A

Almond Cheesecake 204
Almond Crab Supreme 137
Ambrosia Crunch 220
Anycolor Punch 11
Appetizers: (*see* Hors D'Oeuvres, Dips)
Apples:
  Apple Cobbler 242
  Apple Pancakes with Cinnamon Cream Syrup 51
  Apple Squares 215
  Apple-Filled Oven French Toast 52
  Crisp Crust Apple Pie 234
  Fried Apple Pies 235
  Pan-Fried June Apples 116
  Pork Chops with Apples, Onions, and Raisins 158
  Quick and Easy Apple Dumplings 244
  Tennessee Ernie Ford's Fresh Apple Nut Cake 197
Apricots, Mrs. Guerry's Baked 108
Asheville Salad 80
Atlanta Baked Ham 160
Augusta's Best Strawberry Bread 48
Aunt Lula's Mud Hen Cookies 213
Authentic Southern Soft Teacakes 207
Avery Island Trout 125
Avocado Shrimp Salad 81
Award-Winning Seafood Gumbo 64

B

Bacon Roll-Ups 29
Bacon Spoon Bread 46
Baked Chicken Breasts 170
Baked Quail with Dressing 180
Baked Shrimp, New Orleans Style 132
Baked Tomatoes Rockefeller 94
Baked Vidalias au Gratin 109
Bananas:
  Banana Bread 48
  Banana Pudding with Meringue 248
  Bananas Nourries 252
  French Banana Èclair 254
  Peachy Keen Banana Smoothie 14
Barbecue:
  Barbecue Ribs 156
  Barbecued Brisket 142
  Barbequed Country Style Pork Ribs 156
  North Carolina Barbecue Sauce 155
  Slow Cooker Barbecued Pot Roast 142
  24-Hour Crockpot Barbecue 141
Bass, Billy's Baked 123
Beans:
  Beans Anchored in Bacon 96
  Boiled Butter Beans/Lima Beans 98
  Country Baked Beans 99
  Green Beans and Stewed Potatoes 96
  Hoppin' John 97
  Red Beans and Rice 160
  Ro-Tel French-Style Green Beans 97
  Sausage, Red Beans and Rice Casserole 161
Beautiful Raspberry Peach Melba Pie 241

Beef:
  Barbecue Ribs 156
  Barbecued Brisket 142
  Beef Stuffed Peppers 150
  Beef Tips Over Rice 153
  Blue Ribbon Chili 146
  Chicken Fried Steak and Cream Gravy 140
  Delicious Beef Roast 141
  Deviled Swiss Steak 140
  Eggplant Parmigiana Barbara 151
  Grillades and Garlic Cheese Grits 163
  Hamburger Potato Bake 149
  Hot Beef Dip 23
  Juicy Hamburgers 149
  Lucy's Spaghetti Meat Sauce 145
  Magic Beef Stew 68
  Meat Balls and Spaghetti 144
  Pizza Pop Up 148
  Railroad Special 143
  Sausage, Red Beans and Rice Casserole 161
  Slow Cooker Barbecued Pot Roast 142
  Sticky Bones 154
  Stuffed Green Peppers 150
  Sunday Supper Snack 165
  Sweet and Sour Meatballs 31
  24-Hour Crockpot Barbecue 141
  World's Last Meatloaf 152
Beignets 49
Bell-Ringer Molasses Cookies 211
Belle Grove Inn Fried Chicken 167
Benne Cookies 209
Best Hot Cakes I Ever Ate 52
Beverages:
  Anycolor Punch 11
  Bloody Mary 15
  Bourbon Punch 12
  Café au Lait 17
  Christmas Eggnog 15
  Coffee Liqueur 16
  Coffee Punch 16
  Hilton Head Freeze 14
  Joy's Bay Pointe Margaritas 12
  Kentucky Mint Julep 13
  Mimosas 13
  Peachy Keen Banana Smoothie 14
  Southern Champagne Punch 11
  Summer Mint Tea 10
  Summertime Citrus Tea 10
Billy's Baked Bass 123
Biscuits:
  Buttermilk Biscuits 36
  Country Fried Ham Biscuits 38
  Derby Breakfast Yeast Biscuits 37
  Mayonnaise Biscuits 38
  Sweet Potato Biscuits 37
Bisque, Corn and Crab 63
Black-Eyed Peas:
  Black-Eyed Susan Salad 74
  Hoppin' John 97
Black-Eyed Susan Salad 74

Blackberries:
  Slice of the South Salad 82
  Super Blackberry Cobbler 242
Blender Mayonnaise 84
Bloody Mary 15
BLT Bites 29
Blue Ribbon Chili 146
Blueberry Glaze 230
Blueberry Pie, Light and Easy 236
Boiled Butter Beans/Lima Beans 98
Boiled Crabs in a Chest 137
Boiled Peanuts 33
Bonbons, Lemon 212
Bourbon Punch 12
Bread and Butter Pickles 86
Bread Pudding, Creole 246
Bread Pudding, Toasted Almond 247
Breads: (*see also* Biscuits, Muffins)
  Augusta's Best Strawberry Bread 48
  Bacon Spoon Bread 46
  Banana Bread 48
  Beignets 49
  Christmas Morning Rolls 50
  Corn Fritters 45
  Granny's Best Dinner Rolls 42
  In-A-Hurry Rolls 43
  Light Corn Bread 47
  Mamean's Buttermilk Corn Bread 47
  Mississippi Hush Puppies 44
  Monkey Bread 41
  Short'nin Bread 44
  Skillet Popover 49
  Southern Popovers 41
  Southern Spoon Bread 46
  Squash Puppies 45
  Tangy Butter Fingers 43
Broccoli:
  Broccoli and Tomato Casserole 95
  Broccoli Dip 23
  Broccoli Rice Quiche 119
Broiled Tomatoes 95
Brownies and Bar Cookies:
  Apple Squares 215
  Aunt Lula's Mud Hen Cookies 213
  Butter Crème Brownies 216
  Caramel Brickle Bars 214
  Chocolate Chip Pizza 214
  Cream Cheese Fudge Brownies 217
  Lemon Sour Cookies 212
  Praline Brownies 217
  Sinful German Chocolate Squares 215
Buckle, Peach 245
Butter Beans, Boiled 98
Butter Cookies 208
Butter Crème Brownies 216
Buttermilk Biscuits 36
Buttermilk Ice Cream 259

Cabbage:
  Hot and Spicy Cabbage 111
  Hot Slaw 77
Café au Lait 17
Cakes: (*see also* Cheesecakes, Pound Cakes)
  Carrot Gold Cake 194
  Elvis Presley Cake 189
  Exquisite Coconut Cake 193
  French Chocolate Cake 192
  Fresh Peach Cake 200
  Hilbert's Turtle Cake 187
  Hummingbird Cake 191
  Jam Cake 195
  Lemon Cake 198
  Lemon Ice Box Cake 199
  Mardi Gras King Cake 184
  Mississippi Mud 186
  Pecan Pie Cake 187
  Pineapple Upside Down Cake 200
  Praline Cake 190
  Red Velvet Cake 188
  Rotten Cake 190
  Strawberry Cream Cake 198
  Strawberry Shortcake 185
  Sunshine Island 196
  Tennessee Ernie Ford's Fresh Apple Nut Cake 197
Candies:
  Ambrosia Crunch 220
  Chocolate-Filled Snowballs 218
  Cornflake Treats 219
  Crazy Cocoa Krisps 220
  Creamy Pralines 223
  Gold Brick Fudge 222
  Hurricane Fudge 222
  Kentucky Bourbon Balls 223
  Old Fashioned Butter Crunch 221
  Old-Fashioned Divinity 224
  Peanut Brittle 221
  Peanut Butter Sticks 218
  Pecan Kisses 224
  Sweet Nothings 219
  Twisted Kisses 219
Caramel Brickle Bars 214
Caramel Icing 195
Carolina Quail 180
Carolyn's Pan-Fried Catfish 122
Carrots:
  Carrot Gold Cake 194
  Carrot Raisin Salad 76
  Marinated Carrots 76
Catahoula Courtbouillon 60
Catfish:
  Carolyn's Pan-Fried Catfish 122
  Delta Baked Catfish 123
  Mississippi Catfish Fillets 122
Charcoal Grilled Chicken 171
Charlotte Russe 251
Cheeky's Chess Pie 229

Cheese Grits 129
Cheese Straws 26
Cheesecakes:
  Almond Cheesecake 204
  Cheesecake 203
  Chocolate Turtle Cheesecake Pie 241
  Praline Cheesecake 202
Cherries Jubilee 252
Cherry Salad Supreme 82
Chicken Fried Steak and Cream Gravy 140
Chicken:
  Baked Chicken Breasts 170
  Belle Grove Inn Fried Chicken 167
  Charcoal Grilled Chicken 171
  Chicken and Dumplings 173
  Chicken à la King 174
  Chicken Key West 169
  Chicken Pie 172
  Chicken Puffs 172
  Chicken Salad in Raspberry Ring 72
  Chicken Salad with Grapes and Almonds 73
  Chicken-Spaghetti Casserole 176
  Chicken Stew Cabanocey 176
  Elegant Chicken 170
  Fried Chicken 166
  Ham and Chicken Casserole 165
  Hot Chicken Salad 73
  Italian Chicken Delight 174
  Lemon Chicken for the Grill 171
  Louisiana Chicken Sauce Piquant 175
  Mississippi State Chicken-on-a-Stick 168
  Parmesan Chicken 169
  Sesame Chicken Nuggets 32
  Shrimp-Chicken Jambalaya 128
  Sour Cream Chicken Breasts 175
  Southern Pecan Chicken 168
  Sunday School Chicken 177
  Tasty Chicken Wings 31
Chili with Dumplings, Chunky Venison 147
Chili, Blue Ribbon 146
Chocolate:
  Ambrosia Crunch 220
  Butter Crème Brownies 216
  Chocolate Chip Pecan Pie 227
  Chocolate Chip Pizza 214
  Chocolate Leaves 238
  Chocolate Mousse Pie 238
  Chocolate Turtle Cheesecake Pie 241
  Chocolate-Dipped Strawberries 253
  Chocolate-Filled Snowballs 218
  Coffee Toffee Pie 239
  Cream Puffs or Èclairs 255
  Crème de Menthe Pie 240
  Double Chocolate Peanut Butter Ice Cream 259
  French Chocolate Cake 192
  Gold Brick Fudge 222
  Great Grandmother's Chocolate Mousse 249
  Hilbert's Turtle Cake 187
  Hurricane Fudge 222
  Louisiana Swamp 256

Mansion Almond Chocolate Mousse 249
Milk Chocolate Crème Brûlée 251
Mississippi Mud 186
Mud Pie 229
My Mother's Chocolate Pie 228
Old Fashioned Butter Crunch 221
Sinful German Chocolate Squares 215
Sweet Nothings 219
Toffee Ice Cream Pie 240
Twisted Kisses 219
Weidman's Bourbon Pie 230
Chowder, Corn and Ham 62
Chowder, Golden Glow Corn 62
Christmas Eggnog 15
Christmas Morning Rolls 50
Chunky Venison Chili with Dumplings 147
Cinnamon Cream Syrup 51
Cobblers:
  Apple Cobbler 242
  Peach Cobbler 243
  Super Blackberry Cobbler 242
Coca-Cola Cranberry Salad, Congealed 83
Coconut:
  Coconut Cream Pie 237
  Exquisite Coconut Cake 193
  No Crust Coconut Pie 237
  Rotten Cake 190
Coffee Cake, Sausage 53
Coffee Toffee Pie 239
Coffees:
  Café au Lait 17
  Coffee Liqueur 16
  Coffee Punch 16
Condiments: (see also Sauces)
  Blender Mayonnaise 84
  Poppy Seed Dressing 84
Congealed Coca-Cola Cranberry Salad 83
Cookies: (see also Brownies and Bar Cookies)
  Authentic Southern Soft Teacakes 207
  Bell-Ringer Molasses Cookies 211
  Benne Cookies 209
  Butter Cookies 208
  Dishpan Cookies 211
  Fruit Cake Cookies 213
  Lemon Bonbons 212
  Mother's Old-Fashioned Sugar Cookies 210
  Oatmeal Cookies 209
  Pecan Crispies 206
  Praline Cookies 207
  Sand Tarts 206
Corn:
  Black-Eyed Susan Salad 74
  Corn and Crab Bisque 63
  Corn and Crabmeat Soup 61
  Corn and Ham Chowder 62
  Corn Fritters 45
  Corn Quiche 120
  Fried Corn 110
  Golden Glow Corn Chowder 62
  Scalloped Okra and Corn 105

Summer Corn Salad 74
White Corn Casserole 110
Zucchini-Corn Casserole 103
Cornflake Treats 219
Courtbouillon, Catahoula 60
Cottage Cheese Salad 80
Cottage-Fried Potatoes 114
Country Baked Beans 99
Country Fried Ham Biscuits with Red-Eye Gravy 38
Country Ham Slices 161
Crabs:
Almond Crab Supreme 137
Boiled Crabs in a Chest 137
Corn and Crab Bisque 63
Corn and Crabmeat Soup 61
Crab Cakes à la Mobile Bay 136
Crabmeat Canapés 18
Hot Crab Dip 19
Marvelous Seafood Mornay 20
Savannah Crab Stew 66
Cranberry Salad, Congealed Coca-Cola 83
Crawfish:
Creole Crawfish Casserole 135
Creamy Crawfish Fettuccini 135
Mini Bite-Size Crawfish Pies 18
Crazy Cocoa Krisps 220
Cream Cheese Frosting 194
Cream Cheese Fudge Brownies 217
Cream Cheese Icing 197
Cream Gravy 140
Cream Puffs or Éclairs 255
Creamy Crawfish Fettuccini 135
Creamy Pralines 223
Crème Brûlée, Milk Chocolate 251
Crème de Menthe Pie 240
Creole Bread Pudding 246
Creole Crawfish Casserole 135
Crisp Crust Apple Pie 234
Crisp, Fresh Peach 244
Cucumber Pickles, South Carolina 86
Cucumber Sandwiches 26
Cumberland Sauce 170

D

Daddy's Baked Duck 181
Dairy Dip with Parmesan Potato Wedges 22
Daughter-in-Law Potato Salad 70
Deep Fried Ice Cream 260
Delicious Beef Roast 141
Delta Baked Catfish 123
Derby Breakfast Yeast Biscuits 37
Desserts: (see also specific dessert)
Bananas Nourries 252
Charlotte Russe 251
Cherries Jubilee 252
Chocolate-Dipped Strawberries 253
Cream Puffs or Èclairs 255
Creole Bread Pudding 246
Floating Isle 246
French Banana Èclair 254

Fresh Peach Crisp 244
Louisiana Swamp 256
Milk Chocolate Crème Brûlée 251
Peach Buckle 245
Pecan Tassies 253
Quick and Easy Apple Dumplings 244
Deviled Swiss Steak 140
Dips:
Broccoli Dip 23
Dairy Dip with Parmesan Potato Wedges 22
Hot Beef Dip 23
Hot Crab Dip 19
Shrimp Dip 21
Spinach in a Bread Bowl 25
Dishpan Cookies 211
Divinity, Old-Fashioned 224
Double Chocolate Peanut Butter Ice Cream 259
Dressing, Squash 101
Dressing, Turkey 178
Duck:
Daddy's Baked Duck 181
Duck Tenders with Mushrooms 182
Mississippi Delta Duck 181
Dumplings:
Chicken and Dumplings 173
Quick and Easy Apple Dumplings 244
Quick Dumplings 147

E

Easy Flounder Fillets 124
Easy-Do Fresh Strawberry Mousse 250
Éclair, French Banana 254
Éclairs, Cream Puffs or 255
Edinburg Mill Restaurant's Sausage Gravy 39
Eggnog, Christmas 15
Eggs:
Broccoli Rice Quiche 119
Corn Quiche 120
Egg in a Nest 55
Ham and Eggs Breakfast 54
Nellie's Pickled Eggs 85
Plantation Casserole 54
Quiche Lorraine 119
Eggplant:
Eggplant Creole 107
Eggplant Parmigiana Barbara 151
Eggplant-Zucchini Parmigiana 106
Elegant Chicken 170
Elvis Presley Cake 189
English Pea Salad 79
Exquisite Coconut Cake 193

F

Field Peas and Okra 98
Fig Preserves, Strawberry 89
Fire and Ice Tomatoes 79
Fish: (see also Catfish)
Avery Island Trout 125
Billy's Baked Bass 123
Catahoula Courtbouillon 60

Easy Flounder Fillets 124
Pecan Crusted Redfish 126
Snapper in Foil 125
Trout Almandine 124
Fix-Ahead Mashed Potatoes 114
Flawless Oyster Stew 66
Floating Isle 247
Florida Sunshine Salad 81
Flounder Fillets, Easy 124
French Banana Éclair 254
French Chocolate Cake 192
French Fried Dill Pickles 32
French Toast, Apple-Filled Oven 52
Fresh Peach Cake 200
Fresh Peach Crisp 244
Fresh Strawberry Pie 236
Fried Apple Pies 235
Fried Chicken 166
Fried Corn 110
Fried Green Tomatoes 92, 93
Fried Shrimp 131
Fried Squirrel 164
Fried Turkey 179
Frostings:
  Butter Icing 193
  Blueberry Glaze 230
  Bourbon Frosting 212
  Caramel Icing 195
  Cream Cheese Frosting 194
  Cream Cheese Icing 197
  Glossy Chocolate Icing 255
  Lemon Glaze 184, 212
  Orange Mountain Icing 196
  Praline Topping 190
Fruit Cake Cookies 213
Fudge, Gold Brick 222
Fudge, Hurricane 222

G
Gingerbread 202
Glamour Mushroom Rice 118
Glazes: (see Frostings)
Glossy Chocolate Icing 255
Gold Brick Fudge 222
Golden Fried Shrimp Batter 131
Golden Glow Corn Chowder 62
Granny Brock's Greens 112
Granny's Best Dinner Rolls 42
Gravies:
  Cream Gravy 140
  Edinburg Mill Restaurant's Sausage Gravy 39
  Great Giblet Gravy 178
  Red-Eye Gravy 38
  Saw Mill Gravy 39
  Tomato Gravy 40
Great Giblet Gravy 178
Great Grandmother's Chocolate Mousse 249
Green Beans and Stewed Potatoes 96
Green Beans, Ro-Tel French-Style 97
Greens, Granny Brock's 112

Greens, Southern-Style 112
Grillades and Garlic Cheese Grits 163
Grits:
  Cheese Grits 129
  Grillades and Garlic Cheese Grits 163
  Sausage Grits 53
  The South's Best Shrimp and Grits 129
Gumbo Soup, Turkey 61
Gumbo, Award-Winning Seafood 64

H
Ham:
  Atlanta Baked Ham 160
  Corn and Ham Chowder 62
  Country Fried Ham Biscuits with Red-Eye Gravy 38
  Country Ham Slices 161
  Ham and Chicken Casserole 165
  Ham and Eggs Breakfast 54
  Jambalaya 162
  Pawleys Island Ham 159
  Picnic Shoulder Ham 159
  Red Beans and Rice 160
Hamburger Potato Bake 149
Hamburgers, Juicy 149
Hilbert's Turtle Cake 187
Hilton Head Freeze 14
Hominy, Hot 108
Hoppin' John 97
Hors D'Oeuvres: (see also Dips)
  Bacon Roll-Ups 29
  BLT Bites 29
  Boiled Peanuts 33
  Cheese Straws 26
  Crabmeat Canapés 18
  Cucumber Sandwiches 26
  French Fried Dill Pickles 32
  Marinated Shrimp Biloxi 20
  Marvelous Seafood Mornay 20
  Mini Bite-Size Crawfish Pies 18
  Perfect Pimento Spread 24
  Potato Skins 27
  Sausage Balls with Jezebel Sauce 30
  Scrumptious Shrimp Appetizer 19
  Sesame Chicken Nuggets 32
  Shrimp Mousse 21
  Spinach Cheese Squares 28
  Spinach in a Bread Bowl 25
  Sweet and Sour Meatballs 31
  Sweet and Sour Sausage 30
  Sweet Potato and Peanut Chips 27
  Tasty Chicken Wings 31
  Trash the Party Mix 34
  Vegetable Sandwiches 25
  Vegetable Spread 24
  Zucchini Bites 28
Hot and Spicy Cabbage 111
Hot Beef Dip 23
Hot Cakes I Ever Ate, The Best 52
Hot Chicken Salad 73
Hot Crab Dip 19

Hot Hominy 108
Hot Pepper Jelly 90
Hot Slaw 77
Hot Tomato Bouillon 59
Hummingbird Cake 191
Hurricane Fudge 222

I

Ice Cream:
  Bananas Nourries 252
  Buttermilk Ice Cream 259
  Cherries Jubilee 252
  Crème de Menthe Pie 240
  Deep Fried Ice Cream 260
  Double Chocolate Peanut Butter Ice Cream 259
  Peach Buttermilk Ice Cream 258
  Peachy Keen Banana Smoothie 14
  Simply Sensational Frozen Strawberry Trifle 257
  Toffee Ice Cream Pie 240
  Vanilla Sunshine Ice Cream 258
Icings: (see Frostings)
In-A-Hurry Rolls 43
Italian Chicken Delight 174

J

Jam Cake 195
Jambalaya 162
Jambalaya, Shrimp 128
Jelly, Hot Pepper 90
Jezebel Sauce 30
Joy's Bay Pointe Margaritas 12
Juicy Hamburgers 149

K

Kentucky Bourbon Balls 223
Kentucky Mint Julep 13
Kum-Back Sauce 138

L

Lemons:
  Lemon Bonbons 212
  Lemon Cake 198
  Lemon Chess Tarts 233
  Lemon Chicken for the Grill 171
  Lemon Glaze 184, 212
  Lemon Ice Box Cake 199
  Lemon Meringue Tarts 233
  Lemon Sour Cookies 212
  Nostalgic Lemon Ice Box Pie 232
Lettuce, Wilted 77
Light and Easy Blueberry Pie 236
Light Corn Bread 47
Light Southern Waffles 56
Lima Beans, Boiled 98
Louisiana Chicken Sauce Piquant 175
Louisiana Swamp 256
Lucy's Spaghetti Meat Sauce 145

M

Macaroni Pie 117
Magic Beef Stew 68
Mamean's Buttermilk Corn Bread 47
Mandarin Spinach Salad with Poppy Seed Dressing 78
Mansion Almond Chocolate Mousse 249
Mardi Gras King Cake 184
Margaritas, Joy's Bay Pointe 12
Marinated Carrots 76
Marinated Shrimp Biloxi 20
Marvelous Seafood Mornay 20
Mayonnaise Biscuits 38
Mayonnaise, Blender 84
Meat Balls and Spaghetti 144
Meatloaf, The World's Last 152
Meringue 228, 248
Microwave Roux (with Vegetables) 65
Milk Chocolate Crème Brûlée 251
Mimosas 13
Mini Bite-Size Crawfish Pies 18
Mint Julep, Kentucky 13
Mississippi Catfish Fillets 122
Mississippi Delta Duck 181
Mississippi Hush Puppies 44
Mississippi Mud 186
Mississippi State Chicken-on-a-Stick 168
Mixed Pasta Salad 75
Monkey Bread 41
Mother's Old-Fashioned Sugar Cookies 210
Mousses:
  Chocolate Mousse Pie 238
  Easy-Do Fresh Strawberry Mousse 250
  Great Grandmother's Chocolate Mousse 249
  The Mansion Almond Chocolate Mousse 249
Mrs. Guerry's Baked Apricots 108
Mrs. Shingleton's Buttermilk Pound Cake 201
Mud Pie 229
Muffins, Pop-in-Your-Mouth Pecan 56
Mushroom Rice, Glamour 118
Mushrooms, Duck Tenders with 182
My Mother's Chocolate Pie 228

N

Nellie's Pickled Eggs 85
New Orleans Shrimp Rémoulade 132
New Potato Salad 71
No Crust Coconut Pie 237
North Carolina Barbecue Sauce 155
Nostalgic Lemon Ice Box Pie 232

O

Oatmeal Cookies 209
Okra:
  Field Peas and Okra 98
  Old-Time Fried Okra 106
  Scalloped Okra and Corn 105
  Southern Okra 105
  Sweet Pickled Okra 88
Old Fashioned Butter Crunch 221

Old-Fashioned Divinity 224
Old-Time Fried Okra 106
Onions:
  Baked Vidalias au Gratin 109
  Pork Chops with Apples, Onions and Raisins 158
  Quick Onion Soup 58
  Vidalia Onion Potato Salad 71
  Vidalia Soufflé 109
Oranges:
  Orange Mountain Icing 196
  Sunshine Island 196
Oyster Po-Boys 136
Oyster Stew, Flawless 66

P
Pan-Fried June Apples 116
Pancakes, Apple 51
Parmesan Chicken 169
Parmesan Potato Wedges 22
Pasta:
  Chicken-Spaghetti Casserole 176
  Creamy Crawfish Fettuccini 135
  Macaroni Pie 117
  Meat Balls and Spaghetti 144
  Mixed Pasta Salad 75
  Shrimp Tetrazzini 127
  Summer Pasta 117
Pawleys Island Ham 159
Pea Salad, English 79
Peach:
  Beautiful Raspberry Peach Melba Pie 241
  Fresh Peach Cake 200
  Fresh Peach Crisp 244
  Peach Buckle 245
  Peach Buttermilk Ice Cream 258
  Peach Cobbler 243
  Peachy Keen Banana Smoothie 14
Peanut Brittle 221
Peanut Butter:
  Double Chocolate Peanut Butter Ice Cream 259
  Peanut Butter Pie 231
  Peanut Butter Sticks 218
Peanut Soup à la Crème 59
Peanuts, Boiled 33
Pear Preserves 89
Peas and Okra, Field 98
Pecans:
  Chocolate Chip Pecan Pie 227
  Creamy Pralines 223
  Pecan Butter 126
  Pecan Crispies 206
  Pecan Crusted Redfish 126
  Pecan Kisses 224
  Pecan Pie Cake 187
  Pecan Tassies 253
  Pop-in-Your-Mouth Pecan Muffins 56
  Praline Brownies 217
  Praline Cake 190
  Praline Cheesecake 202
  Praline Cookies 207

Praline Pie 227
Sand Tarts 206
Southern Pecan Chicken 168
Southern Pecan Pie 226
Peppers:
  Beef Stuffed Peppers 150
  Shrimp Stuffed Peppers 133
  Stuffed Green Peppers 150
Perfect Pimento Spread 24
Pickles:
  Bread and Butter Pickles 86
  French Fried Dill Pickles 32
  Nellie's Pickled Eggs 85
  Seven Minute Microwave Dills 87
  South Carolina Cucumber Pickles 86
  Sweet Pickled Okra 88
  Watermelon Rind Pickles 87
Picnic Shoulder Ham 159
Pies:
  Beautiful Raspberry Peach Melba Pie 241
  Cheeky's Chess Pie 229
  Chocolate Chip Pecan Pie 227
  Chocolate Mousse Pie 238
  Chocolate Turtle Cheesecake Pie 241
  Coconut Cream Pie 237
  Coffee Toffee Pie 239
  Crème de Menthe Pie 240
  Crisp Crust Apple Pie 234
  Fresh Strawberry Pie 236
  Fried Apple Pies 235
  Light and Easy Blueberry Pie 236
  Mud Pie 229
  My Mother's Chocolate Pie 228
  No Crust Coconut Pie 237
  Nostalgic Lemon Ice Box Pie 232
  Peanut Butter Pie 231
  Praline Pie 227
  Southern Pecan Pie 226
  Summertime Pie 232
  Sweet Potato Pie 226
  Tanglewood Manor House Restaurant's
    Tar Heel Pie 230
  Toffee Ice Cream Pie 240
  Weidman's Bourbon Pie 230
Pineapple Soufflé 116
Pineapple Upside Down Cake 200
Pink House Trifle 257
Pizza Pop Up 148
Pizza, Chocolate Chip 214
Plantation Casserole 54
Pop-in-Your-Mouth Pecan Muffins 56
Poppy Seed Dressing 84
Pork: (*see also* Ham, Sausage)
  Barbequed Country Style Pork Ribs 156
  Pork Chops and Cheesy Potatoes 157
  Pork Chops with Apples, Onions, and Raisins 158
  Rose Davidson's Pork Chops 157
  Southern Shredded Pork 154
  Sweet 'n Sour Chops 158

INDEX

Potatoes:
　Cottage-Fried Potatoes 114
　Dairy Dip with Parmesan Potato Wedges 22
　Daughter-in-Law Potato Salad 70
　Fix-Ahead Mashed Potatoes 114
　Green Beans and Stewed Potatoes 96
　Hamburger Potato Bake 149
　New Potato Salad 71
　Parmesan Potato Wedges 22
　Pork Chops and Cheesy Potatoes 157
　Potato Skins 27
　Ro-Tel Potatoes 113
　Seasoned Potato Slices 113
　Sweet Potato and Peanut Chips 27
　Sweet Potato Biscuits 37
　Sweet Potato Casserole 115
　Vidalia Onion Potato Salad 71
Pound Cake, Mrs. Shingleton's Buttermilk 201
Pound Cake, Rum 201
Pralines:
　Creamy Pralines 223
　Praline Brownies 217
　Praline Cake 190
　Praline Cheesecake 202
　Praline Cookies 207
　Praline Pie 227
　Praline Topping 190
Preserves, Pear 89
Preserves, Strawberry Fig 89
Puddings: (*see also* Mousses)
　Banana Pudding with Meringue 248
　Creole Bread Pudding 246
　Floating Isle 247
　Toasted Almond Bread Pudding 247
Punches:
　Anycolor Punch 11
　Bourbon Punch 12
　Coffee Punch 16
　Southern Champagne Punch 11

Q

Quail with Dressing, Baked 180
Quail, Carolina 180
Quiches:
　Broccoli Rice Quiche 119
　Corn Quiche 120
　Quiche Lorraine 119
Quick and Easy Apple Dumplings 244
Quick Dumplings 147
Quick Onion Soup 58

R

Railroad Special 143
Raspberry Peach Melba Pie, Beautiful 241
Red Beans and Rice 160
Red Beans and Rice Casserole, Sausage 161
Red Rice 118
Red Velvet Cake 188
Redfish, Pecan Crusted 126
Rémoulade Sauce 132

Rice:
　Beef Tips Over Rice 153
　Broccoli Rice Quiche 119
　Glamour Mushroom Rice 118
　Red Beans and Rice 160
　Red Rice 118
　Sausage, Red Beans and Rice Casserole 161
　Shrimp and Rice Casserole 128
Ro-Tel French-Style Green Beans 97
Ro-Tel Potatoes 113
Roast, Venison 153
Rose Davidson's Pork Chops 157
Rotten Cake 190
Roux 65
Roux (with Vegetables), Microwave 65
Rum Pound Cake 201
Rum Sauce 246

S

Salad Dressings:
　Kum-Back Sauce 138
　Poppy Seed Dressing 78, 84
Salads:
　Asheville Salad 80
　Avocado Shrimp Salad 81
　Black-Eyed Susan Salad 74
　Carrot Raisin Salad 76
　Cherry Salad Supreme 82
　Chicken Salad in Raspberry Ring 72
　Chicken Salad with Grapes and Almonds 73
　Congealed Coca-Cola Cranberry Salad 83
　Cottage Cheese Salad 80
　Daughter-in-Law Potato Salad 70
　English Pea Salad 79
　Fire and Ice Tomatoes 79
　Florida Sunshine Salad 81
　Hot Chicken Salad 73
　Hot Slaw 77
　Mandarin Spinach Salad with Poppy Seed Dressing 78
　Marinated Carrots 76
　Mixed Pasta Salad 75
　New Potato Salad 71
　Slice of the South Salad 82
　Spinach Strawberry Salad 78
　Summer Corn Salad 74
　Vidalia Onion Potato Salad 71
　Wilted Lettuce 77
Sand Tarts 206
Sandwiches, Cucumber 26
Sandwiches, Vegetable 25
Sauces:
　Barbecue Sauce 156
　Cumberland Sauce 170
　Jezebel Sauce 30
　Kum-Back Sauce 138
　North Carolina Barbecue Sauce 155
　Rémoulade Sauce 132
　Rum Sauce 246
　Sauce Piquant 32
　Shrimp Sauce 129

Tartar Sauce 138
Sausages:
    Bacon Roll-Ups 29
    Edinburg Mill Restaurant's Sausage Gravy 39
    Red Beans and Rice 160
    Sausage Balls with Jezebel Sauce 30
    Sausage Coffee Cake 53
    Sausage Grits 53
    Sausage, Red Beans and Rice Casserole 161
    Saw Mill Gravy 39
    Sweet and Sour Sausage 30
Savannah Crab Stew 66
Saw Mill Gravy 39
Scalloped Okra and Corn 105
Scalloped Tomatoes 93
Scrumptious Shrimp Appetizer 19
Seafood: (see also Crabs, Crawfish, Fish, Shrimp)
    Award-Winning Seafood Gumbo 64
    Marvelous Seafood Mornay 20
Seaside Stuffed Squash 101
Seasoned Potato Slices 113
Sesame Chicken Nuggets 32
Seven Minute Microwave Dills 87
Shortcake, Strawberry 185
Short'nin Bread 44
Shrimp:
    Avocado Shrimp Salad 81
    Baked Shrimp, New Orleans Style 132
    Fried Shrimp 131
    Golden Fried Shrimp Batter 131
    Marinated Shrimp Biloxi 20
    Marvelous Seafood Mornay 20
    New Orleans Shrimp Rémoulade 132
    Scrumptious Shrimp Appetizer 19
    Shrimp and Rice Casserole 128
    Shrimp Boil Dinner 133
    Shrimp Creole 130
    Shrimp Dip 21
    Shrimp Étouffée 127
    Shrimp Mousse 21
    Shrimp Sauce 129
    Shrimp Stew 67
    Shrimp Stuffed Peppers 133
    Shrimp Tetrazzini 127
    Shrimp-Chicken Jambalaya 128
    The South's Best Shrimp and Grits 129
    Stuffed Shrimp 134
Simply Sensational Frozen Strawberry Trifle 257
Sinful German Chocolate Squares 215
Skillet Squash 100
Skillet Popover 49
Slice of the South Salad 82
Slow Cooker Barbecued Pot Roast 142
Smoothie, Peachy Keen Banana 14
Snapper in Foil 125
Snowballs, Chocolate-Filled 218
Soups:
    Catahoula Courtbouillon 60
    Corn and Crabmeat Soup 61
    Hot Tomato Bouillon 59

Peanut Soup à la Crème 59
    Quick Onion Soup 58
    Turkey Gumbo Soup 61
    Vegetable Soup 58
Sour Cream Chicken Breasts 175
South Carolina Cucumber Pickles 86
Southern Champagne Punch 11
Southern Okra 105
Southern Pecan Chicken 168
Southern Pecan Pie 226
Southern Popovers 41
Southern Shredded Pork 154
Southern Spoon Bread 46
Southern Tomato Pie 94
Southern-Style Greens 112
South's Best Shrimp and Grits 129
Spaghetti, Meatballs and 144
Spinach:
    Mandarin Spinach Salad 78
    Spinach Cheese Squares 28
    Spinach in a Bread Bowl 25
    Spinach Madeline 104
    Spinach Soufflé 103
    Spinach Strawberry Salad 78
Squash:
    Seaside Stuffed Squash 101
    Skillet Squash 100
    Squash Dressing 101
    Squash Morelle 102
    Squash Puppies 45
    Squash Soufflé 100
Squirrel, Fried 164
Sticky Bones 154
Strawberries:
    Augusta's Best Strawberry Bread 48
    Chocolate-Dipped Strawberries 253
    Easy-Do Fresh Strawberry Mousse 250
    Fresh Strawberry Pie 236
    Pink House Trifle 257
    Simply Sensational Frozen Strawberry Trifle 257
    Spinach Strawberry Salad 78
    Strawberry Cream Cake 198
    Strawberry Fig Preserves 89
    Strawberry Shortcake 185
Stews:
    Flawless Oyster Stew 66
    Magic Beef Stew 68
    Savannah Crab Stew 66
    Shrimp Stew 67
Stuffed Green Peppers 150
Stuffed Shrimp 134
Succotash 111
Summer Corn Salad 74
Summer Mint Tea 10
Summer Pasta 117
Summertime Citrus Tea 10
Summertime Pie 232
Sunday School Chicken 177
Sunday Supper Snack 165
Sunshine Island 196

Super Blackberry Cobbler 242
Sweet and Sour Meatballs 31
Sweet and Sour Sausage 30
Sweet Nothings 219
Sweet 'n Sour Chops 158
Sweet Pickled Okra 88
Sweet Potato and Peanut Chips 27
Sweet Potato Biscuits 37
Sweet Potato Casserole 115
Sweet Potato Pie 226
Syrup, Cinnamon Cream 51

T

Tanglewood Manor House Restaurant's
  Tar Heel Pie 230
Tangy Butter Fingers 43
Tartar Sauce 138
Tarts, Lemon Chess 233
Tarts, Lemon Meringue 233
Tasty Chicken Wings 31
Tea, Summer Mint 10
Tea, Summertime Citrus 10
Teacakes, Authentic Southern Soft 207
Tennessee Ernie Ford's Fresh Apple Nut Cake 197
Toasted Almond Bread Pudding 247
Toffee Ice Cream Pie 240
Tomatoes:
  Baked Tomatoes Rockefeller 94
  Broccoli and Tomato Casserole 95
  Broiled Tomatoes 95
  Fire and Ice Tomatoes 79
  Fried Green Tomatoes 92, 93
  Hot Tomato Bouillon 59
  Scalloped Tomatoes 93
  Southern Tomato Pie 94
  Tomato Gravy 40
Trash the Party Mix 34
Trifle, Pink House 257
Trifle, Simply Sensational Frozen Strawberry 257

Trout Almandine 124
Trout, Avery Island 125
Turkey:
  Turkey Dressing 178
  Turkey Gumbo Soup 61
  Fried Turkey 179
24-Hour Crockpot Barbecue 141
Twisted Kisses 219

V

Vanilla Sunshine Ice Cream 258
Vegetables: *(see also specific vegetable)*
  Succotash 111
  Vegetable Sandwiches 25
  Vegetable Soup 58
  Vegetable Spread 24
Venison Chili with Dumplings, Chunky 147
Venison Roast 153
Vidalia Onion Potato Salad 71
Vidalia Soufflé 109

W

Waffles, Light Southern 56
Watermelon Rind Pickles 87
Weidman's Bourbon Pie 230
White Corn Casserole 110
Wilted Lettuce 77
World's Last Meatloaf 152

Z

Zucchini:
  Eggplant-Zucchini Parmigiana 106
  Zucchini Bites 28
  Zucchini Deluxe 102
  Zucchini-Corn Casserole 103

BEST OF THE BEST STATE COOKBOOK SERIES

EACH COOKBOOK IN THIS RENOWNED SERIES INCLUDES:

- 350 to 500 of the state's most popular recipes—tested and easy-to-follow
- A Catalog of Contributing Cookbooks provides a description and ordering information on each contributing cookbook—a treasure for cookbook collectors
- Interesting facts about each state along with pictures and illustrations
- Easy-to-use, cross-referenced index

Preserving America's Food Heritage

BEST OF THE BEST
STATE COOKBOOK SERIES

BEST OF THE BEST STATE COOKBOOKS listed here have been completed as of December 31, 2003.

Best of the Best from
ALABAMA
288 pages

Best of the Best from
ALASKA
288 pages

Best of the Best from
ARIZONA
288 pages

Best of the Best from
ARKANSAS
288 pages

Best of the Best from
BIG SKY
(Montana and Wyoming)
288 pages

Best of the Best from
CALIFORNIA
384 pages

Best of the Best from
COLORADO
288 pages

Best of the Best from
FLORIDA
288 pages

Best of the Best from
GEORGIA
336 pages

Best of the Best from the
GREAT PLAINS
(North and South Dakotas,
Nebraska, and Kansas)
288 pages

Best of the Best from
IDAHO
288 pages

Best of the Best from
ILLINOIS
288 pages

Best of the Best from
INDIANA
288 pages

Best of the Best from
IOWA
288 pages

Best of the Best from
KENTUCKY
288 pages

Best of the Best from
LOUISIANA
288 pages

Best of the Best from
LOUISIANA II
288 pages

Best of the Best from
MICHIGAN
288 pages

Best of the Best from the
MID-ATLANTIC
(Maryland, Delaware, New
Jersey, and Washington, D.C.)
288 pages

Best of the Best from
MINNESOTA
288 pages

Best of the Best from
MISSISSIPPI
288 pages

Best of the Best from
MISSOURI
304 pages

Best of the Best from
NEW ENGLAND
(Rhode Island, Connecticut,
Massachusetts, Vermont,
New Hampshire, and Maine)
368 pages

Best of the Best from
NEW MEXICO
288 pages

Best of the Best from
NEW YORK
288 pages

Best of the Best from
NO. CAROLINA
288 pages

Best of the Best from
OHIO
352 pages

Best of the Best from
OKLAHOMA
288 pages

Best of the Best from
OREGON
288 pages

Best of the Best from
PENNSYLVANIA
320 pages

Best of the Best from
SO. CAROLINA
288 pages

Best of the Best from
TENNESSEE
288 pages

Best of the Best from
TEXAS
352 pages

Best of the Best from
TEXAS II
352 pages

Best of the Best from
VIRGINIA
320 pages

Best of the Best from
WASHINGTON
288 pages

Best of the Best from
WEST VIRGINIA
288 pages

Best of the Best from
WISCONSIN
288 pages

Note: All BEST cookbooks
are comb bound.

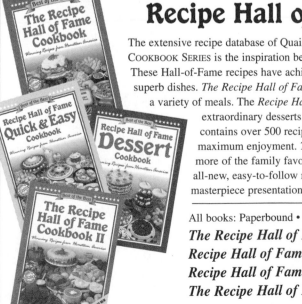

Recipe Hall of Fame Collection

The extensive recipe database of Quail Ridge Press' acclaimed BEST OF THE BEST STATE COOKBOOK SERIES is the inspiration behind the RECIPE HALL OF FAME COLLECTION. These Hall-of-Fame recipes have achieved extra distinction for consistently producing superb dishes. *The Recipe Hall of Fame Cookbook* features over 400 choice dishes for a variety of meals. The *Recipe Hall of Fame Dessert Cookbook* consists entirely of extraordinary desserts. The *Recipe Hall of Fame Quick & Easy Cookbook* contains over 500 recipes that require minimum effort but produce maximum enjoyment. *The Recipe Hall of Fame Cookbook II* brings you more of the family favorites you've come to expect with over 400 all-new, easy-to-follow recipes. Appetizers to desserts, quick dishes to masterpiece presentations, the RECIPE HALL OF FAME COLLECTION has it all.

All books: Paperbound • 7x10 • Illustrations • Index
The Recipe Hall of Fame Cookbook • 304 pages
Recipe Hall of Fame Dessert Cookbook • 240 pages
Recipe Hall of Fame Quick & Easy Cookbook • 304 pages
The Recipe Hall of Fame Cookbook II • 304 pages